Jacob's Ladder
Missional Church in the 1970s

Steen Olsen

Published by Steen and Ruth Olsen

First published in November 2020

www.jakes1970s.net

ISBN 978-0-6489968-0-4

Unless otherwise stated all text copyright © Steen Olsen 2020

Illustrations copyright © Knarelle Beard 2020

Printed by Openbook Howden
2–14 Paul Street, St Marys SA 5042 Australia

All rights reserved
No part of this book may be sold or contracted to any third party
without the prior written permission of the author.
steen.olsen@lca.org.au

Category: 1. Missional Church. 2. Jesus Movement. 3. Lutheran Church Renewal.

The cover design is adapted from the cover of *Servant*, Vol 1 No 2, July 1977.

Scripture quotations are from the New Revised Standard Version Bible (NRSV), copyright © 1989 the Division of Christian Education of the National Council of Churches of Christ in the United States of America. Used by permission.
All rights reserved.

Dedicated to Julie Anne McBride nee Lambert
23/12/1951–4/08/2019

She wanted to write a book like this
and gathered many documents.
She kept in touch with many of us.
She constantly prayed for
our reconciliation,
restoration and healing.

About the Author

Steen Olsen is a retired Lutheran Pastor, who after his time with Jacob's Ladder served three parishes in Australia and New Zealand and then as bishop of the Lutheran Church of New Zealand and finally as director for mission for the Lutheran Church in South Australia and the Northern Territory. His publications include *Spirit Filled: Normal Christian Living* (with Noel Due); *bring Jesus: Making Sense of Mission;* and *125 Years of Grace: St Luke's Lutheran Church Palmerston North 1882–2007*. He was co-founder of the *Kogudus Retreat Ministry* in Australia and New Zealand. A post-war Danish migrant, Steen has a special interest in helping the church to be more missional in its culture, theology and practice. He can be contacted at steen.olsen@lca.org.au

How to read this book

You can obviously read the story in the order in which it was written. In any case, I suggest you read the brief Preface and Introduction first. After that, you might find it more helpful to get to know some of the key participants first. You could do that by beginning with chapter 28 and so hearing how being a part of Jakes has influenced the rest of our lives. Chapter 20 on devotional articles and testimonies also introduces the flavour of the community. On the other hand, if your bent is more theological, you might find it helpful to begin with chapter 27 and then come back to story after that. However you approach it, I hope that you are blessed and edified.

CONTENTS

Preface	vi
Introduction	1
Section I: Jacob's Ladder Coffee Lounge 1970–1973	**5**
1. A Vision is Born	5
2. Up and Running	11
3. The Partnership with St Stephen's	19
Section II: Jacob's Ladder Coffee House 1974	**26**
4. Expanded Premises and Vision	26
5. The Kairos '74 Festival	31
6. New Ministries Emerge	39
7. The Old Wineskins Burst!	47
Section III: Jacob's Ladder Christian Community 1975–1976	**54**
8. Growing a Community at 'Street Level'	54
9. A Week in the Life of the Community	62
10. The Growth of Nurture Houses	71
11. Outreach and Rehabilitation	81
12. Worship, Music, Drama and the Arts	89
13. Lutheran Renewal, Interstate and Overseas Connections	99
14. Fitting into the Lutheran Church	109
Section IV: Servants of Christ Community 1977–1979	**116**
15. A New Direction	116
16. A Covenant for the Community	125
17. Servant Enterprises and Nurture	133
18. Lutheran Charismatic Renewal and Manoah	141
19. From Gawler Place to Torrens Road	148
20. Devotional Articles and Testimonies	155
21. The 1979 AGM	163
22. The End of Jakes	169
23. Epilogue	176
Section V: Further Background to Our Story	**182**
24. The Dorian Society—by Geoff Strelan	182
25. Kerux Apostles Motorcycle Club—by Marty Rosenberg	184
26. Music and Drama—by Colin Smith	188
27. Theology and Teaching	192
Section VI: The Lasting Impact on Our Lives	**217**
28. Our Individual Stories	217
Bibliography	241

PREFACE

This account of the life and mission of Jacob's Ladder has been crafted by those who were participants in this community more than forty years ago. Although we found quite a lot of written materials, they are not a complete record. We discovered that archiving documents, or even putting a date on them, was not a priority back then. Sometimes dating a document therefore involved some guesswork. Consequently, this is our story as recorded in the documents we have found and as we remember it.

While it is 'our' story, it is also true that I wrote it, and so made many decisions about what to include, what to leave out, and how to express things. From time to time, I have reflected on events and expressed opinions that are obviously mine and may not be shared by the whole community. I have also tried to look back on the story from the perspective of 2020, and sometimes I have commented on how our understanding of things has changed, or how things the Lord led us to grapple with have been affirmed by subsequent developments in our understanding of missiology and theology.

After all these years memories begin to fade and people who lived in those times remember different things. We asked all those who were willing to write down their recollections of their participation in the community. Together with the remaining written records, these memories have formed the raw material from which this story was fashioned. These sources, together with conversations with the writers, are simply referred to by the name of the person concerned: "Karl Brettig remembers the time when…" Where individuals other than me have drafted substantial sections, this is acknowledged.

I also want to acknowledge and thank the many people who have contributed to this volume, including those who read the manuscript, and made corrections and suggestions for improvements. In particular, Marty Rosenberg initiated the project and has acted as secretary, writing up his memories, collecting photographs, keeping things together, sending out some updates and responding to emails. Karl Brettig and the late Julie Anne McBride (nee Lambert), had collected a lot of written materials. My thanks to Karl and to Neville McBride for allowing me access to them. Thanks also to the many others who have sent in their recollections or taken the time to speak with me in person or by phone. Not everything could be included. I hope I have managed to do justice to your contributions. The Lutheran Archives had a lot of relevant material, which filled the gaps in our memories and allowed me to document much of this history. My thanks to their staff for finding things even when I did not really know what I was looking for.

My wife Ruth has helped my memory and provided much good advice and proofreading. Karl Brettig, Stephen Haar, Marty Rosenberg and Doug Vogelsang have reviewed the chapters as they appeared and made suggestions. Thanks also to Bev Schneider, Marty

Rosenberg and Knarelle Beard for proofreading the manuscript, and to Knarelle for doing the covers and the layout of the text, adding illustrations and photos, and generally getting it ready for the printers. The illustrations are also Knarelle's work and mostly come from *Jacob's Letter* and *Servant* magazines. They show that we had a sense of humour and could laugh at ourselves. Any remaining errors are of course mine. At times, I have edited quotes for clarity while seeking to retain the writer's meaning. In doing this, I have sought to standardise the formatting as much as possible. I have used the modern convention of not capitalising pronouns referring to God. Where there are obvious typos and grammatical errors I have simply corrected them, rather than letting them stand and then adding the rather superior sounding "(sic)" after the mistake. Comments in [square brackets] in quotations are my additions or observations. Finally, the name of the community was changed to Servants of Christ in early 1977. However, even when writing about the time that followed, I sometimes continue to refer to the community simply as "Jakes", as people still do, even today.

I was a student at Luther Seminary in Adelaide during the time of Jakes. I was involved from early 1971 until the end of 1976, having worked full-time on the staff of the community during 1976. At the beginning of 1977 we moved to Toowoomba Queensland for me to do my 'internship'. Returning to Adelaide for final year seminary in 1978, we were still involved in the community, but no longer in leadership roles. At the end of that year, we left Adelaide for the Hunter Valley in New South Wales and our first parish. We were therefore no longer involved when the community folded.

Steen Olsen

INTRODUCTION

In the 1970s in Adelaide, South Australia, the Holy Spirit gathered a group of young people together into a community that is now generally referred to as Jacob's Ladder or simply as Jakes. This is our story.

The story began with a decision by the Dorian Society and the South Metropolitan Zone of the Lutheran Youth of South Australia to establish a coffee lounge to bring the gospel that is Jesus to the youth of Adelaide. It opened its doors in late 1970 and the community was wound up by the end of 1979. No individual was involved from the conception until the final days. Karl Brettig comes closest, being involved from soon after the Coffee Lounge opened and still being there at the end. People came and went, sometimes moving on for work or other opportunities.

Throughout we were a young community. Most were teenagers or in their twenties. A small handful was in their thirties. We had a lot of energy but could hardly claim huge reserves of acquired wisdom. The Spirit was at work in our midst but our discernment skills were often rudimentary. We were also children of the times, inherently suspicious of 'outside' authority and too confident in our own knowledge and wisdom. The Jesus Movement was in full swing, the Devil had no right to all the good music, and we constantly saw God at work in the lives of kids who came off the street, from outlaw bikie gangs and from among those dabbling in drugs and Eastern Religions and philosophies.

Missional Church

With the perspective of hindsight, we can see that we understood ourselves to be sent by God out into our community with the good news that is a person, Jesus Christ. It wasn't just that we had a mission or two, or even that we were focused on mission, but that our community was shaped by the mission of God, and therefore, in that sense, missional. As the risen Jesus said to his disciples:

> 'Peace be with you. As the Father has sent me, so I send you.'

John then adds:

> When he had said this, he breathed on them and said to them, 'Receive the Holy Spirit. If you forgive the sins of any, they are forgiven them; if you retain the sins of any, they are retained.'   John 20:21–23

We also increasingly understood ourselves to be 'church', and not a parachurch agency. The initial vision was to serve as an outreach arm of existing congregations, but that soon changed as the demands of nurturing new Christians constantly threatened to overwhelm us. We came to see that we needed to form 'church', in the full sense of the word, among the people God had sent us to, and not attempt to bring them back into existing congregations where they simply didn't fit. Our approach needed to be incarnational, not just attractional. In the much later words, 'The church doesn't have a mission; God's mission has a church.'

Much has been learnt and much written about missional church in the last forty years. We didn't have the benefit of that, but the Spirit led us into many of the key concepts. God was at work; he was acting in and through us. In spite of our youthful naivety, and at times arrogance, God was able to work with our broken vessels. As Paul said:

> But we have this treasure in clay jars, so that it may be made clear that this extraordinary power belongs to God and does not come from us. We are afflicted in every way, but not crushed; perplexed, but not driven to despair; persecuted, but not forsaken; struck down, but not destroyed; always carrying in the body the death of Jesus, so that the life of Jesus may also be made visible in our bodies. For while we live, we are always being given up to death for Jesus' sake, so that the life of Jesus may be made visible in our mortal flesh.   2 Corinthians 4:7–11

Good fruit

In researching this story, I have heard from many who were blessed, often beyond their wildest expectations. I have also discovered that some were deeply hurt and, of those, some carry significant scars to this day. It is easier to tell the story of blessings, but I acknowledge that at times, some acted contrary to what Jesus taught, trust was betrayed and as a result, people suffered. In telling the story, I have tried to be real, without pretending that everything was a success and there were never any problems. However, neither have I turned the book into an exposé of the failures. For those who were blessed in those days, I trust that reading this book may lead you to relive and continue to enjoy that sense of blessing. For those who carry wounds, I pray that perhaps even now, this book may be a further step towards healing and reconciliation.

We all went on to other things and while we cannot include those stories, we have asked our people to describe briefly the lasting impact of Jakes on their lives. That forms the final section of this book. In order to keep the main story flowing, we have written in greater detail about some key aspects of our life together in section five.

The structure of the story

The story of Jakes divides somewhat neatly into four phases, each characterised by the name of the community at the time. At least, it seems that way to me!

The first phase is the story of **Jacob's Ladder Coffee Lounge**, which runs from the beginning in 1970 through to the end of 1973. It includes significant planning for what was to follow. Over time, a stable group of workers formed and there was less reliance on volunteers from Lutheran youth groups.

The second phase is **Jacob's Ladder Coffee House** in 1974. The name change is small but significant. This was a time of rapid growth and development. The dreams of those who initiated this work were being realised, often in unexpected ways. The floor area of the coffee house at 102 Gawler Place doubled at the start of the year. The first staff were appointed and the scope of the ministry grew rapidly. A stream of people came to faith and joined the community. The old structures with outside committees being responsible for the work no longer functioned well, and eventually the growing Jacob's Ladder community assumed responsibility for running its own affairs.

The name changed again for the third phase, to **Jacob's Ladder Christian Community**. This covers 1975 and 1976. The expansion continued, but it was also a time of consolidation. Some Government funding was obtained. More staff were employed. Community nurture houses were established. The relationship of the community with the Lutheran Church was strained, with many meetings and much correspondence.

The final phase, **Servants of Christ Community** runs from 1977 to the eventual close in 1979. Community houses gradually relocated to the Brompton-Renown Park area of Adelaide, and the Gawler Place Centre was closed when new premises were rented at 122 Torrens Road Renown Park. The community was clearly ecumenical with a strong Lutheran flavour, with members having come from different Christian backgrounds, or none. Other associated groups were established, such as the Manoah Community and Lutheran Charismatic Renewal Australia.

Choosing to write the story chronologically in four segments, rather than thematically, means that many things are mentioned more than once. Community nurture houses feature in each of the sections from 1974 onwards, our relationship with the Lutheran Church of Australia is dealt with throughout, and key aspects of our ministry like evangelism, worship, teaching and counselling are tracked through the various stages of the community. Hopefully, there is not too much repetition.

In writing up this story, we especially want to reflect on some key issues. What did we learn about issues such as being missional church, community discernment and planning, relational evangelism, nurturing new converts, growing as disciples, and leadership? Why did Jakes come to a fairly sudden end? Our relationship with the Lutheran Church of Australia, which gave birth to us, also leads us to ask what we have learned about relationships with the wider church.

It was quite a journey! Much more happened than we can record here. Some is known only to God and to those who were involved. Much will only be manifest on that day when Jesus returns, for

> With all wisdom and insight [God] has made known to us the mystery of his will, according to his good pleasure that he set forth in Christ, as a plan for the fullness of time, to gather up all things in him, things in heaven and things on earth. In Christ we have also obtained an inheritance, having been destined according to the purpose of him who accomplishes all things according to his counsel and will, so that we, who were the first to set our hope on Christ, might live for the praise of his glory. In him you also, when you had heard the word of truth, the gospel of your salvation, and had believed in him, were marked with the seal of the promised Holy Spirit; this is the pledge of our inheritance toward redemption as God's own people, to the praise of his glory.
> Ephesians 1:8–14 NRSV

Waddya mean there's only one table?! I'm gonna sit with only Jacob's Ladder freaks or none at all!!

JACOB'S LADDER COFFEE LOUNGE 1970–1973

A Vision is Born

The Spirit of God stirs in a generation of young Christians

In the late 60s and early 70s, across the western world, mainly young people worked together across denominational lines to bring Jesus to the world. It came to be called *The Jesus Movement*. The focus was not on feeding the poor and hungry, but people were fed and given a place to stay. The focus was not on justice, but the oppressed were set free. The focus was not on human rights, but God-given dignity and freedom were proclaimed. It was not about welfare, but unapologetically evangelistic: bringing Jesus to those who did not yet know him.

It's all about Jesus! The good news is not a story or a teaching about Jesus; it is Jesus. He is the Word made flesh. By the power of the Spirit at work in God's people, Jesus is still coming to people today, giving them the gifts of repentance, faith, life and salvation. The promise of Pentecost is still at work in the world:

> In the last days it will be, God declares, that I will pour out my Spirit upon all flesh, and your sons and your daughters shall prophesy, and your young men shall see visions, and your old men shall dream dreams. ... Then everyone who calls on the name of the Lord shall be saved.' Acts 2:17, 21

Larry Norman sang, "Why should the devil have all the good music?" and on the 21st June 1971 Time's cover story was *The Jesus Revolution*. In the city of Adelaide in South Australia, a group of young Christians had a vision. At that time they were not the only people in Adelaide, let alone in Australia and the rest of the world, to see such visions. They were just a small part of a much larger story. However, forty to fifty years on, with most of the participants still alive, this is their story of how God worked in their midst during the 1970s.[1]

---

[1] Apart from our memories we have a few early written sources of information about the beginnings of Jakes:
Greg Box, **Drop-in Centres**, Service to Youth Council Inc, Parkside SA, March 1974;
David Graebner, **Christ Conversation Coffee**, The Lutheran, (9 August 1971), 21–23;
Steen Olsen, **History**, Jacob's Letter (October 1975), 2–3;
Steen Olsen, **The Growth of Jacob's Ladder Christian Community as a part of the Lutheran Church of**

Conception and Pregnancy

How did it all begin? In the 1960s coffee lounges were the place to go after you had been out to another event such as a concert, a film, ten pin bowling, or maybe out to dinner. It was natural that Christian young people started to open their own coffee lounges. The first reference I found was in the minutes of the Metro South Zone of the Lutheran Youth of South Australia (LYSA), where on the 22nd October 1967 they noted that, "Tim Fisher told the Executive of the Bethlehem fellowship of the idea of a coffee lounge where youth can meet and talk." In due course, the Zone established a Coffee Lounge Committee to investigate possible locations.

Meanwhile another group of young people had a vision for a coffee lounge that would be a means of bringing Jesus to the youth of the city. On 27th May 1970 Geoff Strelan, Milton Eckermann and Monica Roehrs (now Monica Christian) met and agreed to form the Dorian Society[2], which soon attracted other like-minded people. Monica remembers:

> We were concerned that young people were leaving the church and we were hopeful that we could encourage the use of young people's gifts in the church. ... Jacob's Ladder was the melding of the two ideas of using gifts and hospitality.[3]

The Dorian Society's Report for 1970–71 stated:

> The Dorian Society exists to provide support for anyone wishing to communicate the Gospel. In particular we wish to support those who are investigating _new_ methods of communication.[4] [Emphasis in original]

In the September-October 1970 *Dorian Society Newsletter* they wrote:

> Perhaps our Coffee Lounge at first would attract mainly Lutheran youth, but its main purpose should be as a mission outreach to young people who are looking for somewhere to go, where they can find more meaning in life, or just where they feel that people are concerned about them.

On the 13th July 1970 Geoff Strelan, Milton Eckermann and Rosemarie Markovic (now Rosemarie Menzel) had met with the Zone executive. The minutes recorded:

Australia, South Australian District, Forum 69 (May 1976), 5–9; *Manager's Report Book* 3/3/1972–13/10/1973.

2. The name 'Dorian' comes from the Greek word for gift, δωρεά, *dorea*.
3. Monica Christian with Leigh Newton, **Jacob's Ladder Retrospective: In the beginning**, The Messenger, St Stephens Lutheran Church, Wakefield Street, Adelaide, vol. 60 no. 5 (September/October 1998), 5.
4. See chapter 24 for more background to the Dorian Society.

JACOB'S LADDER COFFEE LOUNGE 1970-1973

SECTION 1

CHAPTER 1

The Chairman of the Dorian Society, Geoff Strelan, outlined the work of the Society and informed us that they are also thinking of setting up a Coffee Lounge. ... It was resolved that we elect the Dorian Society as our Coffee Lounge Committee and that they use the Zone channels for gaining support of Fellowship members wherever and whenever needed.

Two days later, on 15 July 1970 the minutes of the Dorian Society Management Committee recorded:

At a recent meeting of the Metro South Zone of LYSA it was resolved that the Dorian Society be their coffee lounge committee. As such, we are to see to the acquisition of premises, their remodelling and the consequent setup and running of the coffee lounge. ... It was decided that it was most important to arrange a coffee lounge group to start working on the idea as soon as possible.

Geoff Strelan recalls the involvement of the Dorian Society:

This was in the era when Coffee Lounges were popular places for young people to gather after an evening out. There'd be lots of conversations, folk singers, non-alcoholic cocktails, toasted sandwiches etc. So the idea came to set up such a place as an outreach centre.

Milton, Roger Burger and I went to visit a Christian drop-in centre in Geelong and that led to further planning by the Dorian Society. We realised we would need the services of Lutheran young people to help to staff the Centre and we therefore approached the South Zone of LYSA to see if we could get their support and make the project an 'official' church activity. They were pleased to endorse the project and set up a Management Committee to look into finding a suitable site. They handed planning for the running of the Centre back to the Dorian Society.

The Dorian Society not only did initial planning but its members put in a great deal of effort once the doors were open. They spent many hours in addition to managing the coffee lounge on Friday and Saturday nights, purchasing and delivering supplies, setting up the place, cleaning it and driving home workers in the early hours of the morning.

Milton Eckermann recalls that after investigating a number of possible venues, they were led to 102 Gawler Place in the centre of the Adelaide CBD:

Several discussions occurred confirming a desire to establish a coffee lounge drop-in centre... Enthusiasm for this type of activity was very high

A Vision is Born // 7

and a regular event was desired. Trouble was, how could we establish a suitable venue that would allow young people to drop in 2–3 times a week. Meetings continued and excitement grew and we were informed by the manager of Lutheran Publishing House (70 Pirie St) a vacant floor in a building in Gawler Place could be available. We met with the owner of the building who was very wary of a gaggle of young people and with a lot of fear and uncertainty we explained what we were intending to do. We were not encouraged or excited by the way he looked at us nor by the body language he displayed. He agreed to meet us again in a couple of days and would then possibly give us a viewing of the space that could be available. At that viewing, he took us in through a narrow door at street level and up two long flights of stairs to second storey level. We entered into a room not much larger than my parents lounge and we looked at each other not too enthused after the stair climb and to arrive at a not very welcoming location. After we danced from foot to foot and obviously showed our doubts he mentioned the price (which I can't remember) we were ready to put our feet one in front of the other and head downstairs. The owner then informed us it was for the whole floor level but we would have to do whatever we needed to make it functional at our cost. Somehow, we came to an arrangement that was suitable and affordable for a twelve month period with the right to extend the lease if both parties agreed. Many people came forward with personal donations that covered a lease for 6 months. What took place then were many working bees and the seeking out of tradesman from congregations to oversee the work. Donations continued so that material and equipment could be purchased. Many people climbed those stairs carrying material in and then down the stairs to remove the rubbish. Wallahhhh! There was the name!! Climbing the stairs/ladder to something worthwhile and better. Jacobs Ladder. First of all it was for our own youth who attended but soon we saw the arrival of 'outside youth, bikers and gangs of misfits' who had nowhere to go. This quickly meant that our volunteer workers in the kitchen and wait staff soon became listeners, counsellors, missionaries and security officers. Things were exciting and scary and intimidating for us and the task of having to ensure that no vandalism or gathering took place on the first floor landing was pretty onerous. As I am writing this, I remember a spin off, visitations to prisons and mental health institutions—that were happening in a small way—grew into something fairly remarkable with regular 'church' services taking place.

Carpet and some furniture were obtained from a hotel that was being refurbished. Coffee tables were made. The kitchen was equipped with fridges and utensils together with other equipment. A sound system was installed and lighting arranged.

JACOB'S LADDER COFFEE LOUNGE 1970–1973

SECTION 1

CHAPTER 1

Anything that didn't move was painted. An army of people gave of their time, talents and treasure to make Jacob's Ladder happen. All their names are now known only to God, but there would be no story for us to tell, if it were not for their efforts.

Birth

The first night Jacob's Ladder Coffee Lounge opened was Saturday 5 September 1970. By the time the September-October *Dorian Society Newsletter* was published, they could report that Jacob's Ladder had been going for just over a month. "The response has been terrific. At first the customers were almost completely Lutherans, but gradually more and more 'outsiders' came in. It looks as good, if not better than most coffee lounges. One night there wasn't enough room for everyone."

On 10 September 1970, a circular from the 'Youth Office' was sent to pastors. It was signed by Geoff Strelan and it is worth quoting some of it at length:

> Dear Pastor,
>
> This circular is intended to give you some basic information about "Jacob's Ladder"—the Coffee Lounge Counselling Centre opened in Adelaide recently. We trust that you will pass this information on to your members. The centre was opened for Lutheran patrons on September 5th, when a program designed to inform them about the aims and work of the Centre, and to encourage our young people to offer their services, was presented to about 110 people from all over Adelaide. For the next three weeks, the Centre will be open on Friday and Saturday nights. … During this period, we will be relying on Lutherans to patronise the Centre to give us a chance to correct faults in equipment, service and so on.
>
> **Aims:** "Jacob's Ladder" is primarily to be a place where contact with unchurched youth can be made. It was felt that a Coffee Lounge would be an effective setting for this (at least initially) as it allows staff and customers to mix freely. The aim is to get to know the young people personally and gradually to bring them to see their need of a Saviour. It is also hoped that the Centre will be a place where young Lutherans can meet to discuss and encourage one another in the faith.
>
> **Methods:** All work will be done voluntarily by Lutheran Youth (including the entertainment). Workers will serve as kitchen helpers (preparing food and coffee), waiters and waitresses, or some as counsellors. Counsellors are asked to join counselling discussion groups under one of a number of pastors who have agreed to help in this way. Entertainment will be spiritually centred.

Regular prayer will continue in the room set aside for this purpose. There will always be a pastor on hand, readily available. The Police have also agreed to check occasionally on their nightly rounds. As a point of interest, the menu will be much the same as at an average Coffee Lounge, but the prices will be slightly reduced.

Relationship to Fellowships: It is hoped that "Jacob's Ladder" will help to provide a way in which fellowshippers can actively witness. We hope and are confident that those who work in the Centre will be taking more active parts in their local Fellowships and congregations as a result of their work at the Centre.

Finances: Our initial expenses in establishing the Centre (equipment, rent etc) will be close to $1,500. At present we have had to rely on loans and some donations. Before the end of this month we need further loans totalling $500. Eventually the Centre will pay for itself. You may care to mention our needs to anyone whom you feel may be interested in supporting our work.

The vision had become reality. The prayers, hopes and hard work of many had reached their initial goal. The doors were open. God's blessing was evident in so many ways. Now the Holy Spirit sent us on a journey that none of us could have anticipated. We look back on some of the early joys and challenges in the next chapter.

JACOB'S LADDER COFFEE LOUNGE 1970-1973

Up and Running

One of the surviving documents from that time is the *Jacob's Ladder Manager's Report Book 3/3/1972 to 13/10/1973*. The coffee lounge opened most Friday and Saturday evenings with a team of workers and one or more managers responsible for overseeing the operation. Those managers recorded their thoughts on the volunteer staff and significant happenings through the evening. Among the managers in the time covered by this Manager's Report book are Milton Eckermann, Neil Geer, Larry Krieg, Malcolm Pech, Peter Bean, Karl Brettig, Manfred Jusaitis, Doug Vogelsang, Steen Olsen (aka 'me'), Glenn Schultz, Maurie Richter, Judi Schultz, Richard Reedy, Leonore Schubert and Chris Rothe. Volunteer staff from that period who later became leaders in the Jacob's Ladder/Servants of Christ Community include Stephen Haar, Peter Schubert, Marty Rosenberg and Anne Sellers.

Each evening the coffee house staff were assigned roles in the kitchen, waiting on tables, or as 'counsellors'. The counsellors and managers, when not otherwise occupied, spent their time talking with those who came to the coffee lounge. The manager's book records some significant conversations. The first duty of managers was to read the reports from previous nights if they had not been present. That way counsellors could be assigned to follow up with regular customers, even if the person they last talked with was not there.

As mentioned above, in the very early days many of the staff were drawn from Lutheran youth groups and most of the customers were also Christian young people. That soon changed and a more experienced volunteer staff team formed. With more and more 'street' kids, outlaw bikies, drug addicts and eastern freaks in attendance, Jakes was often not a safe environment for young and inexperienced youth fellowship members. We needed to make reports to the police on more than one occasion. David Graebner quotes one parent, "I'm not letting my daughter work at Jacob's Ladder any more. The wrong sort of people are going there."

Geoff Strelan recalls:

> The problems with difficult street kids was present already in the early days. There were times the police had to be called. I vividly remember the big, intimidating police officer who arrived a couple times to sort out the threatening situations. A couple times we had to delay opening. I remember Karl getting whacked on the forehead down on the landing, and the stunned look on his face—in typical Karl fashion he just kept going!

David Graebner also reports that already by early 1971 unruly behaviour by drunk customers (some as young as 14 or 15) was a major problem. There had been fights and damage to property, and every night was rowdy. The friendly atmosphere disappeared and effective discussion became impossible. As a result anyone showing signs of intoxication was turned away (no small task) and the relaxed, informal environment was restored.

That is important, because as Graebner says, "In the relaxed atmosphere, it is usually quite easy for a counsellor to invite himself [or herself] to a table, join in or start a conversation." The sign at the door on the street said, "Christ—Conversation Coffee Jacob's Ladder." People knew it was a Christian coffee lounge. The customers were diverse. Graebner continues:

> Many are youngsters searching for meaning in life. Some of them look for satisfaction of their needs in their groups; some are lonely; some have stolen or used drugs and been in trouble with the police; many of them have problems with home, school or society; most are willing to talk and responsive to real friendship—Jacob's Ladder is where they get it.
>
> What other endeavour associated with the [Lutheran] Church in Australia offers such an opportunity to explain Jesus Christ to so many boys and girls prepared to listen, discuss and question? Making the most of this opportunity is a challenge which Jacob's Ladder has no intention of refusing.[5]

For those of us who were part of this in the early days, it was already beginning to shape our lives in Christ. It was a foundation that has served us well in our Christian lives and service. To quote David Graebner once again:

> A different form of success has come to Jacob's Ladder in a wonderful way. Many of the workers are finding that their faith is stronger, their enthusiasm is keener, their happiness in their faith is more zestful, and their confidence

---

5 David Graebner, **Christ Conversation Coffee**, The Lutheran, (9 August 1971), 21.

JACOB'S LADDER COFFEE LOUNGE 1970–1973

in facing up to life is more abundant. They are going to their Bibles and to prayer with lively purpose; in the confident expectation God will supply their answers and the strength they need. Whatever they give to Jacob's Ladder is returning multiplied to them.[6]

Already in the first year of operation, some workers had opened their homes to troubled young people. Some were visited in prison. It was hard work. Many worked at Jakes from 7.30pm–1.30am after a day at work or study. Graebner also stated that Jacob's Ladder needed a full-time worker. The committee was working towards this. It was finally achieved more than two years later. Graebner concludes, "Jacob's Ladder Coffee Lounge, born of faith and nourished by hard work in the power of God, is here to stay."

Anne Sellers also recalls the early days when she was secretary of the Warradale Lutheran Youth Group:

> I remember volunteering at the Jacob's Ladder Coffee House with youth from Warradale and other congregations from around the Adelaide metro area. ... I remember preparing food in the kitchen and serving it. There was music and interesting people, including cute boys. I was a teenager, in high school. Jacob's Ladder was the most interesting part of my life. Jacob's Ladder leaders had a sense of purpose, and were actively seeking ways to reach out to non-Christians. There was an effort to do more than entertain the church youth. There was a sense of activism in the city in the early 1970s. The Vietnam War was a focus and many young people including my cousin were protesting in the streets. Young people were looking for new ways of thinking, of government, of living, of being. Jacob's Ladder Coffee House offered a focus to reach out to people, and to make a difference. St Stephens Lutheran Church partnered with Jacob's Ladder and I remember attending youth services at St Stephens. I participated in a musical group called Sing Out. We rehearsed, we prayed, we sang, we travelled to perform concerts, and along the way, we formed caring relationships. I felt safe. I enjoyed friendships and picnics featuring watermelon.

Reports from the Time

The surviving Manager's book begins half a year after David Graebner's article in *The Lutheran*. It reports many incidents, both good and bad. Here is a sampling from 1972–73:

---

6   ibid., 23.

1972

Fri 17/6   Very quiet night on the whole. … Steen's "good news" was ripped up. Bibles being used more.

Fri 23/6   Started late (8.30–8.40) due to a lack of workers. Started with 8. About 6 more arrived during the night following emergency calls to LTC and the Girls' Hostel.

Sat 1/7   The response to the "purple letter" brought many workers to the coffee lounge—approx. 35 workers. Hence all could not be utilised fully as the evening was rather quiet. It appears many were able to chat with many of the folk and some serious discussion took place. A few new contacts made.

Sat 28/10   Evening began very quietly—our twenty-odd workers outnumbered customers. At about 9.30pm Neil and Judi took two pairs to canvas in the streets. Nev, Steve and Chris also went street witnessing and counselling. Dejected truckie walked out with a grin on his face and a Bible under his arm.

Sat 18/11   Quiet night. Leonore and Steen walked the street—Bill a Greek chap came back with us. Some difficulty with language.

Fri 24/11   S's[7] gang smashed a hole in a wall on the landing.
Several interesting newcomers. Revd Zinnbauer brought in a girl who was searching.

Sat 2/12   Judi, Bev and Chris walked the street early in the evening. Evening disrupted greatly by T.

Fri 8/12   Karl talked seriously with R + G. They wish to receive Jesus. We are out of pocket New Testaments. They are proving popular.

Sat 9/12   T and gang were present but well controlled by Doug (a lot of noise though). A visit by Christian police officers very helpful. Prayer circle met.

Sat 23/12   Exceptionally good number of workers. Sent out eight in pairs. Good results—8 contacts. T and gang playful. No bad trouble. Some spiritual progress with gang members.

---

[7] Some names have been abbreviated to protect the guilty.

JACOB'S LADDER COFFEE LOUNGE 1970-1973

1973

Sat 27/1 Pastor Ern Heyne came in to look us over and was impressed with the effort but disappointed with the number of regulars. Closed the door at 1am when we had sold nearly everything.

Sat 10/2 Turned out to be one of the busiest nights on record for quite a while. The lounge was full from about 10pm and several customers had to stand and wait before finding seats. Counselling for the night was reasonably active.

Difficult Customers

1973

Fri 16/3 Quite a night. Even our wealth of talent found it difficult to cope. T's boys upended two fire extinguishers.

Fri 23/3 T was downstairs but never came in. As arranged three plain clothes police dropped in at about 10.30. They stayed for 20 minutes and were very helpful. It was arranged for them to drop in from time to time. None of the gangs were in at the time but the word spread.

Sat 24/3 Tonight was the climax and culmination of the problems with T and his gang. Mally was assaulted as T2 was preparing to hurl a fire extinguisher across the coffee lounge. A round table discussion of managers (including Milton) decided that charges should be laid against four people, which was done later in the evening.

Fri 30/3 The complaint against T & Co had not yet been followed up by the police. They arrived drunk and tried to assault a customer. Steen asked them to leave and thought it advisable to tell them charges had been laid. T then hit Steen three times and tore his shirt (No structural damage to Steen, but there was to a toilet door). They returned later and Steen was again assaulted. Police had been called but only arrived after the gang had left. They suggested we talk with CIB once again, which Steen did on Saturday morning. The Police thought that in view of all the circumstances additional charges should be laid. This was done. The gang would be rounded up that afternoon. If any came to the coffee lounge that evening the CIB mobile crime squad should be called. Finished night with a prayer circle debrief with workers.

Up and Running // 15

Fri 6/4   T came and sent up a message asking Steen to come down to the street to talk with him. He went down and explained why the action had been taken. T said he understood. His parting words are worth recording, "I guess I have learned my lesson."

Sat 7/4   No visit from CIB during the evening and no disturbances. However, there appeared to be a lot of serious talking going on at various tables.

Sat 14/3   Talked with P (one of T's gang) for quite a while. Was still rather mad at Steen—or seemed so at first, but after talking it seems he is more puzzled as to why Steen is willing to give him a character reference after laying the complaint with the police.

Fri 27/4   P came in and approached Steen and said he bore no grudges. He asked if Steen would be at court on Tuesday and was assured he would be. P said that he had learned his lesson but that T had not.

That was all from the Manager's book. I attended court with T & his gang. Since it was Children's Court their duty lawyer needed to ask the magistrate for permission for me to be present as a support person. The magistrate asked my name, looked down, and then said, "But you made the complaint." I said, "Yes, I did." He smiled slightly and allowed me to stay. Doug Vogelsang talked with them on the Friday and wrote the following comments in the Manager's Book:

Both Ts [yes there are two of them in T's gang] were good. I chatted with them and also took them home. Both appreciated Steen being in Court and all that he said and did for them—this appreciation was really genuine. Both lads said they slept very badly the Monday evening before going to Court. T2 told me his father said he would smash his head in if he ever got into trouble again. Both boys said we would not have any more trouble with them in the future.
... Steen's action makes him a 'good guy' as far as T and T goes.

No more trouble? If only! I have recorded these incidents at some length since I was the manager primarily involved and therefore have some memory of it as well as the written record. There were many other difficult times with other individuals and groups, but through them the Spirit worked to build relationships that managed to survive the hard calls we sometimes needed to make. While punches were thrown at times and furniture

JACOB'S LADDER COFFEE LOUNGE 1970–1973

flew across the room, for the most part, by the grace of God, we were able to handle the situations and keep talking.

The Observations of an Outsider

As mentioned already, the access to the coffee lounge was by two narrow staircases to the second floor, with a landing halfway, so the name Jacob's Ladder was apt and memorable. The location in the city centre, just one block off Rundle Mall was ideal. There were other similar Christian ventures in Adelaide including the One Way Coffee Lounge in Hindley Street, sponsored by the Assemblies of God, and the One Way Inn in Melbourne Street North Adelaide, both of which began in January 1973.[8]

During this time, Greg Box did a study of drop-in centres in Adelaide, which was published by the *Service to Youth Council Inc* early in 1974. He reported on his two visits to Jacob's Ladder:

> I called at 'Jakes' on two occasions between June and July, staying for approximately an hour or so on each visit. The centre is appropriately named because of the large, steep flight of stairs needed to reach the entrance.
>
> Similarly to the Hindley Street One-way Centre, Jacob's Ladder has a high worker-user ratio in order that individuals or groups of individuals can be met and made feel welcome shortly after their arrival. The centre is spacious, carpeted and has seating and table arrangements to cater for 80 or more people. The interior was warmly lit and background music added to the relaxing atmosphere of the centre.
>
> On my first visit, I mainly just sat and chatted at a table with Karl Brettig, my original contact. On both occasions, it was not long after groups of people (mainly teenagers) had taken their seats, that they were met and engaged in friendly, yet meaningful conversation with individual workers. It was obvious, however, that there was a large proportion of regular users at the centre on the two occasions when I visited.
>
> On my second visit, sitting by myself and just drinking coffee, I was met by one of the workers who sat and chatted with me for some time about the aims and nature of her work at the centre.
>
> I had arrived early when I called the second time and prior to opening at approximately 8.30pm, the group, led by one of the workers, held a small

---

8   Greg Box, ***Drop In Centres***, Service to Youth Council Inc, Parkside SA (March 1974), 14–15.

session during which there was prayer and a small discussion from a passage in the Bible. The group of seven or eight workers were only in their late teens and although they seemed somewhat apprehensive about their night's work, showed that they were very enthusiastic.[9]

Box grouped Jakes together with the two one-way centres mentioned above. He noted that there were few rules except that alcohol and drugs were not to be brought onto the premises. He said that while there was no pressure on people to converse with a staff member, they were approached when they arrived, welcomed, and offered conversation. Customers who returned numbers of times were generally looking for someone to talk with about their needs. He concluded this summary by saying:

> All three centres see God as the ultimate need for individuals, regardless of their particular problems, but all are quick to recognise that problems of a serious nature ... are best met with the added assistance of specialised bodies and in this way they also see that they have a role in referring people.[10]

Summary

During the 'coffee lounge' phase of Jacobs Ladder, which lasted until the end of 1973, there were no paid staff and we were open only on Friday and Saturday evenings. Gradually a fairly stable 'workforce' formed. When new workers arrived they started in the kitchen. Some saw that as their calling. Others moved on to waiting on tables and if they showed aptitude in relating to our customers, and had a reasonably in-depth understanding of the Christian faith, they might become counsellors and eventually managers, if that was also their gifting and call.

Volunteers needed to order and store food and drink each week and to keep the premises, including the kitchen, clean. The menu included coffee, tea, hot chocolate, 'spiders' and toasted sandwiches as well as other long forgotten items. After the coffee lounge closed for the night, the cleaning needed to be done and there was often a team meeting to debrief. It was not unusual for workers to only get home after 2am. I started sleeping to late mornings on weekends and attending Sunday evening worship services.

There were also many times when we provided additional contact and support for our customers during the week. The need for paid staff had been identified early on. Already by the end of 1972, this had gained some momentum and negotiations had begun.

---

9 Greg Box, **Drop In Centres**, Service to Youth Council Inc, Parkside SA (March 1974), 42–43.

10 ibid., 22–23.

JACOB'S LADDER COFFEE LOUNGE 1970-1973

The Partnership with St Stephen's

As previously mentioned, the need for paid staff was recognised in the earliest days of Jacob's Ladder. Already in August 1971 David Graebner wrote:

> To make the most of its follow-up work and to widen its outreach, there can be no doubt that Jacob's Ladder needs a full-time worker. To the committee, this is more than just a nice idea. It is a real goal that they are beginning to work towards.[11]

At the beginning, Jacob's Ladder Coffee Lounge was managed by a committee appointed by the Lutheran Youth of South Australia Metro South Zone, comprised of the youth director Pastor Ted Prenzler, representatives of the South and North LYSA Zones, ET Dutschke as the business manager, Milton Eckermann as the personnel manager and Geoff Strelan as the program manager. The Metro South Zone had assumed full legal and financial responsibility on the 10th May 1970.

On the 14th October 1970 the Metro South Zone added Roger Burger as chair, Neil Geer from the Metro South Zone and David Kaesler of the Metro North Zone, Laurie Hartwig from the Lutheran Publishing House and Jenny Strelan as secretary. Others who attended meetings included Robin Stelzer from the 'old' committee, Monica Christian representing the kitchen, and Anne Zweck who was in charge of ordering supplies.

The committee worked well in those days because most of the members were regularly involved in the ministry. The outreach ministry was blessed and the need for a fulltime worker grew more urgent as each month rolled by. A request for such a worker was made to the LCA SA District Church Council. Many discussions took place. St Stephen's Lutheran Church, Wakefield Street, Adelaide got involved and embraced the opportunity. In late 1972, their newsletter reported:

> *Associate Pastor/Youth Worker to replace Deaconess at St Stephen's*
>
> Deaconess Ruth Presser [later Ruth Olsen], who has faithfully served St Stephen's on a part-time basis for the last two years, will terminate her services here at the end of January, since she has accepted a call to Brisbane. Coinciding with this announcement, the District Church Council has given the green light to the proposal for St Stephen's to call an Associate

---

11 David Graebner, **Christ Conversation Coffee**, The Lutheran, (9 August 1971), 21.

Pastor/Youth Worker. It is anticipated that the associate pastor will spend about 25% of his time assisting in the regular ministry of the congregation, while the rest of his time will be focused on special youth ministry centred on the activities of Jacob's Ladder. He will be expected to spearhead a ministry to the unchurched youth of Adelaide, but he will also try to involve members of the congregation in this ministry. In other words, his special youth ministry is not to be considered a mere appendage to the ministry of the congregation, but an integral part of the congregation's outreach. Every congregation has the responsibility to reach out with the saving Gospel of Jesus Christ, and a full-time youth worker should assist in making this outreach work more effective.

Terms of Reference

On the 22nd August 1972, St Stephen's Lutheran Church in Wakefield Street, Adelaide, had adopted terms of reference for an associate pastor / youth worker. (See footnote p. 42.) This pastor was to be called by St Stephens from nominations put forward by a committee, with equal representation from the congregation, the SA District of the Lutheran Church and the Jacob's Ladder Management Committee. As stated above, it was expected that 25% of his time would be spent in 'regular' congregational work, and 75% in youth mission outreach. Other key points from these terms of reference include:

- ▶ The congregation would appoint a Youth Ministry Committee to "plan, guide and supervise his activities and to be concerned with the well-being of his person and work." This may include representatives of other groups who have an interest in the work.

- ▶ As a general rule, he would preach once a month in the morning and 2–3 times a month at the evening service.

- ▶ He was to work closely with the pastor of the congregation in areas such as youth fellowships and pastoral care, but all with a focus on youth evangelism.

JACOB'S LADDER COFFEE LOUNGE 1970-1973

- His work with Jacob's Ladder was to be "conducted as an integral part of the ministry of St Stephen's congregation".

- Specifically he was to provide "spiritual assistance to the leaders and workers of Jacob's Ladder Coffee Lounge"; "work among the unchurched young people of Adelaide, especially those who visit Jacob's Ladder"; and "work among young Lutherans, living and working in the city, who are not attached to a city or suburban congregation."

The budget for this joint position for 1974 was proposed to be $6,453, [c.$62,000 in 2020] including a less-than-commercial amount for rent of the manse, which had been bought by St Stephen's. This was divided up between a number of bodies:

Jacob's Ladder	24.8%
St Stephen's	21.7% + rental subsidy
Lutheran Youth of South Australia	6.2%
St John's, Unley	1.5%
Lutheran Church, SA District	45.8%

Each of these groups was asked to consider if they could contribute more. This was a significant financial commitment by all parties. The contribution required from Jacob's Ladder was above and beyond our other costs.

Rex Lohmeyer reports:

> Following several [3] unsuccessful calls, a call was issued to Pastor Doug Kuhl [on 1 April 1973], who at the time was located at Swan Hill, Vic. Pastor Kuhl accepted the call, and was duly inducted into our church on 13 January 1974. St Stephen's pastor at the time was Kevin Schmidt. St Stephen's also purchased the manse at Vine Street, Klemzig for Pastor Kuhl and his family.[12]

Geoff Strelan remembers:

> I found God's timing in this very significant. As we started working at Jakes we quickly became aware that no lives were going to be changed unless the Holy Spirit was at work. We began to have Bible studies on the Holy Spirit. I remember we even invited a Pentecostal guy to speak to us (shock horror!) and a hunger to know the Holy Spirit grew in us. Unknown to us, at that time Doug Kuhl in Swan Reach had experienced an infilling with the Spirit and so came to us bringing that understanding and teaching. That became a point of tension in the relationship between the LCA and Jakes.

---

12 Rex Lohmeyer, *Jacob's Ladder Retrospective*, The Messenger, St Stephens Lutheran Church, Wakefield Street, Adelaide, vol 60 no. 4 (July/August 1998), 5.

Working with the McNally Training Centre[13]

During this time new mission opportunities were embraced, including visiting the young inmates and leading worship services at the McNally Training Centre. The relationship developed because some of our customers found themselves detained at McNally from time to time. It was therefore an extension of the Coffee Lounge ministry. Leonore Schubert asked:

> Is it a waste of time to hold services at the McNally Training Centre and to talk with the guys there? It's a matter of attitudes: some see them as no-good kids and not worth bothering with, while others see them as potential members of Christ's kingdom and part of the church's untapped resource.

At first, I felt afraid of these kids but I soon found that apart from their gang, they are lonely and insecure. More than anything, they want love and attention. ... Join us every 2nd Sunday of the month at 11am at McNally. If you can't make it then please pray for us. If anyone is able to open their home for a weekend for one of these guys, then it is very much appreciated, especially by those whose families are no longer interested in them. Ask a manager for details.

A letter of thanks was received from the Institutional Missions Committee of the LCA SA District (IMC):

> Recently the IMC met with the various chaplains under its control to hear their reports and discuss their work. Mr Heyne told us of the very fine help he is receiving from the youth of Jacob's Ladder at the McNally Training Centre. The IMC wishes to convey thanks to all those youth who have given their time and energy in service of their Lord by helping those at McNally. You can be assured that the Church and Chaplain appreciate your efforts of the past and look forward to continued support in the future. With every good wish in your Christian endeavours, Hedley Krieg (Sec, IMC).[14]

Beyond the Coffee Lounge Walls

In the September 1973 *Jacob's Ladder Newsletter* Doug Vogelsang wrote of the home visiting that had been done:

---

13   The McNally Training Centre opened at Magill in 1967 in new buildings on the site of the Boys' Reformatory, Magill. Run by the government, it provided secure care for boys aged 15 to 18 sentenced by the Juvenile Court for committing offences. Younger boys were sent to Brookway Park. In the 1970s McNally also took in boys on remand. In 1979 the McNally Training Centre became the South Australian Youth Training Centre.

14   *Jacob's Ladder Newsletter* (November–December 1973), 6.

JACOB'S LADDER COFFEE LOUNGE 1970-1973

Young people 'off the streets' and others over the past three years have had the opportunity to come to Jacob's Ladder and talk over specific areas of concern and conflict in their lives. Counsellors and other committed Christian young people have sat down and listened to many young people from all walks of life, giving witness to their faith in Christ.

Perhaps for some Jacob's Ladder is just a few hours each Friday and Saturday night. It cannot be denied that much good, by God's grace and with his blessing, can be done in these hours. But I may be voicing the feeling of some workers at Jacob's Ladder when I say that wonderful opportunities are open to us when we are able to visit the homes of some of the contacts made at Jacob's Ladder and meet them on their home ground. To sit down with people in their own homes, in the billiard hall or anywhere else and talking with them, gaining their confidence outside Jacob's Ladder. The opportunity to talk with parents and brothers and sisters often places many things in their right perspective.

After Jacob's Ladder! What? Throws out a big challenge! We are fortunate in having a site, which acts as a nucleus for our outreach work. People come to Jacob's Ladder for various reasons, and this is good, but when we move out amongst them, perhaps causing us inconvenience, we grow in a more genuine concern for people. ...

We have to be geared up for this outreach work, especially when Pastor Doug Kuhl comes to Adelaide to work with us. Note that he will work with us, not for us. One man cannot visit hundreds of young people but a team of workers from Jacob's Ladder can. Will you take one contact under your care?[15]

Ministry Developments

By the end of 1973, it was reported that Jacob's Ladder had introduced fairly regular use of Christian singers and singing groups, as well as film and sound presentations of Christ, into the coffee lounge. Broadsheets [locally produced tracts] and pub and jail visits were being used. A call also went out for anyone interested in forming a drama group or singing in the street. All were indications of things to come.

The January 1974 edition of *Jacob's Ladder Newsletter* was obviously published before Pastor Doug's installation on the thirteenth—it advertises the event, rather than reporting on it. The editorial is almost prophetic in places:

---

15 ***After Jacob's Ladder What?***, *Jacob's Ladder Newsletter* (September 1973), 2.

> All that will be done at Jacob's Ladder, no matter what form the outreach programme will take, must be firmly and confidently placed in Christ's hands. He alone will guide us along the path we are to take. This does not mean that we must sit with prayer-clasped hands and breathe deep sighs of yearning and not budge from this position. We all must be up and doing and up and saying. Our hands and elbows must get dirty, our knees bruised, our feet become sore, sweat must break out on our brows, and our lives must show an even greater witness to the Christ of Christmas—New Year—Easter; the Christ for all people of all time.
>
> Together with Christ, we take up Jacob's Ladder's work with renewed vigour and dedication. … We must lift our horizons to new challenges and ideas; to innovations and perhaps radical schemes (in the eyes of the establishment). …
>
> Christ wants to reach the lives of so many people here in little old Adelaide, through us. Christ will use us. Christ will open areas of concern. Christ will close doors for us and then open new ones. As workers at Jacob's Ladder we go forward into 1974 with Christ as the helmsman of our life and let him lead us wherever he will. We must bury our egos and hang-ups and self-created images and let him take over. We put our lives totally in his hands, especially in this Jacob's Ladder work.
>
> The Holy Spirit will breathe into our lives new power to be daily born anew, to take up new challenges through prayer and trust in him.[16]

Looking Forward

Under the heading *Excitement—Weakness—Urgency* the same writer, this time using the initials K.B. writes:

> It is exciting to think what the Lord would have us do in 1974 at Jacob's Ladder. During the past three and a half years he has shown us many things and above all uncovered our many weaknesses as his children. We have learnt to come to him for guidance, to trust him and obey his directions for the building of his kingdom. Yet there are still many times when we fail him—we certainly do not deserve the love and grace he continues to give us. There are however, things he has taught us and as we look forward to 1974 it is our prayer that we would remember and act on them—because there are just as many people right here in Adelaide in so much trouble and confusion because they do not know the Father through Jesus Christ. …

---

16   Karl Brettig, *Jacob's Ladder Newsletter*, (January 1974), 2.

JACOB'S LADDER COFFEE LOUNGE 1970–1973

CHAPTER 3

What is Jacob's Ladder's future in 1974? It is a place, or rather a community of Christians, which provides an avenue for you to serve the Lord in special areas of ministry to both brothers and sisters in Christ and more specifically to those who do not know Jesus Christ. We are looking forward to having Doug Kuhl among us in 1974, and we are looking forward to your involvement.[17]

And so, the stage was set for the next phase of this community that had simply come to be known as *Jakes*.

What did the Holy Spirit have in store for us?

---

17 ibid., 3–4.

CHAPTER 4: Expanded Premises and Vision

Geoff Turner (Scrooge)

1974 brought many changes to Jacob's Ladder. In partnership with St Stephen's Lutheran Church, Wakefield Street, Adelaide we installed Pastor Doug Kuhl. At the same time we accepted the offer of our landlord to double our floor area, opening up new possibilities for ministry and mission. An archway near the street joined the two spaces. Along the way the name changed from *Lounge* to *House*. A small thing, but also one that indicated new things.

Writing in *Lutheran Student* in March 1974, Karl Brettig described what happened.

> A hole in the northern wall of the 102 Gawler Place premises revealed a nicely done-out section of large rooms; right next door... Since then amateur carpenters, painters, designers, sloggers and foremen have set to work. A pretty expensive sound system has arrived and a resource library of books, magazines, tapes and records is beginning to form. A media workshop is in the offing (actually, it is to be at the back of the new area). But that is just by the way, the real vision for the house has to do with people. I guess the physical environment of the place is fairly important. Kids and others shouldn't feel threatened by bright lights and gleaming cultural baggage. They need to feel at home if they want to become a part of the family—and I guess that is about the vision of the place. A family centred around Jesus and his good news—a loving and caring community of Christians giving out his light and being the salt of his earth to the alienated people around Adelaide. Sounds quite simple but the implications are really heavy.[18]

The Coffee Lounge, which had only opened on Friday and Saturday evenings, was being transformed into a Coffee House that was also a Drop-in Centre, open during the week. As well as the resource and media centres mentioned by Karl, there were offices for workers and private spaces for conversations. Change happened very

---

18 Karl Brettig. *Jacob's Ladder—A New Foundation*, Lutheran Student Vol 1/1 (March 1974), 20–21.

JACOB'S LADDER COFFEE HOUSE 1974

quickly. More people got involved and relationships in the community deepened yet again. The vision expanded as opportunities presented themselves. Yet the vision, in one sense, also remained the same as that proposed by the Dorian Society in 1970. It is worth repeating the quote from their newsletter of September that year, where we read:

> Perhaps our Coffee Lounge at first would attract mainly Lutheran youth, but its main purpose should be as a mission outreach to young people who are looking for somewhere to go, where they can find more meaning in life, or just where they feel that people are concerned about them.

An Additional Worker

A major emphasis in the community during the last months of 1973 was that Pastor Doug was coming to work with us, not for us. The September 1973 *Jacob's Ladder Newsletter* anticipates this:

> Jacob's Ladder is planning to expand its activities in the future. Pastor Doug Kuhl will be arriving after Christmas to work with us. If you have any ideas for other activities and programmes we could be engaged in—in fact if you have any ideas at all—please see the managers. One final thought—this is going to cost money!!! Can we do it???? [Emphasis in the original]

Pastor Doug Kuhl arrived from Swan Hill with his wife Erna and their three young children, Heidi, Ingrid and Kurt. His installation at St Stephens was at 10am on the 13th January 1974. I was busy with other things at the time, in New Zealand introducing a lovely young woman to my parents and siblings, so I have no memory of the event. Nor have I found others who can recall the day with any clarity.

However, the St Stephen's February 1974 newsletter included a report by Senior Pastor Kevin Schmidt on the installation and the early days of Pastor Doug's ministry:

> Looking to the Future: We look to the future with a great deal of confidence and expectation, since the Lord has both led and enabled us to expand our ministry at St Stephen's through the acceptance by Pastor D Kuhl of the Call to become our associate pastor/youth worker. Pastor Kuhl was inducted into his office on January 13 in the presence of a congregation numbering 330. Many members may not yet realise the full significance of this move, but I am convinced that it is the most significant thing that has happened in St Stephen's for many years. The new ministry may not result in a sudden great increase in membership, but it will result in a new thrust in the direction of

the congregation's ministry, and I trust, in the increasing involvement of the congregation in this ministry.

St Stephen's has a commendable record of mission interest and support. Members have always generously and ungrudgingly supported mission projects in Central Australia and New Guinea as well as helping in suburban missions. Many of our members have gone to serve on mission fields. However, we now face a new challenge; the mission on our own doorsteps! Supporting this mission may be less comfortable than supporting one hundreds of miles away, for we will get involved—perhaps more deeply than our present level of commitment to Christ would wish, but I am sure this is the challenge of the day. The Lord surely is calling upon each one of us to go and work in his vineyard and this we will be able to do by personal interest in and support of this new ministry that is now our great opportunity.

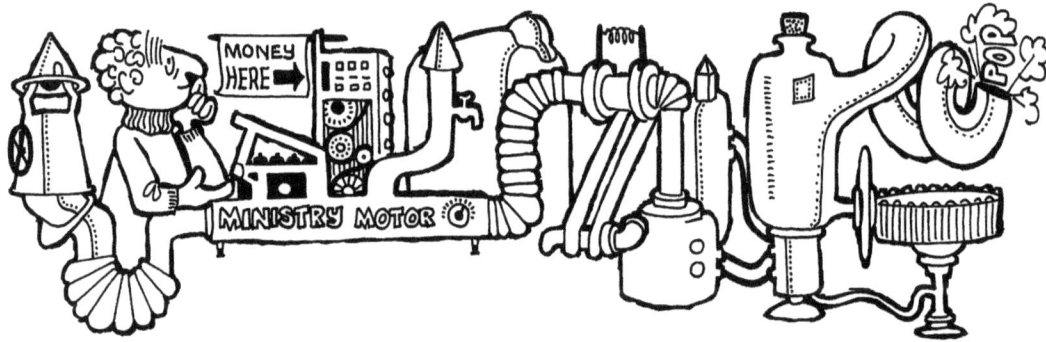

Some remarkable things have happened since Pastor Kuhl's induction, such as the sudden availability of additional space at 102 Gawler Place for the enlargement of Jacob's Ladder to include an activity centre for youth as well as an anonymous donation of $2,500 to underwrite the rental for the first year. [c.$24,000 in 2020]

May God continue to bless St Stephen's with members who will willingly serve the Lord, dedicating not only their time, talents and treasures to him, but by first giving themselves to the Lord.

Yours in Christ Jesus,
Kevin J Schmidt.[19]

The importance of the willingness of the St Stephen's congregation to embrace this new venture should not be underestimated. It required faith, courage and the

---

19 Kevin Schmidt, **The Messenger**, St Stephens Lutheran Church, Wakefield Street, Adelaide (February 1974).

JACOB'S LADDER COFFEE HOUSE 1974

investment of significant resources. As Kevin said, that has been seen again and again in their history. They don't just talk the talk, they walk the walk. In more recent times that has included hosting a Sudanese ministry and integrating a worshipping Chinese community into their congregation, as well as including a season of creation in their worship calendar and working towards the full integration of the ministry of women in the life of the Church. Without the support of St Stephen's and the South Australian District of the Lutheran Church, including the youth, much of that which followed would not have happened. Jacob's Ladder could not have called a pastor on their own; not financially, nor under the rules of the LCA.

As we will see, it did not work out quite as the late Pastor Kevin had anticipated, and there was a parting of the ways in our relationship with St Stephen's after just one year, no doubt causing much hurt and confusion. St Stephen's undoubtedly did not "get their money's worth" and would have had reason to complain, but they played an essential role in birthing a ministry that would bless many.

A Renewed Vision for Mission

If the change during the first two months of 1974 was far reaching, then the changes that occurred during March proved to be revolutionary. That is the subject of the next chapter, but it was already foreshadowed in late 1973. Karl Brettig writes of a meeting held at the Nunyara Chapel, Belair where about thirty people gathered

> to hear from three interstate brothers who had been involved in a Christian happening in the streets of Canberra—called "Kairos 1973". The aim was to get Eastern States brothers and sisters together to see whether the different communities could work together for Christ. It worked fairly well, they told us. It was decided to go ahead with something similar during the Adelaide Festival of Arts in March 1974 and a festival of street culture was born. In a couple of meetings that followed, some of its aims and areas were discussed and a coordinating committee has been convened. Some of the possible happenings in the air at this stage are such things as street drama, music, crafts, broadsheets, Jesus festival marches etc. For Jacob's Ladder it will probably mean a step up from what we plan on doing anyway with the possibility of opening on most nights during the festival. This will require lots of people and suggestions from you are welcome.[20]

Were we ready? Not by a long shot. We were young and inexperienced. What we lacked in maturity and wisdom, we made up for in confidence. Not exactly a recipe

---

20 Karl Brettig, **Climbing Jacob's Ladder**, Jacob's Ladder Newsletter (January 1974), 3.

for a great future! However, the Spirit of God was at work. Jesus was doing a new/old thing and in spite of our weaknesses and failings, great things were about to happen. In a recent letter Pastor Doug spoke for the rest of us as well, when he wrote:

> A young Lutheran Pastor was called out of a country parish to come to Adelaide to walk amongst the Anti Viet Nam War Protest Movement, to debate with advocates of the free speech movements in the middle of Adelaide's Universities and also to live within the emerging Counter Culture. To say he was bewildered would be an understatement. ... This Pastor wounded, broken, untrained in the ways of Counter Culture Street Cred was now faced with the task of being a Pastor of the Good News of Jesus in the middle of a mess. He was out of his depth with only his very basic understanding of Jesus to cling to. ...
>
> This might have been a recipe for complete disaster, but for the pillar that stood in the middle of the Jacob's Ladder Camp. The Pillar was Jesus. He, Jesus, was actually there in the midst of Jacob's Ladder, but why would he choose to come into the middle of a mess like Jakes? I don't know, but only to say that Jesus is really real, and that just as the Scriptures describe him, he really does love the lost and lonely, even if it should kill him in doing so.
>
> As the gospel's picture him, he came and comes among the broken and wounded to bring his healing—healing of hearts, minds, souls, spirits, bodies and of past, of present and future—healing of relationships of families and broken friends—just as the Bible says he would do. So at the very heart of it all, Jesus now, here among us, is the story of Jakes.

After such significant changes in January 1974, perhaps a time of consolidation and careful planning was in order, to lay a solid foundation for the future. We might have thought that, but the Spirit of God had other ideas. One after another, new doors opened. Doors that we didn't even know existed.

The stage was set. The Spirit was at work and about to bring many gifted sisters and brothers from other places to walk with us for a short couple of weeks. We were never the same again.

JACOB'S LADDER COFFEE HOUSE 1974

The Kairos '74 Festival

CHAPTER 5

Near the beginning of 1976 I looked back on the events of two years earlier and wrote:

> During 1974 the ministry of Jacob's Ladder exploded. Initially the movement was slower—the area of the coffee house itself was enlarged ... training nights for workers were established and the ministry began to creep further out into the city. March saw us become the headquarters for Kairos '74, a nation-wide "Jesus People" happening in conjunction with the Adelaide Festival of Arts. In the space of two short weeks Jacob's Ladder was transformed. There were thirty new converts who looked to us and whom we had to nurture. We had another 80 positive contacts, and we had become known to a great number of people in Adelaide and beyond. Our coffee house was packed to capacity (up to 150 people) each night. A steady stream of people began to come to the centre during the week for counselling, friendship or other help.[21]

Christian Leaders and their teams had come from around Australia. John Smith from the *God's Squad* and *Truth and Liberation Concern* in Melbourne, Athol Gill from the *House of the Gentle Bunyip*, also in Melbourne, John Hirt and his surfie mates from the *House of the New World* in Sydney, and people from many other communities including *Teen Challenge* in Brisbane, *The Glebe Zoo* in Sydney, *The House of Freedom*, *Agape House* and *Theos Coffee Shop*; to name some of them.

The Program

Kairos '74 ran from the 9–16 March. A poster describes it as a 'Jesus Family Festival of Street Culture'. The program included:

Sun 10th 1.30pm Elder Park	Jesus Celebration
Fri 15th	Jesus Rock Concert
Sat 16th 11.30am	Street March
12.30pm	Rock Concert
Mon 11th–Wed 13th	University Rallies
Mon 11th–Fri 15th	High School Happenings

---

21 Steen Olsen, *The Growth of Jacob's Ladder Christian Community as a part of the Lutheran Church of Australia, South Australian District*, Forum 69 (May 1976), 5.

Each Day: Theatre, Music, Arts, Crafts and Witness Teams in shopping centres including the City, Tea Tree Plaza, Marion, Arndale and Clovercrest.

There were youth services with *Kindekrist* at St Stephens and Scots Church, concerts, plays, an art exhibition by Judith Heidenreich and much more.

Four Coffee Houses were listed as being open each evening from 8 o'clock: *Jacob's Ladder* in Gawler Place, *Scots Hall* in North Terrace, *Scripture Union* in Grenfell Street and *One Way* in Hindley Street.

Jacob's Ladder's contact details were then listed for those who wanted more information.

The News Media Prepared the Way

The Adelaide newspapers prepared the way with a number of articles in the weeks before Kairos '74. (My, how times have changed!) In one story, the afternoon daily tabloid The News, on 22nd February, with a large photo of God's Squad members Neil McRae, Kevin Smith and John Smith, the heading proclaimed, "God squad bikies will 'chase' converts". They wrote:

> A group of leather-jacketed Eastern States bikies will roar into Adelaide schools and campuses during the Festival of Arts in search of converts. About 12 members of the Melbourne-based God's Squad Christian bikie group would visit 20 schools and both Adelaide and Flinders Universities, their leader, 32-year-old Mr John Smith said when he flew in today. ...
> "Our members include ex-bikie outlaws, who would be well known on Police files, university students, teachers and kids from the street level, who have been drawn together within the bikie sub-culture by the need to help others," Mr Smith said. ... On their visits to SA schools, the bikies would hold group discussions with the children and give testimony of their own experience of rehabilitation through the Jesus Movement. Some 5,000 Jesus followers are expected to take part in the climax of the festival—a march of witness from Victoria Square through the city to Rymill Park on March 16.

On the next day the *Adelaide Advertiser*, with a photo that also included John Hirt, the heading was "Guerrilla love groups to assault Festival city." It said:

> "Urban guerrilla love groups" will take to the streets during the Adelaide Festival of Arts next month. Members of the Jesus Movement will launch a cultural and Christian assault, Kairos '74, on the city. ... Jesus people, the Rev John Hirt and Mr Kevin Smith of Melbourne, said on arrival in Adelaide

JACOB'S LADDER COFFEE HOUSE 1974

yesterday, "We give expression to our Christianity through our art forms." "A lot of the street theatre will be mime and comment about society." ... One of the Adelaide organisers of the Jesus Movement Festival programme, Mr Doug Kuhl, said about 3,000 members from SA and other States would take part. Mr Hirt said: "The Jesus family see themselves as catalysts in all levels of society working for human liberation. We don't just live for possessions or material values."

Taking the Festival to the People

A free newspaper was produced and distributed. In an article titled *Who are we? What are we doing?* Kairos '74 explained what it was all about:

> The people involved in these activities have come together from all over Australia to join with the brothers and sisters in Adelaide to share the truth about Jesus. You may see them on a street corner, at a bus stop, in one of the city's main streets, at a tertiary institution, at a High School or at a shopping centre. They may give you a paper, a broadsheet, a flower and a smile from a heart full of Jesus' incredible love. Many of them know what it is like to have been on drugs, or drunk on booze, or hung up on sex. They try to understand people—they accept them for what they really are—because that's what Jesus did!

> And they won't be just on the street but they will be in coffee houses each night working late—and they'll love every minute of what they are doing because they love God and are convinced God loves you! ...

> All through this week, if you meet any Jesus People, be as open as they are and let them share with you the love and Good News that burns in their hearts. Listen to what they have to say about Jesus' Life Style. Read the rest of this paper and give God a chance to speak to you. You may be pleasantly surprised!

The *Australian Church Record* of 2nd May 1974 reports that people came from interstate at their own expense:

> Most of the demonstrations were given by young people coming from interstate, many had made personal sacrifices in order to undertake the trip. One had been given the week off without pay, others had taken time off their annual holidays, and all paid their own travelling and accommodation expenses. Local young people also played an active part. ... The culmination was the Jesus March on the final day of the Adelaide Festival. On arrival

at Rymill Park the marchers gathered for a simple program of music and speakers, the main message coming from the Rev John Hirt of Sydney.[22]

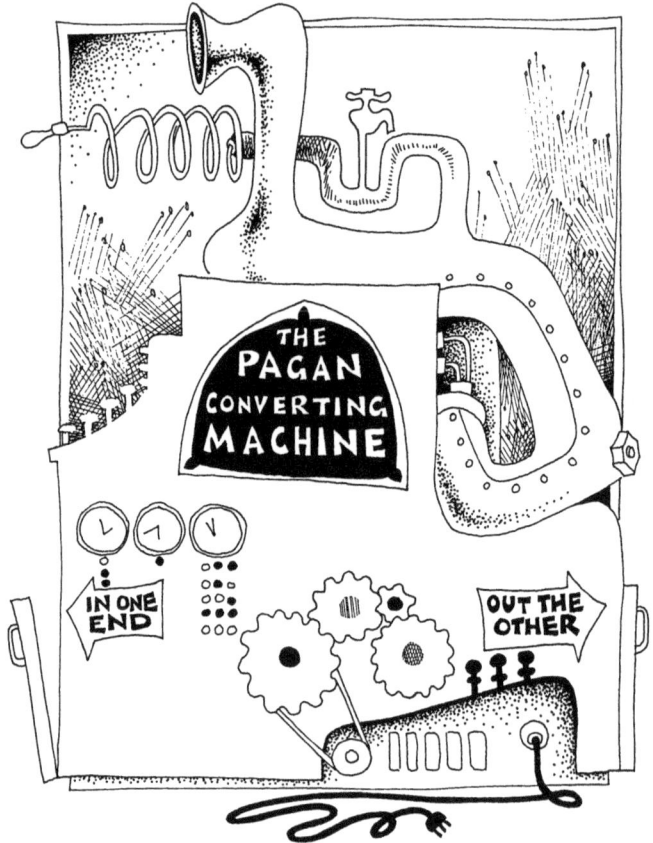

The Impact on Jacob's Ladder

This was an ecumenical city-wide (and indeed nation-wide) effort, but because Jacob's Ladder was centrally located with large premises, we became the hub, and many of those contacted on the streets came back there for further conversation and follow-up. After the two weeks the interstate visitors went home and others returned to their churches and ministries in different parts of the city. The new Christians and those with more questions kept coming to Jacob's Ladder. Now that is a great problem to have! But it did raise issues, because as someone once said, "The harvest is plentiful, but the workers are few." Yes, we prayed to the Lord of the harvest, and more workers were sent, but at times it would have been helpful to our well-being if they would have arrived before they were so desperately needed. [See Luke 10:2]

---

22 *Australian Church Record* Issue no. 1561, 8.

JACOB'S LADDER COFFEE HOUSE 1974

Reflecting on this I wrote:

> To meet the needs the existing small band of workers were cemented closer together and the formation of a community began in earnest. The pressure of such a ministry is intense, and in order to survive we needed to be a group of people who were deeply committed to the Lord and to each other. Those who had recently been converted needed to be part of such a community if they were to withstand the pressures to return to the street.[23]

Marty Rosenberg remembers:

> 1974 and the Kairos event had left the Jacob's Ladder members reeling with a huge influx of new Christians, and many visitors asking questions about Jesus and the church and so many other related topics. The coffee shop was buzzing each Friday and Saturday evening and discussions about these matters were becoming the norm.
>
> These visitors to Jakes were from all walks of life, but we tended to generalise one group by referring to them as being "off the street" or "street kids" and this was because many of them did not have very appealing places to stay overnight. They ranged from sleeping rough (a more current term), to couch surfing (another current term), to house sharing with others in pretty squalid conditions.
>
> It quickly became obvious, very early in 1974, that many of those who did make any sort of commitment to follow Jesus, soon reverted back to their old ways, simply because they had no support for their faith at "home". The need to nurture these babes in Christ more effectively, was fast becoming our next challenge, and the level of commitment that was needed suddenly escalated to involve our private lives in our homes.

Some would no doubt suggest that the new converts should be integrated into existing churches, just as people today suggest that those who come to faith in our schools should become members of neighbouring congregations. That doesn't work today and it didn't in the 1970s. The cultural gap is simply too great and, sadly, most congregations are not equipped to care for infants who yell a lot and mess their pants. Not that we were much better equipped, mind you, but at least we were out there with them and already part of their journey. It also became a journey for us. We had to unlearn some things and then learn many new things. Our students also became our teachers and that is one of the reasons why many of us look back

---

23 ibid., 5–6.

on Jacob's Ladder as a time that played a key role in shaping the rest of our lives of Christian ministry.

Reflecting on Kairos '74

The President of the Metro South Zone of the Lutheran Youth of South Australia [unnamed] commented on Kairos '74 in his report to the annual zone rally held on 25 April 1974. He said:

> Jacob's Ladder continues to be a challenging area of work where we constantly become aware of the need to trust in Jesus for his guidance. Kairos '74 made us painfully aware of our lack of knowledge and means of presenting the Gospel to 'kids' from off the street and also our lack of knowledge of God's Word. We can have an ultimate relationship with Jesus Christ, we can have a great deal of enthusiasm, but unless this is related to knowing who Jesus Christ is, what he has done for us, what God's Word has to say to me (us), we will not be able to share fully with other people. I am only asking those of you hearing this report to pray long and hard for the workers at Jacob's Ladder and Doug Kuhl who has God's responsibility of leading and guiding the workers.

Commenting on this report, Noel Hartwig wrote:

> Here there appears to be a rather heavy burden on the president… The Spirit is stirring something among the people of Jacob's Ladder, to the extent that a gross inadequacy is admitted. Deep reflection and searching, together with continual prayer is at the core of the report. Again Kairos '74, which brought the witness of people from all over Australia, is mentioned as the touchstone for this deep and heartfelt concern. The president pours out his heart.[24]

Kairos '74 was the decisive event that shaped much of what was to follow. It linked us with other ministries across Australia, many of whom were further down the track than we were. We were able to observe others witnessing to Jesus on the street. We heard how they addressed crowds in coffee houses and rallies. We saw how they organised prayer support. In short, we learned much about discipleship, not by attending courses or seminars, but through an intense—albeit very brief—apprenticeship. The boldest witnesses often included those who had most recently come to faith themselves. Someone who came to know Jesus one night might well be in the pub witnessing to mates the next. So they quickly became our teachers

---

24 Noel Hartwig, ***The Story of Jacob's Ladder***, unpublished Thesis (1978), 25. Accessed at Lutheran Archives, 25.

JACOB'S LADDER COFFEE HOUSE 1974

and helped us to understand how best to communicate with those who were not yet Christians.

The Ecumenical Issue

Kairos '74 also raised issues we needed to face. We engaged ecumenically, and allowed that to help shape us and think through our Lutheran convictions, at a time when our church was still railing against "sinful unionism". Less than a decade earlier, in 1966, the new Lutheran Church of Australia adopted as its founding document, The Theses of Agreement, which included, among many good things, Thesis II on Joint Prayer and Worship. This did not exclude prayer, fellowship and working with other Christians, but it was obviously something to be avoided. Joint prayer could not "under all circumstances be identified with unionistic prayer or church fellowship." At times it is "permissible" or cannot "be avoided" and has to be "endured". Sometimes it may be possible to join in such prayer "with a good conscience". It is summarised as follows:

> We agree to the general rule that Lutherans, pastors and lay people, should avoid services conducted by Churches not in fellowship of faith, since loyalty to Christ and obedience to his Word require a Christian to avoid promiscuous worship. ... Since much of this whole matter lies in the sphere of casuistics[25], something will have to be left to individual consciences. Care must, however, be taken not to create offence or to weaken the witness of the Church against sinful unionism.[26]

In 1976, the LCA General Synod adopted a statement that began, "In the exercise of their teaching function ... pastors of the LCA should not run counter to the letter and the spirit of the Thesis of Agreement."[27] If changes were needed the Theses were meant to be amended; which has never happened. However, in 1993 the LCA's Commission on Theology and Inter-Church Relations adopted a statement that tries to soften the original without actually amending it, but treating it as "an important historical document."[28] This pleased neither those who wanted to see

---

25 Odd wording. I guess it means something like 'it depends on circumstances from case to case'.

26 **Thesis II: Joint Prayer and Worship**, Articles 4+10, Theses of Agreement. LCA Doctrinal Statements and Theological Opinions (DSTO Volume IA).
Accessed at www.lca.org.au/departments/commissions/cticr on 14/08/2020.

27 **The Permanent Status of the Theses of Agreement**.
Accessed at www.lca.org.au/departments/commissions/cticr on 14/08/2020.

28 **Theses of Agreement II: Joint Prayer and Worship** (DSTO Volume IIA).
Accessed at www.lca.org.au/departments/commissions/cticr on 14/08/2020.

Thesis II strictly enforced; nor those who wanted to repent of it and move in a new direction.[29]

I have included considerable detail here because it is important to understand the controversies that follow in their original context. When Jacob's Ladder Coffee Lounge opened, all workers were required to be Lutheran. Against this background, it is easy to understand why Jacob's Ladder caused much angst in the Lutheran Church, especially after Kairos '74. There were some who wanted Jacob's Ladder to remain purely Lutheran (whatever that means). It was even suggested that if Jacob's Ladder was to leave the Lutheran Church, then Jacob's Ladder should be closed and its equipment sold and the money given back to the original donors, or at least that they be given the option of getting their money back. The other option canvased at the time, was essentially to let Jakes continue on its merry way, and that was what happened.[30] So, the story continued…

---

[29] It should be noted that the LCA is now a member of Australia's main ecumenical bodies and works extensively with other churches. We have also established formal written agreements on many topics with other denominations, especially in our ongoing dialogues with the Catholic, Uniting and Anglican Churches. I am currently the Lutheran co-chair of the Anglican-Lutheran Dialogue in Australia, and our Anglican colleagues say that over the last thirty years this has been the most productive of their various dialogues.

[30] *Report and appraisal from the Metro South Zone LYSA on the future structure of administration and aims of Jacob's Ladder* (28/11/1974).

JACOB'S LADDER COFFEE HOUSE 1974

New Ministries Emerge

During 1974 the Kerux Apostles Motorcycle Club had been formed, the first community nurture houses had been established, two extra full-time workers had been employed, a resource centre and library had been established, training and teaching programs had begun and the community had been restructured with its own elders and internal management arrangements.[31]

I wrote those words in early 1976 in an article for the *Forum 69* magazine that has been quoted previously. Let's unpack some of those things. We were now at the point where Kairos '74 was over. Our interstate visitors had gone home, but people continued to come. Some who had come to faith were lost back to the street. We had to grapple with how our small team of workers was to survive the pressures and tensions that grew every day. How do we live an authentic, though far from perfect, Christian life in the context in which we now found ourselves? As with much of life, we did not choose the issues we needed to face, they chose us. Or better, the Holy Spirit dropped them in our laps and said, "OK, let's get on with it."

By August of 1974 the Drop-in Centre was opened to the public each weekday, except Wednesday, from 1.00–5.00pm and on Saturdays from 10am–5.00pm. Other regular activities included:

Monday	Team Training 7.30–10.45pm
Tuesday	Confirmation lessons 6.45–8.00pm
	Growth Group for new Christians 8.15–9.30pm
Wednesday	Every second week a bikie meeting was held
Thursday	Prayer Breakfast 6.45am
	Bible Study and Prayer 7.30–10.00pm
Friday	Coffee House 7.00pm–12.30am
Saturday	Coffee House 7.30pm–12.30am
Sunday	Jesus Celebration 3.00–5.00pm[32]

In addition, much time was spent each week counselling, providing welfare assistance, visiting homes and gaols, permanent chaplaincy at the McNally Training Centre, sometimes attending court, and engaging in street evangelism. There were

---

31 Steen Olsen, ***The Growth of Jacob's Ladder Christian Community as a part of the Lutheran Church of Australia, South Australian District***, Forum 69 (May 1976), 7.

32 Douglas Kuhl, ***Report to the Department for Community Welfare*** (9 August 1974), 2.

speaking engagements and religious instruction seminars at Nuriootpa and Jamestown High Schools. Other needs were identified such as a rehabilitation centre where drug addicts, drop-outs, social misfits and criminals could have a secure place to stay and receive nurture and support. As a consequence, there was also a constant stream of phone calls to deal with and requests for other assistance. Life had become very busy indeed.

Equipping the Saints

Workshops and training courses for Coffee Lounge staff had of course been conducted from before Jakes opened. Among other things, Pastor Ted Prenzler had led his course in *Basic Youth Conflicts*, and we did *Dynamic Christian Witness: A Series of Studies to Edify and to Equip Christians for Evangelism* by Pastor Clem Koch. Now Pastor Doug Kuhl and others in the community also got busy 'equipping the saints for the work of ministry'.

In an August 1974 report to the Department for Community Welfare, Doug Kuhl wrote:

> With the expansion of floor space came an expansion of the vision of the work to be attempted through Jacob's Ladder. ... At the time, I considered the implementation of this vision would take some considerable time to develop. Little could I foresee what lay ahead. As I arrived, one of the most urgent needs of the work of Jacob's Ladder was the intensification of the training and nurture programs for the workers of the coffee house. This task was tackled immediately. Training nights were established on each Monday night and Bible Study on each Tuesday night.[33]

Community Nurture Houses

As we worked with new Christians who had come from various gangs, the drug culture and bikie clubs, we found that seeing them a few times a week was not meeting their needs and as mentioned earlier, we began to lose people back to

---

33 Douglas Kuhl, *Report to the Department for Community Welfare* (9 August 1974), 1.

JACOB'S LADDER COFFEE HOUSE 1974

the street. Many were living in very unstable and at times dangerous situations. Sometimes there was a short-term need where a person didn't have anywhere to stay for the night or had been kicked out of home. Married couples and singles who were flatting then began to invite some of the kids to come home with them, but soon the pressures became too great and so established Christians became part of households as team members to help support the street kids.

The Kuhl household in Vine Terrace, Klemzig, probably began the move. Erna remembers it as a very difficult time. They were doing the right sort of things and looking after people but this was in ways they had never attempted before and there was a heavy price to pay. Doug would bring home bikies and others to stay, often late at night. One rode his bike right into the living room on the new carpet. The bikies stayed in the garage, which was also the laundry, and the Kuhls had three kids, two in nappies, at the time. With cloth nappies in those days, access to the laundry was very important, often early in the morning. Most of their 'guests' were economical with the truth when it suited them, and, shall we say, exhibited some less than desirable personal habits. Erna remembers that Chrissy George (now Chris Wills) came to stay to help with the kids. Chris remembers Erna as being the backbone of every house they were in, who somehow even found time to befriend the neighbours. She recalls that there were almost constant interruptions, with people ringing the doorbell, even during mealtimes, demanding to see Doug. Because Doug was so busy, he was often not home and the pressures were immense. This was before the other households were established, so for most of the first year the Kuhls bore the brunt of this ministry on their own.

A girls' house was established in Goodwood with Ruth and myself as the house parents. Ruth remembers:

> Steen and I were married in May 1974, and we lived in half a house (friends in the other half, all separate and self-contained) in Prospect. Steen was a student at seminary while also involved with Jacob's Ladder, and he had a very healthy veggie garden out the back of our flat. We had a marvellous 6 months there. During November, while Steen was at a Jakes Elders/Leaders meeting, in my personal time with the Lord I received the impression that we were going to be moving into a different setting. I don't recall details about that, except that Steen came home from the meeting saying that "house elders are needed for a community house with a small group of young women at Goodwood; that we can't live just inwards for ourselves but outwards for others...", and I told him what I had been sensing that same evening. I am so grateful the Lord prepared me for leaving what had been a thoroughly enjoyable cosy nest time! In Deuteronomy 24:5, one year is granted to a new

husband to be at home; but the Lord had prepared me for extending that nest after only six months.

There is also mention of houses in St Morris and Richmond, but we have not been able to find more information about them. In North Terrace, Highgate, four young men were sharing a house while they were studying their different courses at University or Teacher's College. Three of them—Karl Brettig, Peter Schubert and Marty Rosenberg—were involved with Jakes and with the need to accommodate some of the new converts or others in need, they began taking them in. Marty remembers:

> When I moved in at the beginning of 1974, it was great to have my own room, sharing with other Christians. We all got on well and I celebrated my 21st in March that year with many others who I had gotten to know through Jakes and the near-by Lutheran Teachers College.
>
> As the year progressed, the need to take in some of those we had met through Jakes became more pressing, so we did. We shared our rooms with some at times and had many late night discussions about many different topics. My study times moved from home to the University library, but we managed. It was not what I expected in my first year flatting with mates.

This boys' house was parallel to our girls' house. Ruth remembers that they had a double mattress, which was much better than the one we had. Since it was a boys' house with no married couple, they obviously had no need of it, so it was 'requisitioned' for our use.

Most of those in these two houses moved into a large two-storey house in Queen Street Norwood in early 1975. It had 15 beds and slept up to 21 people on occasion. Ruth and I, together with Karl Brettig, were the house parents. At the same time, a two-house household was established in Highgate with Val and Trevor Brooks as the house parents. More will be said about this later.

The Kerux Apostles MC

Discussions were held with the God's Squad Motorcycle Club in Melbourne with a view to establishing a chapter in Adelaide that would be associated with Jacob's Ladder. That did not eventuate but a number of smaller groups came together and formed the *Kerux Apostles Motorcycle Club*.

JACOB'S LADDER COFFEE HOUSE 1974

Geoff (Scrooge) Turner therefore reports that "'Kerux Apostles' seeks to bring our outlaw brothers and sisters into the saving knowledge and freedom experience of Jesus Christ. We fly Christ's colours as a banner uplifting Jesus within the bike scene."[34] This was already in the embryonic stage in 1974 and developed into a fully-fledged ministry in the years that followed.

This significant mission field is reported on in greater detail in Chapter 25.

Ian Wade was Appointed

Pastor Doug was our only paid staff member, working much more than full time. Some government funding was obtained and another worker needed to be appointed. There was some controversy over the appointment of Ian Wade because they were not members of the Lutheran Church. However, Ian brought much needed expertise to Jakes. Helen was also a valuable addition to the community, as were her articles of spiritual encouragement in the newsletters.

Helen and Ian had established a post-release residential facility for prisoners called "Freedom House" on Greenhill Road, which Helen was managing, while Ian also did relief teaching, including tech studies. One of their residents went up to Jacob's Ladder and met Doug Kuhl and rang Helen from there, putting Doug on the phone. Following their talk Doug visited, and in due course Ian was invited to join the staff.

Their experience in working with ex-prisoners and Ian's background in teaching technical and other courses, brought much needed relief for the situation at Jakes. We now had two capable workers who could handle most situations. It didn't solve the problem of course, because the work continued to grow, and so more staff were needed.

An Eldership was Established

We had a pastor, but as the community was developing it was decided to establish an eldership, taking more of a team approach to leadership. There had of course

---

34 Geoff (Scrooge) Turner, **Bike and Street,** Jacob's Letter (October 1975), 11.

The First Eleven
Steen Olsen // Steve Haar // Ian & Helen Wade // Karl & Ruth Brettig // Doug & Erna Kuhl
Absent: Ruth Olsen // Jan Haar // Doug Vogelsang

been various committees, some of which were still in existence, but they were external to the community, albeit with some Jakes representation. But that is the story of the next chapter. The eldership was a team, who together with Pastor Doug, would exercise spiritual oversight and provide leadership for the community. Since it eventually comprised eleven people (after a few marriages), it came to be known as the 'first eleven'. The 1st XI comprised Erna and Pastor Doug Kuhl, Ruth and Karl Brettig, Jan and Steve Haar, Ruth and Steen Olsen, Doug Vogelsang who was not married during his time with Jakes, and Helen and Ian Wade.

This represented a development of the identity of Jacob's Ladder. From a group of people running a parachurch outreach ministry, it had evolved into a community that saw itself as 'church'. More and more people now looked to Jakes as their primary church identity. That was of course true of the people who had recently come to faith, but increasingly it was also true of those who previously saw themselves as members of another congregation. The recognition of leadership within the community—in addition to the pastor—was one of the signs along that road. Previously there had been managers whose role was to run the coffee house. Now we appointed an eldership who shared oversight and leadership with the pastor of the community.

JACOB'S LADDER COFFEE HOUSE 1974

Sunday Afternoon Worship

The original idea had been that the Jacob's Ladder ministry should be incorporated into the St Stephen's Congregation. Pastor Doug was to preach there once a month at morning services and a couple of times at evening services. It turned out that the expectations of what these services would be like differed considerably. Doug pulled no punches in a report to the St Stephen's Youth Ministry Committee on 3 April 1974:

> In conclusion, I am worried and constantly disturbed by the slowness, and in certain quarters, the utter inability of the church members to comprehend what is involved in a street ministry. The gossip reports that have filtered back to me have been both hurtful and vicious, and certainly haven't helped me to feel any affinity with the church's attitude to those whom we call "street people". ... I personally have become utterly disappointed at the unwillingness of the St Stephen's congregation to allow me to conduct "contemporary services", of such a nature as to communicate with these people and to help them feel at home and to meet their specific needs. Our liturgical services are hopelessly out of touch with the feel and needs of unchurched people. I cannot build bridges from Jacob's Ladder to the church unless you allow me to begin construction work from both banks of the chasm. The gap between Jacob's Ladder and the church is so large at present, I have almost despaired of ever bridging it. I trust that with God's help and guidance a solution may be found to this dilemma.[35]

There was clearly a clash of cultures, and indeed, at the time, the chasm was too wide. Yes, there were well-intentioned people in the Church who thought it could be done, but they didn't have first-hand experience of the people being drawn to Jakes. This was made worse when during one service some of our ratbags managed to get into the vestry at St Stephen's and empty Pastor Kevin's wallet. He was very good about it, but for us such things were part of the territory.

I described some aspects of our worship services in the article in *Forum 69*:

> Slowly the new life of individuals begins to be expressed in the worship life of the community. Someone quietly sobs as he is released from a burden of guilt that he has carried for many years. Someone is healed, a steady stream of people is converted, and the community finds that its worship times are gradually getting longer as its desire to worship God grows. We are still growing. God has lots to teach us and lots more to do through us. We have

---

35 Noel Hartwig, *The Story of Jacob's Ladder*, unpublished Thesis (1978), 28. Accessed at Lutheran Archives.

only experienced a small part of the worship and praise, the life and faith that he could lead us into. We sin much and are disobedient often. The Lord has had to lead us to repent as our worship has tended towards the mere repetition of a new form; but somehow, through it all, the Lord has slowly led us towards his goal.

I'm not saying that this isn't happening elsewhere in the church, nor am I commenting on the worship and life of the church generally, but just seeking to portray what the Lord has led Jacob's Ladder community through.[36]

Services were begun in the Coffee House on Sunday afternoons. This represented a decisive break with the dream of Jakes being fully integrated into St Stephen's. From that point on, the formation of a new worshipping community, or church, was inevitable. New ministries had become a new community.

All that remained was for the break with St Stephen's to be finalised. That is the story of the next chapter.

---

[36] Steen Olsen, *The Growth of Jacob's Ladder Christian Community as a part of the Lutheran Church of Australia, South Australian District*, Forum 69 (May 1976), 7.

JACOB'S LADDER COFFEE HOUSE 1974

The Old Wineskins Burst!

CHAPTER 7

We need, briefly, to revisit parts of the story that have already been told. When Jacob's Ladder Coffee Lounge opened its doors in September 1970, the Metro South Zone of The Lutheran Youth of South Australia had established a Management Committee, which by October also included representation from the Metro North Zone and Lutheran Publishing House. LCA Youth Pastor Ted Prenzler was also a member. A number of Managers were appointed to run the place when it was open. The Metro South Zone had assumed 'legal and financial' responsibility for the project. The committee was responsible for policy, staff, equipment, finance and major decisions. The managers were responsible for seeing that the coffee lounge ran as smoothly as possible, and for the spiritual welfare of all concerned.

That seemed to work well enough at the time, though a report from the Metro South Zone in November 1974 looked back and noted that up until the expansion in the first months of 1974,

> the management committee still had a fairly good "working" relationship with the Jacob's Ladder community, although strains on the relationship were beginning to show (e.g. new name for Jacob's Ladder became a major issue, whereas it should have played a minor role).

> Managers of Jacob's Ladder had begun to say that the Management Committee members should be more involved with the activities of the coffee lounge rather than being a body that met once a month, but were not able to share the joys and frustrations of the work with the workers.[37]

Meanwhile the St Stephen's congregation had agreed to partner with the district, Metro South Zone and Jacob's Ladder, to call a pastor to work a quarter time in the congregation and the rest of his time in youth ministry centred on Jacob's Ladder. He was to be responsible to the St Stephen's Congregation with regular reports to be made to the SA District. The congregation appointed

> a youth ministry committee of which the pastor of the congregation is a member, to plan, guide and supervise his [the associate pastor / youth worker] activities and to be concerned with the well-being of his person and work. The congregation may include in the membership of this committee

---

37 *Report and Appraisal from the Metro South Zone on the Future Structure of Administration and Aims of Jacob's Ladder* (28/11/1974), 2.

representatives of other groups and congregations, which have an interest in the work.[38]

Therefore, we now had two committees to deal with! Jakes reported to the Metro South Zone, but the pastor reported to the St Stephen's Congregation, regarding all his work, not just the work at St Stephens. That was not an ideal structure. It is also worth noting that it was intended that the pastor's work should be "conducted as an integral part of the ministry of St Stephen's congregation." How exactly that was meant to work, I am not sure.

The report quoted above expresses the hope that Jacob's Ladder can stay within the framework of the Lutheran Church. The report notes:

> The management committee began to realise that activity in the coffee lounge was heightened and expanding but were not always made aware of which directions the Jacob's Ladder community was moving. Jacob's Ladder community believed that because they were working with a constantly changing society, they had to make decisions quickly. The management committee believed that because they were representing many sections of the "body of Christ", decisions should be thought out carefully, especially in the area of larger policy changes.

The report then notes that two issues emerged:

- That the Lutheran Church was too structure-oriented and did not allow enough flexibility. For example, Jacob's Ladder had to be administered by a board of control.

- That the Lutheran Church has not always, in the past, allowed active fellowship and participation with other denominations.[39]

After summarising the two-committee structure, I added the following comment when writing in *Forum 69* in early 1976:

> There was already a community of people who were bearing the heat of the day in the ministry and so quite rightly felt that they should be involved in the decisions that were made. The monthly meetings of the management committee were largely spent catching up on the previous month's activity and more and more basic decisions were made at the grassroots level.

---

38   *Terms of Reference for Associate Pastor / Youth Worker*, point 4.

39   Steen Olsen, *The Growth of Jacob's Ladder Christian Community as a part of the Lutheran Church of Australia, South Australian District*, Forum 69 (May 1976), 2.

JACOB'S LADDER COFFEE HOUSE 1974

SECTION ii

CHAPTER 7

The Pastor's Ministry

As reported earlier, the ministry of Jacob's Ladder irrevocably changed during a few short weeks after Pastor Doug's installation. Doug himself wrote:

> I must point out most strongly that the situation, which existed at Jacob's Ladder at the time my terms of reference were drawn up, changed dramatically at the very outset of my ministry in Adelaide. I mentioned to Pastor Schmidt very early in the year that I envisaged a situation in the near future when these terms of reference would have to be investigated in the light of these new developments and most probably revised.[40]

It quickly became clear that St Stephen's were not 'getting their money's worth'. Yet, there are only so many hours in each day. No one could criticise the amount of time and effort put in by the pastor. Add to this the inability of the St Stephen's congregation to make the changes to their worship services that the Jakes community felt were essential, and the relationship very soon collapsed totally. By 10 July 1974, Pastor Schmidt wrote a letter to the Youth Ministry Committee in which he stated that, in his opinion, a team ministry with an associate pastor had not worked and that Pastor Kuhl had breached his letter of call on several counts.[41]

A meeting was held on 25 July 1974. The notes from that meeting begin:

> Following on from Discussions with the Jacob's Ladder Team members and members of SA District Church Council and the Metropolitan Mission Committee, the following proposals have been considered by representatives of the Jacob's Ladder Team, and we now wish to present these to the [St Stephen's] Youth Ministry Committee for their consideration.

Six proposals were listed. They are summarised below:

1. That the formal connection between Jakes and the Metro South Zone of the Youth be severed and the management committee dissolved. Jacob's Ladder should be allowed to manage its own affairs.

2. The St Stephen's Youth Ministry Committee become advisory to Jakes and act as a liaison with St Stephen's and the District.

---

40   Douglas Kuhl, *Report to the Department for Community Welfare* (9 August 1974), 2.
41   Noel Hartwig, *The Story of Jacob's Ladder*, unpublished Thesis (1978), 29. Accessed at Lutheran Archives.

3. That Jakes manage their own affairs, but that they do so under the advice of the Youth Ministry Committee.

4. That Ian Wade be employed as a full-time worker.

5. That contemporary worship services be commenced at 7pm on Sundays at St Stephens, with the Youth Ministry Committee to petition the St Stephen's Church Council with this proposal.

6. That all means possible be used to integrate the St Stephen's youth fellowships and their Pub Outreach, with the Jacob's Ladder outreach ministries.[42]

We have the minutes of a meeting of the Management Committee held on 28th November 1974. The membership is listed as Doug Vogelsang, Pr John Sabel (Tertiary Chaplain), Graham Lienert, Pr Ted Prenzler (LCA Youth Director), Ian Zimmermann, Jim Pietsch, Pr Kevin Schmidt and Steen Olsen. Mr ET Dutschke apologised. Visitors were Pr Artie Schirmer (District Church Development Director), District President Clem Koch and Pr Doug Kuhl. The following points give a good indication of the state of the Jakes ministry at the time (following the numbering of the minutes):

1. Doug Kuhl presented his report and stressed verbally that the issues were not just organisational, nor was it that Jacob's Ladder didn't like authority, but that the issues were theological. The report was discussed and received with thanks.

2. It was decided to take up a mission at Henley Beach this summer. [That became the *Sonshine Centre*.]

3. Friday lunchtime concerts have been held at Victoria Square between noon and 2pm, involving music and street theatre, together with various displays. They have been very well received.

4. A Newsletter is to come out as soon as possible.

5. The Kerux Bike Club is growing in maturity.

6. Ian Wade's report was received with thanks.

7. Services are held at the McNally Training Centre every six weeks.

8. The media workshop is currently being set up.

---

42 Notes of the meeting—since it was an informal gathering these are not minutes as such.

JACOB'S LADDER COFFEE HOUSE 1974

SECTION ii

CHAPTER 7

9. The Treasurer's report indicated a healthy balance of over $4,000: $760 in the general operating account; $600 in the rent account and $2,756 in the staff fund.

10. The auditor's certificate had been received.

11. A report from the Metro South Zone was received with thanks.

12. "Doug Kuhl announced his intention to resign his call to St Stephens. This involves his work at Jacob's Ladder. Considerable discussion ensued on the future of the ministry at Jakes."

13. The following motion was passed: *That the management committee favours the ministry of Jacob's Ladder to continue within the framework of the LCA SA District.*

The Pastor resigns his Call

Pastor Doug immediately submitted a letter of resignation, dated 1 December 1974. It was presented to a meeting of the Youth Ministry Committee on the same date. In his letter he notes that the reasons for this decision have been discussed over a long period of time and that it had become impossible for him to fulfil his responsibilities at both St Stephen's and Jakes. He stated that he was prepared to continue to minister at Jakes, "however I acknowledge the difficulties the District may have in allowing such a move to take place. I place my future into God's hands." He then thanked the congregation for their love, consideration and effort over the past year.

It should be noted that when an LCA pastor resigns his call, he does that in its totality. It is not possible to resign part of a call. A new call would need to be issued. This means the pastor becomes a 'pastor without a call', which is a vulnerable place to be, and means that he can more easily be removed from the LCA roll of pastors. The Jacob's Ladder Community was not allowed to call under the rules of the LCA. To do so it would need to be constituted as a congregation of the Church.

At the Youth Ministry Committee meeting I moved that the resignation be received, and Doug Vogelsang moved that we recommend to the St Stephen's Church Council that the resignation be accepted. Both were carried unanimously. Subsequent motions recommended that the control of Jakes be vested in one body and that it continued to operate within the framework of the LCA SA District. Recommendations were then made concerning termination arrangements. President Clem Koch was also present as an observer.

There was simply no other way forward. The old wineskin had burst and was not capable of holding the new wine. Looking back it is easy to see that there was fault on both sides. The structure of an external management committee was also used for new congregations in growing suburbs. Various 'home mission committees' fulfilled such a role. It was the way the LCA operated at the time.

To quote once again from my article in *Forum 69*:

> Many hours were spent at meetings. Since there were now three different committees and the Jacob's Ladder Community involved [yes, the District had established another 'interim committee'], the same points were talked through many times. The pressure of the continuing ministry at Jacob's Ladder, and our general slackness in administration, caused much frustration to those who desired written reports and statements concerning the work. We were doing and saying things that were not in keeping with the current practice of the Church, and so naturally suspicions arose. Since we were learning and working through issues as we went, our statements and explanations were not always as clear as they might have been.
>
> Sensitive feelings were aroused as people were threatened by our different approach. Since we steadfastly refused to follow some of the guidelines established within the church for such a ministry, we were disagreeing with the way the church does things and therefore judging the brethren. Some criticism was of course implied, for we were sifting through the general trends in our church and discarding some of them, but such criticism is vital to the health of a body like the LCA. God was doing something in Jacob's Ladder and both we and the rest of the LCA had to come to terms with it.
>
> Within the community, changes were continuing to occur. There was a shift from a special ministry, which was task-oriented to the development of a community, which was "complete" in the sense that it was concerned with all that is involved in being a Christian. Weekly worship celebrations were held as well as teaching and nurture programs. The regular celebration of the Lord's Supper was yet to come, not because it wasn't desired—it was. But it was delayed so as not to cause offense to other brothers and sisters in the church. The few occasions when it was celebrated caused a considerable stream of protest.[43]

Jacob's Ladder now became responsible for Pastor Doug's salary and accommodation. St Stephen's kindly allowed the Kuhls to stay in the Vine Terrace house for

---

43 Steen Olsen, *The Growth of Jacob's Ladder Christian Community as a part of the Lutheran Church of Australia, South Australian District*, Forum 69 (May 1976), 7–8.

JACOB'S LADDER COFFEE HOUSE 1974

CHAPTER 7

some months while an alternative was found. During that time rent was paid. The first year's rent of the Gawler Place premises had been donated—$2,500—a significant sum at the time. Now that also needed to be raised. We had also been successful in obtaining some government grants towards our costs. Way too much time was spent trying to work with a cumbersome administrative system—time that could have been put to much more productive use.

While recognising that we were far from perfect, I still want to make the point that the system was built around control and was 'low trust' in the extreme. It wasn't even that we were suspected of wasting money, or not being good stewards of the funds raised by others. The fruit was there for all to see. It is not my right to question the motives or intentions of others, but writing as one who was subsequently involved at the most senior levels in national and state church leadership for more than two decades before I retired, it is clear that the confusing structure, constant criticism and obstructive behaviour we were faced with then, left a lot to be desired.

The old wineskins had burst, and new wineskins needed to be found.

CHAPTER 8 *Growing a Community at 'Street Level'*

On 11 May 1975 Jakes was legally incorporated as "Jacob's Ladder Christian Community Inc".

Jakes began as an outreach to those who were not generally finding their way into existing churches, with a focus on the various youth cultures of the 1970s. At first, we all belonged to other congregations. We came together on Friday and Saturday nights to run a coffee house where people might hear about Jesus and come to meet him. Gradually a team began to form and more and more activities took place at other times during the week.

In a paper for his Social Work course Kevin Lieschke later wrote:

> Servants of Christ [the name of Jakes from early 1977] became a community out of the need to have an established Christian lifestyle into which the poor and oppressed could come and experience the presence and love of Jesus. … The vision of community … saw the development of committed relationships between those who felt called to do this, and this has developed into not only commitment to each other for the sake of ministry, but also for the whole of life.[44]

By 1975, some lived in community houses, relationships deepened, we prayed together more. The team became a community. The community began to gather for worship. It was a perfectly natural progression, but it caused a lot of controversy. In the October 1975 edition of *Jacob's Letter*, Peter Muller wrote an explanation, or perhaps even a defence, of what we were doing. Here are some excerpts:

> Community is not a kinky idea borrowed from the Counter Culture hippie freaks of the late 1960s. Community is as old as God's chosen people, lately seen in the form of the Christian Church… See Acts 4:32, where the community held all things in common. Note that it follows immediately after the statement, "They were filled with the Holy Spirit". We have discovered that such living can be truly successful only with the empowering of the Holy Spirit. Such a radical lifestyle is not new. It is not weird or, as commonly stated, an alternative to this society. We yearn to live as normal human beings, that is, as children of God.

---

[44] Kevin Lieschke, *Case Study of an Organisation: Servants of Christ Community*, unpublished paper (15/6/1979).

JACOB'S LADDER CHRISTIAN COMMUNITY 1975-1976

Community is not just living with one another (although this helps immensely); it is living for one another. It is not a question of whether one is living in community or not, because as Christians we are automatically living in community when we confess we are a member of Christ's body. ... It is then a question of how much you are willing to let it be a reality in your life. To live truly in a community of love and commitment and sharing isn't something you bind yourself to in a legalistic way, but it is a blessed release in Christ from the bondage and alienation we suffer living in Western society, which is based on selfish principles of private gain and accumulation of goods...

We recognise that we are all still enslaved to some degree by the systems of this world. We recognise the source of our growing freedom—Christ in the Holy Spirit. It is our slavery to the will of God through the power of his grace, that is our life now. We have been called by Jesus to be released from the systems of this world, made to be truly his children, and thus truly normal human beings as God originally intended us to be.[45]

Writing about this emerging community, Karl Brettig said:

Central to the ministry is the principle of a caring and sharing community of believers devoted to teaching, fellowship and prayer. (Acts 2:42) We are learning what it means to be a Christian community living in a world that has lost its experience of community. (John 13:34–35) We are seeking to support one another in order that we may fulfil the ministry that Christ has called us to fulfil. ... There are many other areas in which we are learning to share our lives together in the Lord and give witness to him in terms of Christian community. By living simply, we are finding that we can give more of our time, our talents and our earnings to his service. Currently, Jakes has five fulltime staff workers and two part-time who are being supported by the community. These are involved in the running of the drop-in centre, making field visits

---

45   Peter Muller, **Questions We Face**, *Jacob's Letter* (October 1975), 15–18.

to homes and hospitals, developing Christian music, art and drama for the presentation of the Gospel, as well as many other areas of ministry.[46]

We were influenced, among many other things, by the writings of Dietrich Bonhoeffer, who in *Life Together* wrote of Christian community being a Divine reality rather than an idealised wish-dream (to use Bonhoeffer's term).[47] It was not heaven on earth, was far from perfect, and could not be enforced by any sort of legalism or coercion. It was characterised by thankfulness and worship, by teaching and mentoring, and by fellowship and care. It could only be received as a gift in the midst of much brokenness. And we had abundant supplies of the latter. That was important, because it was our failings and weaknesses, our struggles and our plain old-fashioned sinfulness, that the Spirit used to grow Christ-likeness in us.

We grow as we live life together in the real world. Our experience was therefore not utopian or cultish. There was leadership and oversight, but no one lived in subservient obedience to another, apart from to God. No one was to control another's life, or make decisions for them. Some lived in community houses, many others did not. Some were established longer-term members of the community; others were testing the waters at the edge. Some only worked in the coffee house, or attended training or worship. In other words, while the community had shape and form, it was also porous. People came and went. This openness was particularly marked towards the street, or if you like, the local non-Christian community around us. There were no rigid boundaries; no clearly defined 'them' and 'us'. In one sense, we lived our lives on the street (not sleeping rough though!) and sought to be part of that scene, so that people felt comfortable to come and check us out.

Dwelling in the World

In hindsight, we had stumbled on to something that is often spoken of today as missional church. We understood the people of God to have been sent into the world by the sending God (*"missio Dei"*), where we lived the Christian life in the midst of the world. Like the earliest disciples in Luke 10, we were sent to receive the hospitality of strangers and not just to offer it to them. We made it our practice to listen carefully to the people we met and got to know. We discovered that there is much we can do together with those who are not yet Christian. Establishing a community that is on and off the street meant that we needed to cross the cultural

---

46 Karl Brettig, **What's Happening Currently at Jakes**, Jacob's Letter (October 1975), 9–10.

47 Other writings that helped shape us included **A New Way of Living** by Michael Harper, **Living together in a World Falling Apart** by Dave & Neta Jackson, **God's Forever Family** by Jack Sparkes and **Repentance the Joy-filled Life** by Basilea Schlink.

JACOB'S LADDER CHRISTIAN COMMUNITY 1975–1976

SECTION III

CHAPTER 8

gap, rather than expect new Christians to make the journey into an established church. We were not there to solve all their problems, but we were there to live honestly together with them. Recently, I wrote about this under the heading *Dwelling in the World*:

> We listen for the signs that God has been at work in his world, preparing people to hear the gospel. As we share in all things with those to whom we have been sent, we are salt and light in the world and the yeast that brings the presence of the kingdom of God into our neighbourhoods and networks. We come as equals, not as those with all the answers. Wherever we go, we bring Jesus, because that is who we are. We can do no other.
>
> We seek to live as Christians and so love and care for others, but we are not there just to create a better world. Sadly, unlike the early church, most churches today spend very little of their money, energy and time on bringing the good news that is Jesus to others. Their focus is on fulfilling the needs of their existing members, with most of what is left, going to various 'community care' efforts. These are good things, but the one thing that only the church can do, is mostly neglected.
>
> Dwelling in the world is not a call to establish ministry initiatives such as cafés and counselling services. Rather we form Christian community out in the world. It is an 'evangelism first' approach to beginning new Christian communities rather than 'service first' or 'worship first'. Our priority is not trying to bring new Christians back to our existing churches, though if some want to come that is OK too. Rather we form Christian communities out in the world, where others feel at home.
>
> Dwelling in the world means that we keep an outward focus. We are in the world, though not of it. We follow the beat of a different drum as we engage with people, grow relationships and form community where they already live, work and play. It is good to put some energy into our 'inward journey' but if we neglect to also go into God's world, we will miss what Christian living is really all about—we are there for others.[48]

While only written recently, in many ways, that reflects what we were trying to do back in the 1970s. We understood ourselves to be the church in the world, sharing life with others who were not yet Christian.

---

48 Steen Olsen, *Six Disruptive Missional Practices: Renewing the Life of our Congregations and Other Communities*, 8 page paper (2019). Available from the author on request.

Looking back on our experience of Community

We all went on to other things after our time in the Jakes community. Writing recently, Anne Sellers, who went from Jakes to a long-term involvement with *Youth With A Mission*, reflects:

Phil Jefferis
Marcia Lieschke (Schutz)
Anne Sellers // Colin Smith

> One helpful concept has been the Biblical idea of "seasons" of life. Pastor Doug taught on this topic several times. The concept was "when the time is ready." I see now that there are some natural patterns that shape our lives such as attending university, marriage, birth and raising children, empty nest years, and finishing paid work/retirement. God wants to lead us in each of these phases of our lives. Some jobs, ministries, hobbies, or places to live are for a season and then it is time to move on. I believe that God knows each person's name and works with each person to shape their life for their good, and for his glory. God also works to move each person towards Christian maturity. We often don't understand what is happening until much later. The question of knowing when to start or stop doing something or move to another location, or pursue something completely new, is often difficult. This was true for the Jakes community towards the end. I didn't understand this concept of stopping/starting as being God's leading when I was younger. I am now able to more fully embrace change, and let go when needed.

Another community member has written, "Living in community does not make you perfect, on the contrary, it makes you aware of just how imperfect you are. This allows you to confess your failures to God and pray for the gift of repentance and renewal." We learnt many things about ourselves, others and God that helped to shape us as people.

A Lesson from Hanging out Washing

Anne remembers some growing experiences:

> P wasn't very good at domestic chores. I shared a house with P and several other Jakes friends. P started a load of laundry and left it in the twin tub machine for a few days, unfinished. The water was dirty. I needed to use the machine and he didn't respond to my request to empty his laundry, so I

JACOB'S LADDER CHRISTIAN COMMUNITY 1975–1976

SECTION iii

CHAPTER 8

removed it from the machine and threw it in a big plastic tub. I was irritated. He shouldn't have left a mess for others to clean up. I then decided that I would finish up his washing. I rinsed the clothing a couple of times and set it aside. It wasn't my responsibility to do anything further. I then washed my clothes and did some chores around the house. P's laundry sat in a heap where I left it. I had a mental argument with myself with all the reasons that I could leave P's laundry and he could deal with it when he got around to it. But, I couldn't let it sit there. I was challenged by the idea that I could do more than the minimum. I muttered to myself as I hung up P's clothing. Someone else arrived home and came out to the backyard and criticized the way I was hanging up the clothes. I became more irritated. About this time, I realized that God wanted me to learn something important and I should pay attention to my attitude. I became more careful in hanging the laundry. I came to see that this was a modern day equivalent of washing a person's feet. This could be an act of service, of honouring the person. I could show care to my friend, and not embarrass him. He already knew he wasn't good at domestic chores, and he was probably helping someone with a broken car, or damaged plumbing. I finished the laundry and went on with my day. Within a few days, we were at Jakes Sunday worship, and Pastor Doug started talking about hanging out washing and how we can show care for our fellow community members. I don't know whether he heard anything about my experience a few days earlier. I had learned that serving is to be done in a way that is meaningful to the recipient even when I may have a different preference. An important life lesson.

Michelle Gibson remembers another time when flexibility and tolerance was needed. It occurred in 1975 in one of the Winchester Street houses led by Val and Trevor Brooks. Michelle recalls:

A man came with his two dogs to live with us for a short time. He came from working on properties out bush. He told me that he wanted to get his own farm one day. He asked Trevor if he could get a few chooks for the back yard to give us some eggs. A great idea. However, he didn't stop there. Each week he would go to a market somewhere and bring home more livestock: different varieties of chickens, ducks, rabbits, there was a box of ferrets in the garage, and a big white turkey who would chase us. One day I did a headcount—53 birds and animals in the back yard. The next week I arrived home from work to find eight sheep grazing on the back lawn under the clothes line—apparently four of them were pregnant. He said that he brought them home in his car, some in the back seat and some in the boot. This was the last straw and Trevor said they would have to go. The following Saturday the man was going fishing. That night we got home at about midnight from Jacob's Ladder Coffee House. I went to the bathroom and collapsed with laughter to find several large redfin fish swimming up and down in the bathtub and laundry sink. He moved on soon after.

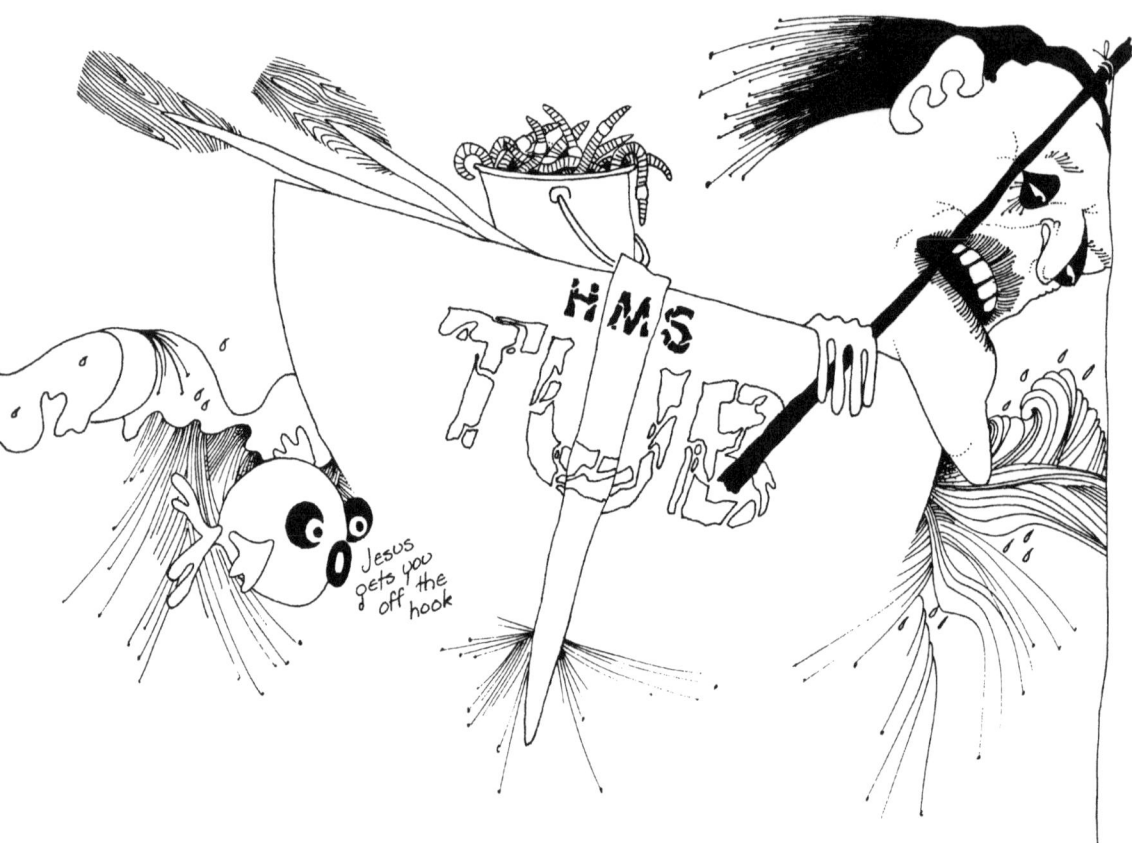

The one that got away...

JACOB'S LADDER
CHRISTIAN COMMUNITY 1975-1976

CHAPTER 8

For all the difficulties and struggles, many of us look back on our experience in the Jakes Community as having played a significant role in shaping the rest of our lives. Michelle Gibson reflects, "For sure there were challenges, scary moments and times when I wondered what God had called me into. But upon reflection, I am grateful that God led me up those stairs as this time became a touchstone of what it means to live in Christian fellowship; to follow God's calling; to be open to his Spirit; to be kind and caring and to share the love of Jesus with others."

CHAPTER 9: A Week in the Life of the Community

It seems that quite a few people would like to see some sort of a description of what exactly goes on at Jacob's Ladder Christian Community. Well here goes an attempt to describe something of the life of the community. So wrote Karl Brettig in the September 1976 issue of *Jacob's Letter*. Here is a summary of what he reported:

Sunday

The week began on Sunday morning with two study groups at 9am. One was a basic introductory course for new Christians and people new to the community. The other was a more intensive course that delved deeper into both the Old and New Testaments. At 10.30am the community gathered for worship, which often extended into the afternoon. The form this took varied:

> Often this is a time of praise and joy as we respond to the Lord's presence among us. Other times there are extended periods of intercession, prayer for healing of relationships, of broken lives and of physical ailments. Order in worship is preserved by the participating leaders (preaching and teaching, liturgical and song leaders). The whole body is very much involved as much as possible in accordance with 1 Corinthians 1:26. These are usually very blessed times and are a focal point of the week's activity.[49]

On Sunday afternoons, there were often various community activities. At 8pm the elders and pastor met to talk and pray about the community and to make joint decisions about issues as required.

Throughout the Week

Mondays were a day off for the staff. Tuesday to Friday the centre at 102 Gawler Place was usually open from 10am to 4.30pm. The week began with a staff meeting to coordinate visiting and other activities and to pray through the week's activities. Karl reported that at the time of writing we had five fulltime and three part time staff as well as some voluntary staff members. During 1975–6 the staff included Pastor Doug Kuhl, Ian Wade, Ruth Olsen, Karl Brettig, Peter Schubert, Ruth Phillipson (later Brettig)—Office, Colin Smith—Music, Phil Jefferis—Drama, Marty Rosenberg—

---

49   Karl Brettig, **Current Happenings**, *Jacob's Letter* (September 1976), 13–14.

JACOB'S LADDER CHRISTIAN COMMUNITY 1975–1976

SECTION iii

CHAPTER 9

Social Work, and Knarelle Beard—Artist and Graphic Design. I replaced my wife Ruth on the staff in 1976, taking a year off studies at Luther Seminary and working fulltime in the Community. A Government grant of $5,000 helped pay for the salary of the director. The rest was raised by worship offerings and donations. Staff lived according to need, not on the basis of having a fixed generous salary. The report for 1975 said, "Staff workers at present working for Jacob's Ladder live on wages ranging from $20 to $100 per week, according to the availability of funds and needs of the staff worker at the time."[50] This was their choice, for the sake of the ministry. There was a job to be done and we were blessed with a strong sense of all being in this together. I guess that would be illegal today. As I wrote then:

> During the first two months of this year [1976], the community found itself particularly short of money and so there was little to pay staff with. Many people were on holidays, but the Lord wasn't. He provided for our needs as our gardens bore fruit and many of his people were moved to bring gifts of food. And so our tables were full and we could invite others to come to share the goodness of the Lord. We simply bring our needs to the Lord and trust him to provide—and he does![51]

Karl reported, "We are in the process of involving various professional workers in social work, medicine etc, who are committed Christians. We are also currently being phoned and visited

---

50   Douglas Kuhl, *Jacob's Ladder Christian Community: Report for Year 1975*, 3.

51   Steen Olsen, *Money Money Everywhere (and not a drop to drink)*, Jacob's Letter (May 76), 8–9.

by numerous social workers." Staff activities during the week included visits to individuals and groups, counselling, preparation of study material, organisation of both community activities and events which embraced the wider Body of Christ, the development of a resource and research centre and other things like producing the *Jacob's Letter* magazine and other materials. The drop-in centre was also staffed by other community members during the week and had a steady stream of visitors.

Week Nights

Karl wrote:

> **Tuesday** nights are devoted to either times of prayer, praise, intercession and teaching, or to in depth studies of contemporary issues. For example, in the past months we have looked at Christianity and 20th Century thought, Christianity and communism, and currently we are looking at the various eastern religions and sects that are invading Western society. (How many of us are aware of the pagan rituals that are involved in Transcendental Meditation?)
>
> On **Wednesday** and **Thursday** nights the community houses hold their own meetings, as required, and there were sharing times for those not living in one of the houses. Music practise and the Kerux Apostles bike group meetings also happen on those nights. These were flexible evenings when things could be arranged or when relationships could be built. Different parts of the community would do different things. Not everyone was involved in everything.

Weekends

On Friday and Saturday nights there continued to be ministry in various places where people gathered. The coffee house had been temporarily closed at the time Karl was writing and was due to reopen the following month. New regulations meant that a second fireproof staircase needed to be constructed. That also meant that the coffee house was redesigned to make it suitable for "things other than making coffee" and the offices needed to be relocated for a time. In the May 76 issue of *Jacob's Letter*, the editor also reported that there was "a lovely new secretary, Ruth Phillipson, who has been on the fulltime staff since about a month ago." [He subsequently married her!]

Karl also reported that a musical had been written by community members and that it would be presented on Saturday evenings as well as at the Youth EXPO at the Adelaide Showground on the October long weekend. He summarised this by saying that people were being reached for Jesus, taught the faith and healed of many wounds from their past.

JACOB'S LADDER CHRISTIAN COMMUNITY 1975–1976

CHAPTER 9

Brian Proeve described a typical Friday evening in the Coffee House:

> At 8pm some 12–15 people meet at 102 Gawler Place for prayer, study and a worship time of about 60 minutes. We find it essential to be at peace with God and one another before going out to bring a message of peace… From about 9.30pm until 12.30am the street team divides into pairs and attends bars, the Pancake Kitchen, pinball parlours and other places in Hindley Street. At 12.30am we meet back at Jakes for a short sharing time and prayer. We don't use tracts. They make contact impersonal. … To tell people about Jesus is just being loving, open and honest. There aren't any formulas, just the Holy Spirit who is the hallmark of the ministry.[52]

Tony's Story

As an example of someone's journey to faith, the September 1976 *Jacob's Letter* included the following testimony:

> Well, let me start at the age of 17. I was a street-fighter. I used to run a pack of skin-heads in one of the many suburbs of Melbourne which I thought was pretty good. My Dad didn't think so—he wanted me to go back to college to learn more. After a while it started to get slack in Melbourne—I came across to Adelaide for some fun. I was over here for a week before I found some more skins—which made me feel at home. The cops over here were more alert. This made me shift from the Leisure Centre, to City Cross, to Jakes. I was mean to people here—not because of the fact that the people worked at Jakes, but because of the fact that they kept on bugging me about Jesus, which was pretty stupid because I knew God but to hand my life to him was like asking the next guy to stab me, which was pretty stupid.
>
> Anyway, I was kicked out of Adelaide for too many assault and shooting charges. For the next two years, I worked for my father in Melbourne because I didn't feel part of the scene anymore. In June 1975 I had a motorbike smash which put me in hospital—I felt there was nothing left for me, even though my family had lots of money to spend. I still felt nothing until one morning I decided to go back to Adelaide to live. I believe the Lord brought me back to him.
>
> The night I got in, I felt as if something was leading me to Jakes because the minute I was in I felt the love that was in these people that I'd never realised

---

52 Brian Proeve, **Stepping out with the Lord**, *Jacob's Letter* (May 1976), 21.

before. I committed my life to Jesus and then I began to see the real face of my problem. I am now living in a community house where I am learning to know the Lord better. As a street kid I learnt never to trust anybody but myself, but now I am learning to love and trust everybody in the community.

The House of Milk and Honey Cooperative

Other things began to develop as regular features of our life together. A Co-op was formed. As John Grimwade and Terry Allen explained, the idea was not just to provide cheap quality food for the community:

> As Christians in the world but not of the world (John 17), it is totally unnecessary to support the materialistic, capitalistic society, which surrounds us. We need not eat and drink the dead foods of a dying society. We at Jakes Co-op believe that by eating 'whole' unprocessed, unrefined foods we lift our physical stamina, which in turn will lift our spiritual and mental dimensions. When you eat wrong, or the processed foods, your body does not get the sufficient vitamins and minerals required to keep your body at its peak. When stamina (physical dimension) drops off, the mental and spiritual dimensions also become affected leaving you weaker. This means you are more vulnerable to the attacks of Satan in many areas of your life.[53]

---

53   John Grimwade and Terry Allen, *House of Milk and Honey Cooperative: The food we eat has been got at*, *Jacob's Letter* (September 1976), 15–17.

JACOB'S LADDER
CHRISTIAN COMMUNITY 1975–1976

By August 1976 they could report:

> Praise the Lord! The Co-op is really coming together at present. Many of our prayers have been answered already and the others are well on the way. We're still going to the market Friday mornings, so if you want to buy your fruit and veg at a cheaper price, all you have to do is write your order on a piece of paper and drop it in to us.[54]

Three weeks later we read:

> The Co-op is hoping to move onto the land! Praise the Lord! The gardens in the houses at the moment are being prepared ready to plant the summer vegetables. With each house planting what they feel like planting, we are likely to end up with an overflow of tomatoes and a shortage of carrots or something else. The idea is for the community houses that are willing, to "give" over their vegetable gardens to the Co-op to be planned.[55]

By 14 September we are told, "As you are aware by now, the Co-op has been floundering under its present system. The level of commitment towards the Co-op has been at a minimum which has caused us to re-structure it." Another undated *Jakes' Epistle* reported that meat is now available through the Co-op.

Developing long term gardens in rented houses was mostly not feasible. In addition, many of those living in the houses had few if any gardening skills. There were many different opinions on what brands to buy and some houses found it was quicker and easier just to buy their own supplies. After all, they were involved in many other things, which kept them busy. At the time of writing, we have been unable to track down Di & John Grimwade or Terry Allen, and have found no further written information.

Kerux Apostles MC

As already mentioned, Kerux Adelaide Motorcycle Club was formed early in 1974 as a merger between a number of small groups and the former *God's Disciples MC*. By May 1975 Geoff (Scrooge) Turner could report that "*Kerux* brothers and sisters realise that whole-hearted commitment to such a ministry requires a lifestyle of sacrifice where the lessons … are learnt if one is prepared to pay the cost of radical discipleship in Jesus."[56] Later that year the name was changed to *Kerux Apostles*

---

54   John and Di Grimwade, and Terry Allen, **Co-op News**, *Jakes' Epistle* (8 August 1976), 2.
55   John Grimwade, **Co-op News**, *Jakes' Epistle* (29 August 1976), 4.
56   Geoff Turner, **Bike and Street**, *Jacob's Letter* (May 1975), 4.

MC. Geoff explains that *Kerux* is a New Testament Greek word for witness or proclaimer and an apostle is a delegate or one sent with the full power of attorney to act on behalf of another.

Establishing relationships with 'outlaw' bikies was not easy. The task was challenging as Geoff explained:

> Kerux Apostles seeks to bring our outlaw brothers and sisters into the saving knowledge and freedom experience of Jesus Christ. We fly Christ's colours as a banner uplifting Jesus within the bike scene, and bound by the truth we know, we wear a cross strung out on our backs.

Love Blossoms

Other things began to happen. There were engagements and then marriages. That led in due course to children being born. It must have been quite a significant emphasis in the community because in October 1976 'name withheld' wrote:

> We seem to have suddenly become a community which is very "marriage fixated", so much so that in the past twelve months I have sat through numerous lectures on preparing for marriage, on courtship and just on girl/boy relationships. Everything seems to be focused on marriage. I am not knocking the marriage institution (how can I because it is quite scriptural) but I am beginning to wonder when we are going to be told how to be fulfilled by just being single. (Paul was single and he seemed quite fulfilled.) I am not married, nor am I planning to get married, and I am not lonely; I don't feel as though a vital part of me is missing, I feel quite fulfilled. I have Jesus as my companion and friend

to whom I can turn and who will be with me for better or for worse. Am I so terribly unusual being like this, or is something radically wrong with me?

Dr Daniel Overduin had written a major article on marriage in the September 1976 edition of *Jacob's Letter*. In many ways it was ahead of its time, using Ephesians 5:21–33 to emphasise mutual subordination in marriage. He devoted more space to the call to husbands to subordinate themselves to their wives by loving them just as Christ loved the church, than he did to the call to wives to subordinate themselves to their husbands. In addressing the word to wives, he corrected many a wrong emphasis in times past, by saying that:

> The call to subordinate is qualified at least three times: first, by the overarching exhortation, which calls for mutual subordination; next, by the unambiguous statement that a woman has to subordinate herself only to her husband (not to men in general); finally, by specifying the wife's subordination in terms of the Church's servant function before Christ.[57]

---

57 Overduin, Daniel, *The Excellent Model of a Marriage Handbook: Some notes on Ephesians 5:21–33*, *Jacob's Letter* (September 1976), 2–5.

In the same magazine it was reported that while the Kuhls and the Heidenreichs were travelling overseas, Doug's mother was looking after her grandchildren. The Editor wrote, "My ideal of community has in it the concept that it should be a community of all ages. For a long time we've had teenagers—they got married and now we've got young 'uns. Now, at last we have a Grandma!"

As more and more of the singles got married and had children, it was inevitable that the life of the community, and its daily/weekly routines, would change. Sadly, we need to recognise that many of those marriages did not last. This is not the place to canvas the reasons for that.

JACOB'S LADDER
CHRISTIAN COMMUNITY 1975-1976

SECTION iii

The Growth of Nurture Houses

CHAPTER 10

As previously mentioned, at the beginning of 1975 a large house was rented at 58 Queen Street, Norwood. It had 15 beds and at times housed up to 21 people. Ruth and I, together with Karl Brettig, were the house parents. A number of previous houses at St Morris (which may have closed earlier), Richmond, Highgate and Goodwood were amalgamated to form this new household. At the same time, we still had the house at 19 Vine Terrace, Klemzig with Erna and Doug Kuhl as house parents, and two houses at 33+37 Winchester Street, Highgate with Val and Trevor Brooks in charge.

On 6 May 1975 I wrote a report for the Lutheran Church of Australia, South Australian District Church Council on our community houses, with an appendix by Trevor Brooks. At the time, that sort of community living was treated as suspicious, if not condemned outright. I presume that the District Church Council had asked for a report. I conclude the report by stating:

> We are young and short of experience in living in extended family or community houses. We are learning new insights all the time as the Lord graciously reveals his will to us. We are attempting to put into practice the principles revealed in Scripture, chiefly those concerning the relationships of God's children in the world (mutual forgiveness etc), being in the world but not of it, the welcoming of strangers into our homes, and being wise stewards of time and money. We believe that the extended family is scripturally valid, if not indeed the scriptural norm for family life. We are not saying that the particular expression of it which is found in our midst, is the only or even the best way of living the Christian Life in this world, but we believe it is a valid way.

> This is in no way intended to be a complete report on our community houses but rather a brief outline of how we got where we are and how we're living at present. We remain open to the Lord that he may lead us further into his will and show us how he would have us live as his people in this world.[58]

---

58 Steen Olsen, with an appendix by Trevor Brooks, **Community Houses: A Report for the Church Council, LCA, SA District** (6 May 1975), 57.

The report explains how our community houses functioned. In summary, they were all an integral part of the ministry of Jacob's Ladder and as such came under the spiritual oversight of its eldership. The household lived together as family, and not as a boarding house, crash pad or whatever, and so each person shared in devotions, prayer, cooking and chores. The purpose of the houses was fourfold:

1. That members of the family may mature in their faith through their corporate study of the Word, prayer, working together and dealing with problems as they occur.

2. To minister through taking in non-Christian or young Christian guests to rehabilitate and nurture them.

3. To minister through taking in 'crashers' overnight.

4. To minister through being bases of outreach, both in media and in witnessing in specific situations.

Each house consisted of the family members who were the ministry team of the house. They were responsible for the ministry and for seeking the Lord's will concerning it. Guests were invited to stay as the Lord led. How long they stayed was reviewed weekly or periodically. In due course guests either joined the family or moved on. If someone wanted to join the family then the existing family prayed together and individually, seeking the Lord's leading. Only if a consensus in prayer was reached could the person become a family member. Guests usually came in through the same consensus process but, if necessary, the house elders could accept someone in as a guest. Any member of the family could agree to a 'crasher' staying for one night, if possible with the knowledge of a house elder. If a person was asked to leave a community house they could not stay in another until they had been reconciled to the household they left.

Marty Rosenberg remembers:

> To make sure there was a "Christian environment" in each Community House we ensured the Christian family members outnumbered the non-Christians. The daily lives and routines of each household flowed to varying degrees of smoothness but in the midst of the seeming chaos at times, lives were being changed. People who wanted to follow Jesus were given an opportunity to ask those difficult questions as they arose, and many a discussion was held late into the night. Group prayer became commonplace. Those who were seeking a new life in Christ received the love, appreciation and acknowledgement of being a worthwhile and much-loved person, and they

JACOB'S LADDER CHRISTIAN COMMUNITY 1975–1976

developed positive, encouraging relationships, which they had not previously experienced. This was the reality in many of the community houses, but of course, not everyone felt this way.

Establishing a New House

Peter Muller remembers setting up a new house in Henry Street, Stepney:

> We had nothing to set up a house. Therefore, I went off to the St Vincent de Paul on Payneham Rd and explained who we were and what we were planning to do as part of a diverse ecumenical community. We had less than $100 between us, after rent and bond. They simply replied, "Leave it to us." The next day a truck arrived with everything needed to set up a three bedroom house: Beds, wardrobes, lounge suite, tables, chairs, cooking utensils, crockery and cutlery. Someone had taken a great deal of care and thought.
>
> After setting up with help from a few others, we were resting late on the first Sunday morning when there was a knock at the door. Two elderly ladies were standing there who said, "We were just walking home from church when we felt compelled to stop and pray with the people in this house". We invited them in and did just that and they soon left. We were a bit stunned. A few seconds after they left, I rushed to the footpath but they were gone. They were very real flesh and blood Baptists but also angels to me. ("They entertained angels unawares" Heb 13:2.)
>
> A few weeks after setting up, I returned to the St Vincent de Paul store to thank them and bought a huge box of artificial flowers. I spread these around the garden with quirky combinations like inserting gardenias into the stem of an Arum Lilly. While some people were peeved, others appreciated the joke and there were many times that the decorations sparked conversations with neighbours and passers-by.

The Growth of Nurture Houses

I had a bit of ground to make up with my neighbours, as one of my first acts was to clean up the garden. This involved burning a lot of waste that was too damp. Consequently, I smoked out several clothes lines of fresh washing in the street. I promptly received an annoyed delegation of neighbours who graciously forgave my youthful inexperience.

While the time there was reasonably pleasant, the system of life required to make an effective house had not yet evolved.

Finances and Practical Arrangements

Each person living in a house was expected to contribute to the cost of rent, utilities, food and other expenses. At the time the report was written that was about $16 per week for each person. Sometimes a family would reduce that if there was a particular need. Each house was financially self-supporting, though in times of particular hardship others naturally helped. Everyone staying in the house, including guests and crashers, were expected to help with cooking, cleaning and gardening, as well as participating in other house activities.

Trevor Brookes reports that at the time of writing their two-house community had nine members, five girls, two guys and Val and Trevor and their two boys, aged 2½ and nine months. Marty Rosenberg and Dianne Nitschke were elders, working together with the house parents. Trevor notes:

> The concept is to try to supply a home environment where a person can come to know the Lord if not saved or grow closer to him if saved. A further ministry of the house is to live in such a way so we can release some of our money to support the work of Jakes. ... Each family member submits to our pastor Doug Kuhl and the elders of Jacob's Ladder. We thus see ourselves as an integral part of Jacob's Ladder ministry. In all this we recognise that we are doing no radical thing but are merely following the principles laid down in the Scriptures... We don't look upon the situation as permanent as there is no permanence in this world, in which we are all pilgrims and strangers.[59]

Problems

Of course, it was a long way from being smooth sailing. As Doug Kuhl notes in his 1975 report, "As would be expected, we face problems in practically every area of

---

59 Steen Olsen, with an appendix by Trevor Brooks, **Community Houses: A Report for the Church Council, LCA, SA District** (6 May 1975), 3.

JACOB'S LADDER CHRISTIAN COMMUNITY 1975–1976

SECTION iii

CHAPTER 10

our involvement in the ministry."⁶⁰ The community houses were meant to run as described above, but of course, this was often not the case. Sometimes chores were left undone, disagreements became arguments, and property was damaged. Sometimes team members were a bigger headache than the guests. Doug Kuhl provides an accurate summary:

> The most fundamental problem is the one of immaturity, over and against the as yet largely untrodden paths of this work. So far, it has been a matter of inching our way along and trying desperately to make the necessary adjustments we see are needed. It is quite possible that there are many problems we are not even recognising. But this is what growth is all about.

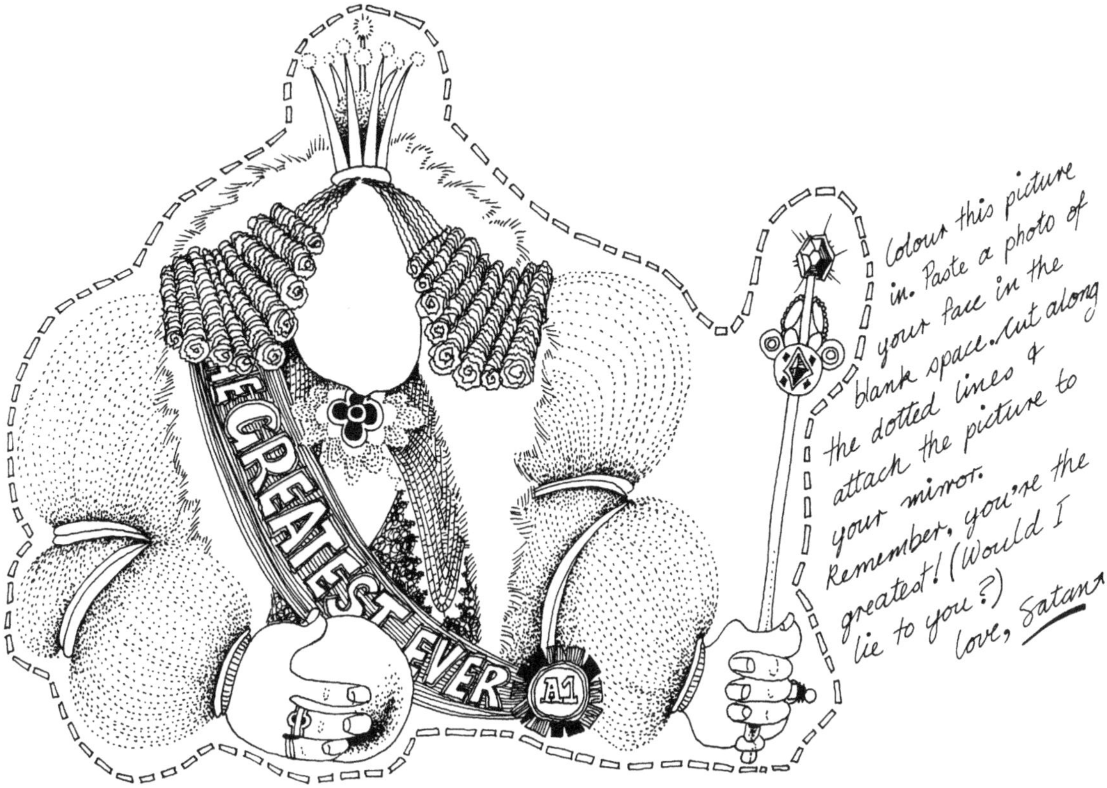

There is a lack of spiritually and emotionally mature leaders to guide the work of the nurture houses. However, within the structure of our community life together, we are endeavouring to train members for leadership roles. But this takes time. In the meantime, we live under the strain of great demands, and few human resources.

---

60 Douglas Kuhl, *Jacob's Ladder Christian Community: Report for Year 1975*, 5.

> There is a great need to form healthy family and community structures, which takes a great deal of time. Coupled with this our society in general is experiencing a constant breakdown of these types of structures. ... There is also great strain on us because our family/community relationships are in the context in which healing therapy (towards healthy attitudes, understandings, emotions and spirituality) takes place.[61]

The difficulty of having small children in community houses

In September 1975, Val and Trevor Brooks decided to move out of their nurture house in Highgate to reform their nuclear family. They had two boys under the age of three at the time. Thereafter, Trevor wrote an explanation to the Jakes community.[62] He said that they sensed that many in the community could not understand their action and some saw it as a betrayal of the ideal of community living. Trevor explains that when they were married they were living in a shared house. When that fell apart, they were alone for about three weeks before others again joined them. Up to the time they established the Jakes nurture house in January 1975, they had had about 30 young people staying with them for various amounts of time. Trevor wrote:

> At the time of our fifth wedding anniversary, we had spent approximately three months alone as husband and wife. Thus we would ask those of our younger unmarried brethren who are still in a nurture situation to try to understand. We weren't pulling out of nurture houses because we tried it, and it didn't work. We were pulling out in one sense to start a marriage. This is the first reason for leaving the nurture house scene. The second is so that we could provide the proper care to our children.[63]

Trevor then went into some detail about how difficult he found it to be the husband and father he wanted to be. "The reasons being the busyness of the house, the lack of privacy and my own sinfulness and laziness." He said that he saw the nuclear family as a norm, without which the extended family is impossible.[64] Too much well-meant advice from young single community members did not help the situation. Trevor continued:

> The second reason I have given earlier in this paper for us leaving the nurture house scene is so that we can spend the proper time with our

---

61 Douglas Kuhl, *Jacob's Ladder Christian Community: Report for Year 1975*, 5.

62 Trevor Brooks, *Why we left Nurture Houses* (undated, but it appears to have been distributed with a letter dated 13 May 1976).

63 ibid., 1.

64 ibid., 3.

JACOB'S LADDER
CHRISTIAN COMMUNITY 1975–1976

SECTION iii

CHAPTER 10

children. I have heard that in some Christian communities, there is a rule that parents with children up to five or six years should not be in a nurture ministry. My experience with my own children and my limited knowledge of the psychology of young children makes me believe that this rule ought to apply in Jakes. You only have to sit and observe a three year old, as my eldest is, to see how much they ape everybody. ... I watched my son sit in our front yard the other day, five metres from a group of boys and ape their every word and action. Their swearing and my son's echo put a stop to the situation. ... At Highgate he stopped saying grace because one of the girls always kept her eyes open and distracted him ... he went around "smoking" leaves and sticking cigarette butts in his mouth. ... On top of this we received numerous attempts at advice on how to bring up our kids handed to us, including one classic that I should sit him down and give him a talking to—when he was two![65]

As we look back, we see plenty of evidence that we were young and inexperienced. With hindsight, some things would have been done differently. Ruth and I moved into a nurture house after we had been married for six months. Our firstborn arrived a month before we moved out of the community house in Frederick Street, Welland to go to Toowoomba, Queensland for me to do my seminary internship through 1977. When we returned to Adelaide for my final year, we shared a house in Brompton with Jan and Steve Haar (who was also doing final year) and their newborn son Nathan. That was a great experience, perhaps also because we were not attempting to be a nurture house for troubled kids and new Christians. There are seasons in life (as Anne Sellers said a couple of chapters back) and we are grateful that we were able to raise our young family without all those extra pressures.

I also agree with Trevor that being newly married in a house of singles is not easy at times. In Queen Street, Ruth and I were fortunate to have a large room by the front door that served us as a small lounge and my study, as well as our bedroom (no ensuite though!) We had private space to which we could withdraw. We also had Karl who shared the house-parent responsibilities with us. He was still unmarried and had a small single room upstairs. The three of us were of one heart and mind, and so spoke with a single voice. That meant Ruth and I could withdraw at times. Having said that, for other reasons, the Queen Street house was probably too large. With up to twenty people coming and going, it was difficult to maintain a family atmosphere. At times decisions had to be made, family meetings were chaotic, and we probably felt more like a dictatorship than an intimate community striving for prayerful consensus. Christian community is not an ideal, but a broken reality that is always in the process of becoming.

---

65 ibid., 5–6.

Bob Lewis

One of our longer-term guests at Queen Street was a young bikie named Bob Lewis. Bob was quite a handful at times and we had our ups and downs. His time with us had begun with him living in a tent at the back of the men's house in Highgate. Later in 1975 Bob left and moved to Sydney. On the morning of Christmas Day that year, a Policeman knocked on our door and told us that Bob had been killed in Sydney. Apparently, he had put Ruth and me down as his next of kin. Between all of us, we managed to narrow down the area of Victoria where Bob's parents lived, so that the Police were able to notify them.

We learned that Bob died in a fire at the Savoy Hotel (backpackers/boarding house) in Kings Cross in Sydney that killed fifteen people. The fire was deliberately lit early on Christmas Eve and a Reginald John Little was subsequently convicted of murdering Bob and three others and sentenced to four life terms and a minimum of 28 years in gaol. He was eventually paroled in 2010, after serving 34 years. Writing almost a year after Bob's death, Ian Wade remembered that "a great deal of prayer, time and love had been given to Bob to build him up in the faith and love of God."[66]

Bob's death was a sobering reminder of why we did what we did. It came as we were preparing to move out of Queen Street. The owner would not renew the lease because he wanted to sell the property. The household therefore split into different houses and Ruth and I moved to Frederick Street, Welland, where a nurture house was established with three young men and three young women.

Nurturing Young Christians

Each house had young Christians and those who had more recently come to faith as 'family members'. One such family member at Queen Street was Peter Jasprizza. Peter recently looked back on his journey to faith and how he first came to be involved with Jakes:

> I asked God to help me one evening as I looked up at the stars above Hillcrest Psychiatric Hospital in Adelaide. I was there because I was a drug user and I had suffered some very nasty experiences on LSD. I had read the Gideons Bible I found in the hospital and I asked God if he really was there, and if he was the one

---

66   Ian Wade, *Jakes' Epistle* (5 December 1976), 6.

JACOB'S LADDER
CHRISTIAN COMMUNITY 1975–1976

SECTION iii

CHAPTER 10

who died so us humans could be born again. If so then could he please help me because otherwise, my life was over. The following morning, I awoke to discover that my heart was filled with great joy and that all I wanted to do was sing. The birds outside my window would come and sit on the windowsill and sing to me.

About a year later Bonny Gibson led me up the stairs that really was Jacob's Ladder. As others have also said, the atmosphere, the smiling faces, the willingness to help was something astonishing to me and something I will never forget. The next 10 years was a slippery ride of highs and lows. I had no idea of how a follower of Jesus should live and I did not buy all of what I saw in churches. It was very confusing.

Peter remained part of the Jakes community until it ended. You can read a little more of his story in chapter 28.

Gradually Stable Patterns Emerged

Peter Muller remembers his time in 59 Frederick Street Welland during 1976:

> Ruth and Steen were the house parents and there were several 'stable' community members in support. At any one time, one or two other contacts were included, depending on the complexity of need. Some combinations worked well, others were disruptive.
>
> This was my first model of a community house that was truly functional, with a disciplined devotional and house chores regime. Margo Pulkinghorne, Marcia Schutz, Anne Sellers, myself, and at one time Peter Jasprizza, were the support. It was a good learning experience.
>
> We had a lot of fun. One time Margo, who was dressed in a Halloween costume with a long black cape and wild hair and makeup, rushed the front door thinking that her ride had arrived only to find that there was no one there. Was it because of how Margo was dressed? Or, the fact that I had followed still carrying the kitchen knife that I was using to chop vegetables. Steen was horrified and demanded that we apologise. However, we never found out who it was.

Other Guests and Issues

I remember that the Christmas of 1975 we had an older alcoholic staying. He came in drunk again

The Growth of Nurture Houses // 79

late on Christmas Eve. I told him that I wanted to see him before he left the next morning, so he was to wait in the house until I got up, or else I would take it that he had moved out. The next morning he was gone. He returned later on Christmas Day and so I simply told him he didn't live here anymore, and he left. It occurred to me that if I could throw someone out on Christmas Day, then I was no longer a pushover. Some months later, someone else in the community ran into him somewhere and reported that he was sober. I have no idea what became of him. That also indicates something of how our houses operated. We did not allow ourselves to be walked over, and people were sometimes asked to leave.

I guess it was inevitable, given the people we were working with, that things would go missing from time to time. In the 29 August 1976 *Jakes' Epistle*, we noted while we were in New Zealand three of our blankets and a tablecloth went missing from Queen Street or during the move to Frederick Street. I also lost nearly all the tools that I had accumulated to that point—they were kept in a shed—and someone (we thought we knew who) took our pressure cooker, which had been a wedding present from my parents. We quietly replaced it and never told them. That was just in the nature of the situation and was not a big deal at the time.

A number of other houses were established in 1976. The Kuhls had moved to a Housing Commission home in Malvern and the Wades were in Dartmouth Street, West Croydon. In his 1975 annual report Doug mentioned that one of the goals that was being worked towards was to gradually move all the nurture houses to the Brompton-Croydon area.[67] That was achieved over time. Community nurture houses remained a core aspect of the life and work of Jacob's Ladder.

---

67 Douglas Kuhl, *Jacob's Ladder Christian Community: Report for Year 1975*, 5.

Outreach and Rehabilitation

Through all our activities, we continued to bring Jesus to those God brought to us. The 1975 annual report tells us that 47 people came to faith through that year, leading to four adult and two child baptisms. The community had 40 core members at the end of 1975, with 14 people being added during the year. A total of 49 other people seriously engaged with the community during the year as associate members. Some helped for a while and then moved on to other things or found work in other places. Another 85 were being nurtured at some stage during the year, either in community houses or through regular engagement with us. It was also reported that 18 people using drugs came to us that year and were now clean.[68]

It is worth pointing out that for Jacob's Ladder, evangelism was not one ministry among many. Everything was working towards, supporting and enabling the bringing of the message of God reconciling us to himself through the forgiveness of sins, in the power of the Spirit, for Jesus' sake. It was not that we would only help someone if they became a Christian—far from it. But our approach to rehabilitation, and all the various caring ministries, included seeking to help them to come into a relationship with Jesus, which was (and is) the best way we could help anyone. There was no one in Jakes whose task was to lead the outreach ministry; that was what we were all doing. God was at work and we were joining him in his mission to his world.

That didn't mean that there was no pastoral care of the community. That happened as well. Without nurturing, supporting and caring for those who were already Christian, there would be no outreach. In fact, when the church focuses on bringing Jesus to those who as yet do not know him, there will always be pastoral care. Sadly, when the church prioritises meeting the needs and wants of those who are already part of their community, there is often little or no evangelism. Often the word 'outreach' and 'mission' are broadened to include all manner of community care and justice concerns, which are not bad things, except when we only care for people's temporal needs, and do not bring them the good news that is both for this world and the one to come. In Jakes at this time, we tried to care for people, stood up for the oppressed and provided practical help, while also talking about Jesus. Everything that we did was focused on the hope and prayer that people would not just be helped in this life, but would also receive the life that lasts for all eternity.

---

68 Douglas Kuhl, *Jacob's Ladder Christian Community: Report for Year 1975*, 4.

Concerts and Street Theatre

Music and drama were an integral part of the life of Jakes, and a core part of our outreach efforts. As well as in worship services and the Coffee House, music and drama were used to raise questions and bring Jesus wherever and whenever we got the opportunity. At that time there was no need to get permits, and permission was only needed if it was a private venue.

David Skeat, who went on to work with *Youth with a Mission* Australia and is now on their National Eldership and is National Director of Australian Mercy, remembers:

> Phil Jefferis and I used to do street theatre together on outreaches and later with the Christian rock band called *Kerygma* who later changed their name to *Strike A light!* Phil and I used to write a lot of stuff and perform it at Jakes and in other coffee shops around the traps, along with Colin Smith and Danny Brauchli who provided the music. Kevin and Marcia were also part of the crew who used to perform. Phil and I called ourselves *Fool Phil* and *Dave the Rave*, but other times we referred to ourselves as the *Acts of the Apostles*. Some of the stuff we did was funny and apt, some stuff I am embarrassed to remember.
>
> One day Phil and I were talking about how that word Xmas was offensive because it took Christ out of Christmas. At that time, John Martins were advertising the John Martins "Xmas" parade. The advertising was everywhere. So Phil and I decided to take action. We constructed a coffin out of materials that were lying around, painted it black, and painted a sign on the sides that said, "Xmas is dead. Christ is alive!" Phil and I (there could have been a few others as well) carried the coffin behind the last float in John Martins Christmas pageant. We were booed, but we figured that we were suffering for the gospel. The other stuff we wrote and performed was better than that, but that is one clear memory I have of those times.
>
> Another time I had a vision whilst praying of a hole in a wall and people crawling through it. The creative juices flowed and about a month later, Phil and I and the team were performing "Hole in the Wall" concerts for youth groups and coffee houses. Colin had helped us put music to a song that I had written, and away we went. I think it would be a fair thing to say that we were very inspired by the writings of CS Lewis and JRR Tolkien whose books the *Chronicles of Narnia* and *The Lord of the Rings* were doing the rounds at the time.
>
> Early on in the piece, a muso came to the community called Neil Reichelt. Neil was a farmer from NSW but ended up at Jakes. He was happy and

JACOB'S LADDER CHRISTIAN COMMUNITY 1975–1976

positive and wrote songs and performed at Jakes a few times. In about 1977 he went to the US to make a record. The record was called *Neil Reichelt Sings "I'm Happy"*. It included two songs from the community: Fireside News by Karl Brettig and *Fairy Tales* by me (I had written the words but Neil really made the tune work).

There was enormous creativity at work in the community. Graphics were done by the gifted Knarelle Beard and later also by Phil Jacobs. The worship band was writing and performing great worship stuff, and then there was the street theatre and other artistic expressions.

The Sonshine Centre

Late in 1974, the Jacob's Ladder Management decided "to take up a beach ministry at Henley Beach this summer."[69] A shopfront on the Square was rented and prepared. Knarelle Beard produced business cards and then painted the logo on the window of the shop. There was a soundshell down towards the beach where Christian musicians were able to perform. We operated it as a summer ministry at the beginning of 1975. "It was later taken over by a local church group, and continued to operate, due to the considerable interest shown by the youth of the area."[70]

There was a fire, which caused extensive damage to the centre. The town clerk blamed gangs and hooligans in the area but Mr JS Walker, the director of the centre at the time, said that the accusation made by the council was misleading. He said that the fire was an accident and the police did not suspect arson.

Julie Anne and the ongoing work of Rehabilitation

Julie Anne Lambert (later McBride) became involved with Jakes through a chance conversation with Trevor Brooks shortly after her brother, and only sibling, died in an accident on their family farm on 1 October 1975. Julie Anne was a bundle of energy and remained so until her death on 4 August 2019. She had been born with cerebral palsy, used a wheelchair all her life, and lived in institutions for twenty years from the age of five. Julie Anne quickly became a part of community life. She and her wheelchair were regularly carried up and down the stairs to the Coffee House. She moved into a community house for a while, where she continued her

---

69 *Jacob's Ladder Management Committee Minutes* (28/11/1974).

70 *Jakes' Epistle* (7 November 1976), 8.

already impressive journey into independence. Soon she was using her skills in caring for others. She continued doing this throughout her life, establishing houses for people, both with disabilities and the able-bodied, including her first house at Oaklands Park in the early 1980s.

> The simple lessons that Julie Anne had learnt at Jacob's Ladder—cooking and washing, independence and meaningful existence—she now passed on to others. Over the next four years, 50 people moved through the house, some staying several months and others up to three years.[71]

Along the way, Julie Anne also worked for various other organisations, speaking to hundreds of meetings. She married Neville McBride in April 1986. They continued the work of outreach and rehabilitation together through Koinonia Trust, which Julie Anne had established. There was a good representation of former Jakes people at her funeral at Clare, South Australia on 14 August 2019. The *Adelaide Advertiser* printed an obituary in which they also recorded the following event, which speaks volumes about Julie Anne's approach and determination.

> In 1983 she decided that entering the Miss Australia Quest would be a good way to challenge people's ideas on what was normal and beautiful. Wheelchair-bound Julie Anne, who was prone to occasional spasms and needed to gasp when speaking, was putting herself out there as a means of disagreeing with the accepted norms. While the disabled in other states had made rowdy protests against the quest and its ideas of beauty, Julie Anne decided it might be more effective if she entered. Her entry threw the organisation into disarray and it embarked on a major learning curve on discrimination. The Adelaide media of the day were similarly challenged. "All organisations need to look at what normal is," Julie Anne said.[72]

A Rural Rehabilitation Facility

The need for a rural rehabilitation facility was already identified by August 1974:

> We feel great pressure upon us to found a rehabilitation centre for dropouts, drug addicts, criminals, and general social misfits. To attempt to push these people out into society, the society which they have already proved that they can't handle by virtue of their misfit behaviours, is frankly being quite unrealistic. We desperately need places to bed people down, spiritual elders

---

71 Anne Bartlett, **Ready, Willing & Disabled**, *Alive* (February 1999), 28.

72 **Adelaide Advertiser** (Saturday 16 November 2019), 54.

JACOB'S LADDER CHRISTIAN COMMUNITY 1975–1976

to nurture these people, workshop facilities to engage these dropouts in creative activities.[73]

Doug Vogelsang remembers that a property was made available to us at Pine Point, 20km south of Ardrossan on Yorke Peninsula, approximately 150km north of Adelaide. On 9 June 1975, John Holberton was employed by Jacob's Ladder to establish and lead a rehabilitation work at that site. It was called *Maranatha*. John had come from Brisbane and before that from the United States. The position was funded by a government grant obtained by the Lutheran Youth of South Australia. A local *Maranatha Community Advisory Committee* was established. Bonny Gibson remembers being there and that there was a lot of physical work involved. They needed to dig a new septic tank and do other work on the house and grounds. He doesn't remember anyone arriving to be rehabilitated, and it may be that the work never really got established.

In any case, on 26 August the Advisory Committee wrote to the Jacob's Ladder Management Committee expressing concern over the 'general inactivity' concerning the project and said that a constitution for Maranatha was urgently needed so that local confidence in the project was not impacted. They expressed confidence in the ability of John Holberton and said that an anonymous donation of $150 had

---

73 Douglas Kuhl, ***Report to the Department for Community Welfare*** (9 August 1974), 3.

been received but that its use was dependent on the establishment of a "stable management structure, comprised mainly of local people." They therefore asked that as many members of the Jakes Management Committee as possible attend their meeting on 9 September.

On 22 September John Holberton wrote to Doug Vogelsang as secretary of the Jacob's Ladder Management Committee, resigning from his position, effective from 9 September. In resigning, it was obvious that John did not intend leaving Maranatha, since he hoped to "be in a position to receive drug cases you feel we may be able to assist you with." He also stated that he strongly felt that "no organisation, religious denomination, or any one person should have controlling interest over the 'Maranatha Community' ministry."

That provoked a fiery response from Doug Kuhl. In a letter dated 30 September he refused to accept John's resignation until outstanding matters had been dealt with. In summary, these included that since John had been employed by Jacob's Ladder and been paid with money from a government grant, it was unclear how John could explain that he had "used this money, time and opportunity to set up his own structure so that he can now do his own thing." Normally when someone resigns, someone else is appointed in their place. For the advisory committee to suddenly take over this ministry which was established by someone else was described as 'piracy' and legal action was threatened. Doug pointed out that the advisory committee was just that, advisory, and legally the ministry was tied to Jacob's Ladder and the Lutheran Church.

The Advisory Committee responded on 2 October. They said that local leadership was vital to the success of the ministry and that John's resignation left them with no option but to choose between John and Jacob's Ladder, and they decided

JACOB'S LADDER CHRISTIAN COMMUNITY 1975–1976

that they would rather have John 'in charge' than Jakes. They felt that doing this would keep faith with the local community "who have supported the ministry so wholeheartedly". They regretted and apologised for the derogatory remarks about Jacob's Ladder.

On 5 October, Doug Vogelsang wrote to the secretary of the Maranatha Community saying that the Jacob's Ladder Management Committee, in view of everything, had decided to accept John's resignation and terminate his employment from 8 October. Even though John had recently returned two cheques, Doug enclosed full payment up until that date. On 10 October, Doug Kuhl wrote to the Advisory Committee stating that at the time of his letter of 29 September the Jakes Management Committee had not yet met and that his letter reflected the great personal concern felt by himself and the elders of Jacob's Ladder. Secondly, he apologised for the general tone of that letter and for 'any offense' caused. He asked for their forgiveness of any unfair inferences in his letter.

So ended this attempt to establish a rural rehabilitation centre. Clearly, we failed in regard to this endeavour. Perhaps we did not do enough background pre-employment checks. Maybe we didn't put enough time into the early stages of the venture. On the other hand, the fact that the situation deteriorated so quickly suggests that there were other agendas at play. While the correspondence referred to above has survived, we don't have any other written records, only our memories, which are getting a bit sketchy.

Yahweh Shalom at Padthaway

Early in 1976 was one of those times when the community found itself particularly short of money. Our gardens were fruitful and people brought gifts of food so we could still invite people to come and share in the goodness of the Lord. After our relationship with Maranatha ended, we still felt the need to have a country property for rehabilitation and to grow food. I pick up the story in *Jacob's Letter*:

> We had no money to buy farms, so we asked the Lord to provide one, if it was his will that we have one at this point of time. A little while later a man [Mr Frank Edsen] got in touch with us to say that he believed that the Lord wanted him to give away his 300 acre farm to be used by a Christian group for rehabilitating drug addicts, alcoholics and others with similar problems. "Thank you Lord!"
>
> The Yahweh Shalom ministry at Padthaway has now gotten under way on this property and a small community has been established to minister to those that

the Lord is leading there. It is legally independent of Jacob's Ladder but works in close fellowship and interdependence with us. The Lord is keen to provide what his people need for ministry purposes. [74]

Ian McLeish, the caretaker/manager of Yahweh Shalom provided more detail:

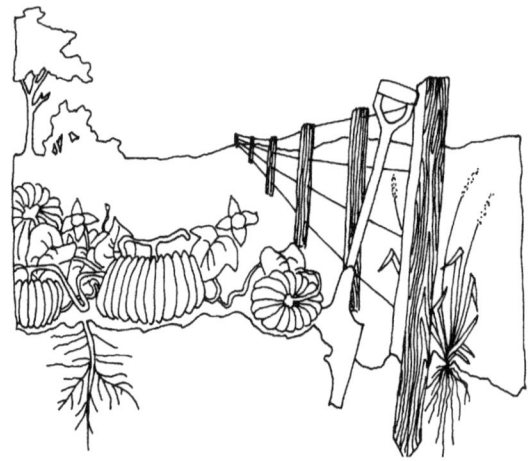

> In January this year a committee of local Christians formed to begin and manage this work. From the beginning we planned to work in close co-operation with groups such as Jacob's Ladder. ... Although we have only the bare fundamentals now, we plan to provide more labour intense farm activities, hobby and craft facilities, which should give folk an opportunity for self-expression and support the community. ... The Council however, is still uncertain of how they should decide to view what we propose to do. It would appear they are caught between severe pressure from influential local people in our area and a sense that what we propose is good and worthwhile. ... The Council recently called a rate-payers meeting to gauge public reaction and we thank God for a response of 2:1 in favour of Yahweh Shalom.[75]

Once again, I don't know what happened after that. None of us can recall anyone being sent there for rehabilitation.

From the viewpoint of Jakes, it was another attempt at establishing the rural rehabilitation centre that did not come to fruition.

---

74 Steen Olsen, **Money Money Everywhere (and not a drop to drink)**, Jacob's Letter (May 76), 9.

75 Ian McLeish, **Yahweh Shalom Christian Community**, Jacob's Letter (May 76), 22.

JACOB'S LADDER CHRISTIAN COMMUNITY 1975–1976

Worship, Music, Drama and the Arts

For many months, we struggled with the whole area of worship. It began among us as a kind of peripheral observance, which we faithfully carried out every Sunday afternoon for an hour or so. We broke free from rigid liturgical forms and substituted choruses, readings, sharing times, prayer and of course a sermon, and yet something was still lacking.[76]

It took a while to work out that the key issue was not just the form of worship, or the language, or the sort of music and instruments we used. It went much deeper than that. Sure, the cultural expressions we used should be appropriate to those who gathered for worship. Pipe organs, classical music, liturgies that were substantially the same each week, vestments and robes and sanctuaries that oozed formality, with fixed pews and ornate fittings, were not our heart language, let alone that of most of those who came to faith. Yet when we changed all those things, we still found that there was something lacking, as Karl said in the quote above.

In coming to understand worship relationally, we first needed to overcome the naturalism that had been deeply ingrained in us from a young age. We needed to recognise the fallacy in the idea that worship is something that we do for God. We needed to come to see that worship flowed out of the relationship God has with us, through the Spirit, and secondly that it has to do with the relationships we have with one another, because it is something we do as a community and not just as individuals. Jesus lives in the midst of the community through his Spirit. He is the host who welcomes us into his presence. He ministers to us through his Word and comes to us under bread and wine as we gather at his table. We respond to him with adoration, praise, confession and prayer. Worship is relational, and God is the main 'actor'.

That means that when relationships in the community are broken, they need to be fixed through confession and forgiveness. As Karl wrote:

> In our community houses, we discovered that we could not come before the Lord in praise and worship, unless our relationships with each other had been put right. Times of ministry, one with another, became an important part of our worship life. Sometimes we found these needed to be incorporated into our worship time. We would come before the Lord to praise him and somehow we

---

76 Karl Brettig., **Worship (or don't make the stones cry!)**, *Jacob's Letter* (September 1975), 11.

would know that there was something wrong among us … "OK brothers and sisters, let's break for a while, pray individually for a time and then minister to one another before we come before the Lord together as one in his Body." The Lord does not entrust too much of his almighty power to a bunch of immature kids with nappy problems![77]

Gradually we grew in worship. Sometimes it was a couple of steps forward, then one step back. At other times we just seemed to be slipping backwards. However, there was a genuine desire to learn and grow. Our services became longer and moved to Sunday mornings. Others, who were not involved in the community, began to come to join us in worship. We made room for people to exercise spiritual gifts, under the oversight of the pastor and the elders. Sometimes we just waited on the Lord. Sometimes people were healed or released from burdens. At times demonic oppressors were driven out and people set free. We came to understand that the Lord inhabits the praises of his people and moves among us to bless us as we gather in his name. At times it was noisy and must have seemed chaotic. We copped a lot of criticism, but then so did Jesus:

> [36]As Jesus rode along, people kept spreading their cloaks on the road.
> [37]As he was now approaching the path down from the Mount of Olives, the whole multitude of the disciples began to praise God joyfully with a loud

---

77 Karl Brettig., **Worship (or don't make the stones cry!)**, *Jacob's Letter* (September 1975), 12.

JACOB'S LADDER
CHRISTIAN COMMUNITY 1975–1976

SECTION iii

CHAPTER 12

voice for all the deeds of power that they had seen, ³⁸saying, "Blessed is the king who comes in the name of the Lord! Peace in heaven, and glory in the highest heaven!" ³⁹Some of the Pharisees in the crowd said to him, "Teacher, order your disciples to stop." ⁴⁰He answered, "I tell you, if these were silent, the stones would shout out." Luke 19:36–40, NRSV

Prayer and Intercession

Prayer was a priority. The Coffee House had a prayer room. When we were on the road, conducting a mission or ministering to Christians at the invitation of a congregation, we established a room or area for prayer. Prayer quite simply was part of every activity. If you were on your own you could pray while washing the dishes or doing laundry. In community houses it was normal to see two people or a small group sitting somewhere and praying. I remember one night in the Coffee House a small team came back and reported that they had been having a difficult time witnessing in a pub. They all came outside and went down a fairly dark alley, gathered in a circle and prayed. Next moment they were bathed in torchlight and a gruff Police Officer's voice said, "What are you doing?" "Praying", they answered. "Don't be smart", he growled. No, really, they were! Because that is what we did.

Preaching and Teaching

Preaching and teaching was another core feature of community life. Pastor Doug Kuhl was of course the main preacher and did much of the teaching, but many others were also involved. We were also privileged to hear from others, both from the Adelaide area, interstate and overseas. Erika Anear wrote:

> I have remembered one of Doug's sermons, on and off, throughout my life, and the message still proves true today. The shortened version went something like this:
>
> "Imagine that one day you go out into your garden and notice a new tiny garden shed in the corner. You open the door and go inside to investigate and once inside, to your astonishment the garden shed inside is somehow bigger than your whole property and looks like a huge basketball stadium. You walk around inside and explore it all the while being amazed at how something like this got to be in your garden. After a while you notice in the corner of this stadium there is another small similar shed. You go over and go inside and this time the area inside is a big oval. You are overwhelmed at the impossibility of this and yet here you stand. How could you be inside something that is bigger than what you saw from the outside? You wander

around for a while taking in the whole scene and yes after a while you notice another small shed…"

The message was about us getting to know God and then at some point thinking we understand him. Then one day He gives us a surprise and all of a sudden, we see so much more of him and his Kingdom and so we proceed to live in that and learn about that. Then some time later, it happens again and again and again. Each time our hearts are thrilled with the wonder of finding out how much more wonderful and loving and amazing and good he is than we had previously known.

Noel Paul Stookey and Barry McGuire

On Sunday morning 2 May 1976, Noel Paul Stookey—'Paul' of *Peter, Paul and Mary* fame—played and sang at our worship celebration. He spoke about how we lose our first love and the need to turn ourselves over to the Lord:

> We take with us those objects that display the fact that we were in love once. They may be photographs in an album, or a ring, or a gift, or a sacred song. Sometimes the object will be a church [or some aspect of our life as Christians]. Then we use the gifts, the ring, and the photograph albums to remind ourselves that we were once in love. That also reminds us that we need to be in love all the time, but I think it is impossible to be in love all the time, unless you are with Jesus all the time.[78]

---

78 *Stookey Visit*, *Jacob's Letter* (May 1976), 23–24.

JACOB'S LADDER CHRISTIAN COMMUNITY 1975–1976

SECTION iii

CHAPTER 12

Barry McGuire performed at the Festival Theatre in Adelaide on 3 July 1976. He walked out on an empty stage with just his guitar, simply dressed in a T-shirt, jeans and boots, and began singing, "I don't know what you came to do, but I came to praise the Lord." He was known for his hit anti-war protest song *Eve of Destruction* and contributed much to the contemporary Christian music scene. Barry was kind enough to give us a day of his time, where some of us shared a BBQ and talked. He shared a new communion song he had recently written and a recorded interview in which he talked about the exciting new wave of Christian music that was emerging across the globe. Encouraging local musicians to use their gifts in worship and proclamation of the good news, he inspired us to take Jesus music into the streets and entertainment venues around the city.

In a taped interview, he shared some key insights behind his striking ability to translate the message of the gospel into the culture of the day. "When Jesus spoke to the street he spoke in parables. He was aware of what was happening in the daily lives of people, especially their worries and fears. You have to find key phrases to which people listen. People come because the topic is interesting to them. Is there life after death? Get familiar with the headlines in the newspaper, speak in parables that they understand and gently introduce Jesus at the end." He also encouraged various branches of the Body of Christ to work together using the same images and words where possible to communicate core messages.

Music and Drama in the Streets

Drama was a regular part of Jakes outreach activities, with Phil Jefferis being on staff to work in this area. But many others were also involved. Marcia Lieschke remembers:

Karl Brettig // Colin Smith // Ann Richter (Drechsler) // Chris Wills (George)

> During 1975 and 1976, street concerts and street evangelism were held during summer months in Victoria Square and on North Terrace out the front of the Museum of SA. We also visited some schools and Universities on a less regular basis.
> Our purpose was to sing songs that might cause people to think about purpose, life, Jesus. Colin wrote many of the songs but we also sang some well-known songs of the time.

Worship, Music, Drama and the Arts // 93

Drama teams performed at these events and would participate in street marches demonstrating against Uranium mining and nuclear war, in an effort to relate to other participants and as an opportunity to evangelise at these events. Sometimes we carried a 'coffin' (which by the way served as a means to carry our costumes or props). I can remember a drama called *The Trouble with Toys* which featured a couple who gave their children toy guns to play with, in effect, giving them opportunity to do their own thing. As they grew up, they became a law unto themselves and in the end turned upon their parents with 'real guns' shooting them down. It was in effect speaking to the 'lawlessness' in society that would end up reaping destruction upon themselves.

Our music group 'Servants' won a recording session in around 1977 or 78 where we were able to record in a professional studio some of our own songs composed by Colin Smith, Alan Muston, Karl Brettig and Marcia Lieschke (Schutz).

As Marcia mentioned, many of the songs and dramas were written by Colin and Phil and members of their teams. There was a great deal of creativity. Anne Sellers remembers Alan Muston (who was also our resident sculptor) and the Rock Opera, and others writing stories, poems and broadsheets. The best of this written material was published with Knarelle Beard's amazing artwork. She also produced letterheads, business cards and illustrated our magazines and newsletters.

We worked with many musicians, bands and groups, both in the Coffee House and in other settings. Among them are Robin and Dorothy Mann and Kindekrist, Rod Boucher, Kerygma, Rob and Sandy McCarthy and the Country Gospel Bluegrass Band, Neil Reichelt and Peter Campbell.

Drama in Adelaide University dining hall

Knarelle Beard remembers:

When he was visiting from the U.K., Os Guiness, an English author and social critic, was asked to do a talk at the University of Adelaide. Before the talk, the Jakes Drama team did some promotion in the Refectory. Most of us stationed ourselves around the hall while Phil Jefferis joined the queue to buy his meal. On his metal tray was a small amount of food (potato chips, I think) and as much metal cutlery and plates as he could fit on his tray. At the end of the queue he paid, then "tripped" as he left the cash register, making an abundance of prolonged clatter as he hit the floor. Everyone in

JACOB'S LADDER CHRISTIAN COMMUNITY 1975–1976

the Refectory looked up. One by one, those of us around the hall yelled out: "Don't look at me! I had nothing to do with it!" or "I was nowhere near him when it happened!" or "It's not my fault!" as we rushed out of the Refectory. Phil picked up himself, his chips, his tray, his cutlery, his plates, and announced in his loudest voice, "Os Guiness is speaking today on *Collective Guilt* at (this place) at (this time)!"

Spontaneous Drama at Tunarama

A Jakes outreach team went to Tunarama in Port Lincoln on Eyre Peninsula in South Australia on the Australia Day long weekend at the end of January in 1976. The Tunarama Festival features a wide array of participation events, arts and cultural displays, local market stalls, as well as celebrating the Tuna fishing industry of the city. Knarelle remembers that not all drama was planned. Sometimes someone got an idea, and there was an opportunity, so the team went to work. Knarelle recounts a couple of examples:

> Some of the drama team was off duty down at the water's edge where a family-friendly amusement area had been set up. One of the tents had gaming machines in it—machines that didn't look like poker machines but functioned in the same way. And this was a family-friendly venue! We decided to do some improvised drama using the props we had at our disposal: a bugle, a 20 cent coin, a cushion, a full-length hooded crushed velvet cape. We paraded into the tent, first the bugler, then the cushion bearer with the 20 cent atop, then the princess in her velvet cape, her courtiers holding her train. Everyone in the tent stopped playing the machines as the princess and her retinue approached. The owner, looking as if he were about to commit murder because we were stopping his money-making concerns, demanded to know what we were doing. The princess indicated the coin on the cushion, picked it up, and fed it into one of the machines. A Jackpot wasn't achieved, and we processed out of the tent, thankful that the presence of young families had prevented a possible homicide.

> On the Sunday a local church hosted an outside communal lunch for everyone following the service. After grace was said, everyone rushed the food tables as if there wasn't enough food to go around. I commented on this to the drama team, and we devised an impromptu performance. All but one of us approached the tables and began loudly bickering about whose turn it was to do the dishes, each of us excusing ourselves and adamant that "It's not my turn!" Then the team member not at the tables stood up and said, "It wasn't Jesus' turn to die

on the cross either." That was the end of our drama, but we had talked ourselves into a corner—we couldn't *not* do the washing up after that!

Dance

Lyn Muller recalls:

> I began to teach some Israeli dances to community members, and soon formed a dance group, which could also perform in the worship services. The constant members of this group were Chris Tierney-Smith, Jenny Mac, and Knarelle Beard. Others were involved at times. Colin Tierney-Smith composed and performed songs for Jacob's Ladder, and we began to rehearse with him and the band, to choreograph and present dances to their songs.

Ecumenical EXPO Outreach

On the 8–11 October 1976 long weekend an EXPO was held at the Adelaide Showground. *Jacob's Letter* reported, "The Christians of Adelaide have been offered a MAZE that presents Christ as the only one worth having, compared to what the commercial world is offering. Jakes is directly responsible for a creative activities area. This needs your prayer support."[79] Knarelle did the art work for the publicity and other materials, as well as for the "I'm Amazed" buttons, which were given to those who successfully completed the maze.

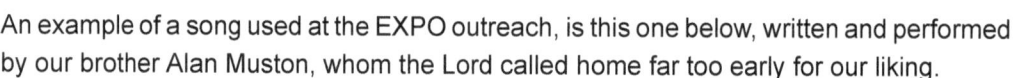

An example of a song used at the EXPO outreach, is this one below, written and performed by our brother Alan Muston, whom the Lord called home far too early for our liking.

> **There's a Man with a Withered Hand**
> by Alan Muston
>
> VERSE 1
> There's a man with a withered hand,
> third left in the picture.
> The man on the right had a fight last night
> with the girl who looks like his sister.
> And the soul of the man who looks old
> is rotting in hell since this picture.

---

79 ***News***, *Jacob's Letter* (September 1976), 22.

JACOB'S LADDER CHRISTIAN COMMUNITY 1975–1976

SECTION iii

CHAPTER 12

VERSE 2
The tall boney man who hardly can stand
is crippled with frustration
while waiting in fear, with a sword and a tear,
for war to take his nation.
And the heart of the man at the rear
is burning with fear for his loved one.

CHORUS
What are we doing here, standin' like we don't care?
The storm is blowin' hard against the shores.
What are we gonna say to the Lord on Judgment Day—
that we didn't see them stray our way?

VERSE 3
Here he comes and he's got no thumbs—
leprosy took them away.
He's lookin' at you and he's startin' to chew
on his fingers. What do you say?
Are you too blind to see his most desperate need
ain't tomorrow it's today?

VERSE 4
Look, ya know, there's Joe
with the flagon he stole from the hotel.
His body's a wreck and the head on his neck
is bleedin'. You say "Oh well.
It's now time to move, I've got shopping to do,
the specials are on at New World."

CHORUS

Alan Muston

Knarelle remembers Alan's audience being so convicted by the words and passion of his song that there was a split second of silence before they were able to gather themselves to show their appreciation in prolonged applause.

This song obviously has a message, but it also prepares the way for a message. Drama and song raise questions in people's minds. They can be confronting in ways that are difficult to do with speech, at least without causing people to stop listening and start walking away. This song is law, that is, it judges our uncaring attitudes and lack of action. Law prepares us to hear the gospel. It opens the way for us to bring the story of Jesus and what God has done for us through him.

The message of forgiveness fits in here; as does the work of the Holy Spirit in making us new—not perfect, but new. A new heart and a new mind, so that we may care for others and not look the other way.

Outreach activities, such as at the EXPO, happened frequently and were usually a collaboration between our musicians, drama teams and artists, as well as preachers/speakers, when that was appropriate. Some were staged as a spontaneous street drama, as already mentioned, others were part of larger projects like EXPO. Many involved cooperation with other groups and ministries in Adelaide. Universities and schools were open to our involvement. The media treated us much more kindly than would be the case today. We were blessed with a deep sense of God being at work in his world. We were just a small part of what God was doing.

The importance of music, drama and the arts in the work of Jakes should not be under-estimated. While the emphasis often fell on the "name" speaker or preacher, it was very much a team effort.

Lutheran Renewal, Interstate and Overseas Connections

Already in 1974, Jakes had become a focal point for Lutherans who had been touched by charismatic renewal. By 1975, a number of people had begun to attend worship and teaching events at the Coffee House. In early 1976, a significant number of Lutherans attended an interdenominational charismatic conference in Adelaide. A loosely structured group formed, involving both people from Jakes and lay members of Lutheran congregations in South Australia.

The beginnings of Lutheran Charismatic Renewal Australia

On 6 February 1976 a letter from Pastor Doug Kuhl was sent to those who were thought to be interested, inviting them to a day-long meeting on 21 February to discuss and plan the formation of a fellowship "that will sponsor in our own church such a charismatic or spiritual renewal." It was held at the El Carim Camp, Stirling, in the Adelaide Hills.

Doug Vogelsang took minutes at the subsequent gathering held at the same place on 3 April. Approximately 120 people attended. There was worship, fellowship and sharing in the morning. In the afternoon, Pastor Daniel Overduin delivered a paper on *New Life in the Spirit*, based on Galatians 5:13–25. Then Pastor John Sims began to present his paper on *Divine Healing*. The program was probably running late and Pastor Sims had another appointment, so he was unable to complete his presentation, but he was invited to do so at a future meeting. (He finished his paper at the gathering held on 1 May.)

In the evening a business meeting was held. The following are the key points from the minutes:

- There was discussion on holding regional meetings in different parts of the State and it was decided that the feasibility of doing that would need to be discussed in consultation with the pastors of local congregations.

- It was decided that Lutheran Spiritual Renewal Meetings would be held monthly on the first Saturday of each month.

- It was noted that this would need to be done properly in the light of the SA District President's Pastoral Letter. "The gathering reaffirmed its desire to stay within the body of the Lutheran Church and to work within the framework of the congregations."

- A steering committee was elected comprising of Pastor Doug Kuhl, Doug Vogelsang, Hans Scholtfeldt, Glen and Judith Heidenreich, Ian McLeish and David Trudinger. The committee was to work "in close consultation with the LCA SA District and the Lutheran Church at large." [Only Doug Kuhl and Doug Vogelsang were members of Jakes.]

- "The gathering asked Pastor Doug Kuhl to be its spiritual leader. Pastor Kuhl stated that this would have to be discussed with the church officials."

- It was decided that a bank account be opened in the name of Lutheran Spiritual Renewal and that a treasurer be appointment from within the steering committee.[80]

Working with the Church

On 18 March Pastor Doug Kuhl reported on his correspondence with the District President, Pastor Clem Koch. He quotes part of his letter to the president:

> The 93 member[81] conference wishes to advise the leaders of the district of their intention to conduct a second meeting to be held at the same venue on 3 April 1976. These members earnestly seek the recognition and blessing of our church leaders for another such meeting. They gave strong voice to their loyalty and willingness to support their church through their respective congregations, working closely together with their pastors, elders and fellow church members. Their desire is to sponsor love, peace and understanding of each person's growth, experience, calling and service in their Lord Jesus Christ, by means of the Gospel. Together with this, the conference members wish to encourage and sponsor among Christian people a deeper acceptance of a further release of the power and influence of the Holy Spirit at work in our lives—realising that the Spirit's work is to empower us towards a deeper acceptance of Christ and his victorious work on the cross and in his rising to life again. Thus we may be further enabled to live Christ-centred lives in today's world.

---

80 Doug Vogelsang, *Minutes of Lutheran Spiritual Renewal Conference, El Carim* (3 April 1976). (The document was found in an Olsen filing cabinet!)

81 I presume this is the number of adults who 'signed up', rather than the total number, including children, who attended.

JACOB'S LADDER CHRISTIAN COMMUNITY 1975–1976

SECTION iii

CHAPTER 13

Doug reports that the reply neither condemned efforts to establish a charismatic renewal fellowship; nor did it encourage or accept such a move. They wished to be assured that these meetings would be run along correct doctrinal and procedural lines before any recognition or blessing would be given. He then quotes from President Koch's reply:

> Spiritual growth should take place basically in the setting of the congregation where the leadership, activities and intentions are clearly spelled out in advance. This is also true concerning the activities that the Church fosters across parish boundaries… For the Church to give it's blessing to any activity without adequate spiritual safeguards would be an act of irresponsibility.
> We would be ready at any time to discuss any aspects of the work in detail with a view to providing the framework in which the involvement of the Church could be rightly sought.

Doug concluded, "We feel therefore, that we can proceed with plans for another Lutheran Spiritual Renewal meeting provided we strive to work toward a deeper understanding and trust between us and the Lutheran Church of Australia." He then said that this would take time, patience, wisdom and the application of Christ's love.

There was a desire to work with the Church and to be under its covering, while still wanting to pursue spiritual gifts and an active understanding of the Spirit's role and work in our lives. That was more than the Church could cope with at the time. More about that later. The selection of teachers does not suggest that the group only wanted to hear from like-minded individuals. Dr Overduin was generally supportive. However, I happened to stumble across my notes from Pastor Sims' talk on 3 April and 1 May 1976. They suggest that he wanted to warn us that the New Testament didn't promise that miracles will and must take place today. Therefore, miracles and the 'spectacular' need to be put in perspective—they served the proclamation of the Word and even the demonic can produce signs and wonders. He said that too many people simply use Pentecostal terminology and thought forms. In other words, I don't think John Sims would have understood himself to be a supporter of the aims of Lutheran Spiritual Renewal.

An underlying problem of control

In a report—not sure to whom—dated 18 March 1976, President Clem Koch wrote:

> It is my view that no pastor should circularise members under the care of another pastor on a question of such spiritual implication without prior consultation and consent of the local pastor. … To ignore the congregational

spiritual relationship of pastor-people would be unethical and spiritually divisive and harmful.[82]

In other words, a pastor should be able to say that his members were not to receive certain material, even if they desired to receive it. There is no question that we should be open and courteous in our communication, but to suggest that a pastor should be able to control what his members are allowed to see, is another matter. It sounds a bit patronising now, and would be quite impossible in the age of the internet, but some believed it was a pastor's duty, not merely to warn people of dangers out there, but to control what they were allowed to read and attend. It didn't work of course, not even in the 1970s, but it was an additional reason for the Church to criticise the renewal movement.

Ecumenical Teamwork

Many have memories of being involved with Lutheran and ecumenical renewal meetings during these years. Marcia Lieschke remembers one night in the Queen Street house when during a prayer meeting, "hands were laid on many of us and many were filled with the Holy Spirit and began to speak in tongues. Around this time the Holy Spirit became more manifest in our Sunday meetings in Jakes at Gawler Place."

Anne Sellers recalls being part of the music group at an ecumenical event held in Maughan Uniting Church in Adelaide. She played the flute. She continues:

> The team was led by a Catholic trumpet player. The other flute player was also Catholic. The pianist was a Uniting Church pastor. The violinist was Anglican. Drums, bass, flute, leader guitar and vocals were all Jacob's Ladder members. There was a strong sense of unity, of prayer and of spiritual breakthrough during that meeting. Many people came forward for prayer and received a touch from God: restoration, understanding, forgiveness, hope, and healing. I had a glimpse of heaven as people from several "tribes" gathered together and worshipped for hours. Because I was on the platform, I could see the worshipping "in one accord." I sensed God was leaping with joy.

The work of Lutheran Spiritual/Charismatic Renewal continued to grow. Groups sprang up in Victoria and the Riverina in New South Wales. While there was obviously some overlap with Jakes, it was a separate movement and involved many people who were not directly involved in our street and community ministry. It's development is another matter and will only be referred to here, insofar as it impacts the story of Jacob's Ladder.

---

82 Clem I Koch, ***Report on Conference on Spiritual Renewal*** 18 March 1976).

JACOB'S LADDER CHRISTIAN COMMUNITY 1975–1976

Interstate and Other Friends

Our interstate connections got a major boost during *Kairos 74*, as has been described in Chapter 5. Kairos linked us into an ecumenical network across Australia. This included ministries such as John Smith and Truth and Liberation Concern, and Athol Gill and the House of the Gentle Bunyip, both in Melbourne, John Hirt and the House of the New World in Sydney, and Charles Ringma and Teen Challenge in Brisbane. There were also Adelaide-based ministries such as the Abode of the Friendly Toad and the Jesus Centre. We visited them and they visited Jakes, and we discussed big and small issues about community living and outreach. There were discussions about authentic Christian living, relating to the established church and denominations, being less materialistic and working with the poor. We also developed connections with groups of Lutheran youth doing similar things in other places. Various trips were made to the Eastern States to visit and see what they were doing and to meet with their leaders.

In July 1976, five of us joined our pilot Vern Taylor (who later established *Outreach Aviation*) in a rented or borrowed six-seater plane for a series of visits. We flew from Adelaide to Essendon in Melbourne on 9 July. On 11 July we were on our way to Sydney when due to deteriorating weather, Sydney was closed to all but instrument rated pilots, which Vern was not, so we turned around and managed to land at Goulburn. We had nowhere to stay, so we contacted a local church for help. They weren't too keen at first, having somehow heard a rumour that we split up fellowships. Eventually they relented and we were allowed to crash at someone's house. (We straightened that out in a meeting with their Adelaide leadership when we got home!) The next day we went by road to Sydney. Then on 15 July it was back to Goulburn to pick up the plane and then on to Brisbane. On 17 July, we started the journey back, stopping overnight in West Maitland NSW, before getting home the next day. We visited our sister ministries in the other cities, as well as groups of Lutheran young people who were engaged in outreach. Helen and Ian Wade were also on that trip but we can't remember who occupied the other two seats. Nor do we remember specifically whom we visited.

That was one of a number of trips that Vern took us on during those years. It must have been cheaper back then than it would be now. We also made a number of road trips, including a visit to the God's Squad and Truth and Liberation Concern in Melbourne. I remember being on the back of Doug Kuhl's motorbike as we headed down to Geelong for a High School ministry time. I had borrowed someone's helmet. I won't reveal how fast we travelled, but I can tell you that it cured me of any desire to join the *Kerux Apostles*. Not that I had that desire in the first place.

Overseas Travel

In the second half of 1976 Erna and Doug Kuhl, together with Judy and Glen Heidenreich travelled to visit people and ministries in the northern hemisphere. I remember preaching for eleven Sundays in a row, so they were obviously away for a substantial amount of time. A letter from Doug Kuhl was published in the 8 August 1976 *Jakes' Epistle*. He reported that they had reached Los Angeles and stayed for a week with Gerry and Cheri Steinker.

Glen and Doug visited Larry Christensen who was pastor at Trinity Lutheran Church in San Pedro, beginning with a 6.00am prayer breakfast with the elders of the congregation. The purpose of the prayer breakfast was to help shape the sermon for the coming Sunday, with each elder sharing insights into the text. Then there was Holy Communion and prayer. Doug continues:

> Larry gave a prophecy for us. "The padlock of fellowship has been removed. We (Australians) can enter through the door. Great things are to be done." There's more but that sums it up pretty well. Then pancake breakfast. Then I shared the principles of community living over and against confession, forgiveness, restoration, reconciliation and healing. They were amazed! Later Larry took us back to his office. We shared together for quite a while. I was able to share with him work done on "righteousness" which excited him. He hadn't approached things from that angle before. He was tremendously helpful in other ways.[83]

Among the other places they visited were Maranatha Village, and Melodyland, and Calvary Chapel, which had a Sunday attendance of 12,000 and was "no longer a Jesus people centre". Regarding the Teen Challenge centres they visited, Doug wrote:

> The work is as you might imagine from all you've read. They are on the ball as far as getting out among the people and sharing the gospel is concerned. We are on the right track with our street patrols. We have mountains to learn though. They sure know how to do it. They're on the streets (dangerous!) and on the beaches. Anything where crowds gather. They watch for public functions and they are there.[84]

While in the United States, they also visited San Francisco and met with John Hirt, formerly of the House of the New World in Sydney. They went to Bethany

---

83 Doug Kuhl, *Jakes' Epistle* (8 August 1976), 4.

84 ibid., 5.

JACOB'S LADDER CHRISTIAN COMMUNITY 1975–1976

SECTION iii

CHAPTER 13

Fellowship and attended the International Lutheran Charismatic Conference in Minneapolis. They then visited the United Kingdom and Europe. Erna recalls visiting many Christian communities and other interesting ministries. In the United Kingdom the Kuhls went as far as Scotland, while the Heidenreichs spent more time in the south. They then crossed the Channel and managed to drive through four or five countries in one day. They only realised they had been in Liechtenstein when they later consulted the map. They spent time with the Sisters of Mary in Darmstadt in Germany, where they also attended a play the Sisters presented. The experiences they brought back to Jakes enriched our understanding of the many different ways Christians were establishing communities. Doug reflected on their experiences in Europe:

> It is notoriously difficult to find 'alive' Christians in Europe. They are rare, rare birds. The atmosphere of post-Christian countries is grossly heavy. Australia seems like a spiritual paradise in comparison. Os Guinness said this and it is true. Australia is a bright spot in the world scene. Let's get rid of this inferiority complex and this 'things are better overseas' syndrome.[85]

Visiting Teachers

Throughout this time, a string of overseas speakers came through Adelaide. We attended their presentations and many spent time with us at Jakes or in our community houses. There were George Patterson, Dave Andrews, Malcolm Muggeridge, Os Guinness, David Du Plessis and Ed Stube.

George Patterson, for example, was a journalist specialising in Asian affairs, who had extensive experience with the Christian Church in the East. He spent time with us at the Queen Street house when he was visiting Adelaide for a Lutheran Student Fellowship Conference held at Luther Seminary. Karl interviewed him for *Jacob's Letter*:

---

85 Karl Brettig, **Lutheran Spiritual Renewal Newsletter** (2 October 1976), 1.

I don't believe that the Spirit of God can become a prisoner of anything or anybody. ... We know that when the [Old Testament] people of God tried to contain God within their imagery—and I am thinking not only of building 'golden calves' and putting them in the Temple, I am thinking of just devitalising the forms themselves so that Temple worship became an end in itself. The purposes of God were lost; so they went through their observances, they killed their bullocks and sheep and their lambs for offerings. However, God said that all this did was to bring a stench in his nostrils, and the Spirit departed from them.

...I see that this is what has happened in the present state of the 20th Century institutional church that the Spirit of God is not amongst them anymore. They have an empty shell and the theology that they have is a systematic accumulation of human thinking, of doctrinal practice which is ... 20 years out of date by the time it is accumulated into a whole systematic theology. In any case it reflects the problems—theological, political, economic and social—of the West.

In Asia they have discovered out of necessity that they have a whole different ball-game going on, and that therefore the God that they discover from the Bible was not contained within the thought forms that they have had imposed on them for a couple of hundred years... The thought forms are very much oriental, and it is this marriage that is producing an exciting new theology ... not a pale imitation of Western theology, though it is still a structured, but much more dynamic approach, to God's work in their generation. ...

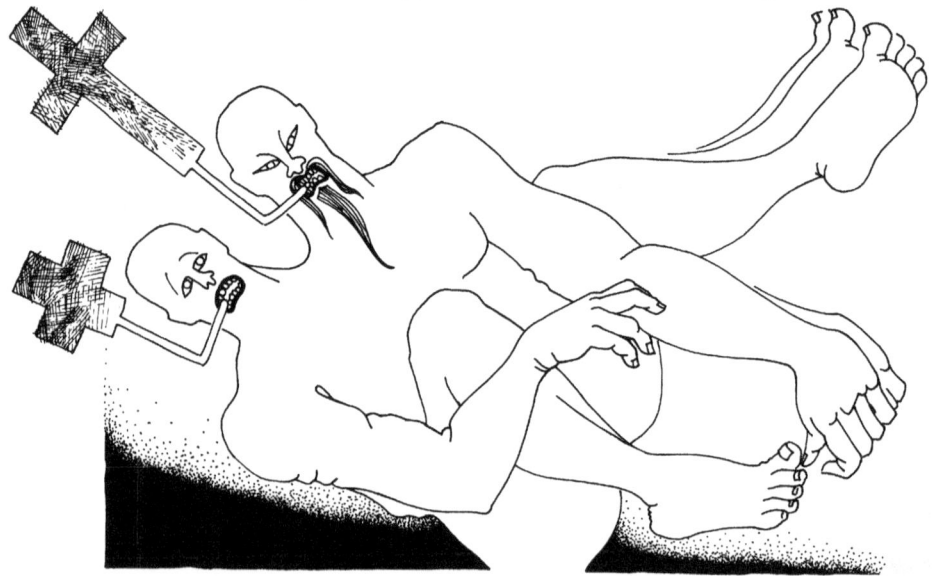

JACOB'S LADDER
CHRISTIAN COMMUNITY 1975–1976

SECTION iii

CHAPTER 13

They come to it and say, "This is the Word of God—how does it apply?" And they find excitingly that it is working out in practice.

Karl continues:

> These comments reflect a growing awareness of our need as Christians, to unlearn, or at least break free from our Westernised ways of thinking and seek to discover what God is doing among his people all over the world and what he is desiring to do with us. God doesn't change, we do. ... What then is to be our reality? Do we like Paul wrestle against the rulers of the darkness of this present age, or are we continuously trying to strive against flesh and blood? ... Are our ears open to hear the small still voice of the Father speaking to us? Do we have the eyes of faith that enable us to walk victoriously over the troubled waters beneath us? ... He waits to receive us and pour his streams of living water upon us. If only we knew how much he longs to do it.[86]

This was well before the time of mobile phones and the internet, so keeping in touch with people was much more difficult, but we tried. Numbers of trips were made by different Jakes people, both around Australia and overseas, and we were blessed by overseas visitors with experience in similar ministries. We had a sense of being part of something much bigger that God was doing around the world.

We wrestled with many of the great thinkers of the time. The July 1977 edition of *Servant* included the feature over the page, where Alexander Solzhenitsyn calls on us not to repeat the lie on which his society is based.[87]

---

86 Karl Brettig, ***Christianity or Western Thinking?*** *Jacob's Letter* (May 1976), 18–19.

87 Alexander Solzhenitsyn, ***Do Not Lie!***, *Servant* (July 1977), 10.

The following quotation is from a book edited by Nobel Peace Prize winner, Alexander Solzhenitsyn in which he examines Christ's call to national repentance and change. Its message has plenty of application to all of us as we live our lives in a world system where truth and honesty have lost their meaning.

Do not lie!
Do not support the lie!
Do not take part in the lie!

because in our country the daily lie is not the whim of corrupt natures but a mode of existence, a condition of the daily welfare of every man. In our country the lie has been incorporated into the state system as the vital link holding everything together, with billions of tiny fasteners, several dozen to each man.

This is precisely why we find life so oppressive… Which is the sacrifice? To go for years without truly breathing, gulping down stench? Or to begin to breathe, as is the prerogative of every man on this earth? What cynic would venture to object aloud to such a policy as non-participation in the lie?

Oh! people will object at once with ingenuity. What is a lie? Who can determine precisely where the lie ends & the truth begins? In every historically concrete dialectical situation, & so on — all the evasions that liars have been using for the past half century…

What does it mean not to lie? It doesn't mean going around preaching the truth at the top of your voice. It doesn't even mean muttering what you think in an undertone. It simply means not saying what you don't think, & that includes not whispering, not opening your mouth, not raising your hand, not casting your vote, not feigning a smile, not lending your presence, not standing up, & not cheering…

People will say how unfair on the young! After all, if you don't utter the obligatory lie at your social science exam, you'll be failed & expelled from your institute, & your education & life will be disrupted.

Be that as it may, educational damage is not the greatest damage one can suffer in life. Damage to the soul & corruption of the soul, to which we carelessly assent from our earliest years, are far more inseparable.

Alexander Solzhenitsyn
"From under the Rubble"

JACOB'S LADDER CHRISTIAN COMMUNITY 1975–1976

SECTION iii

Fitting into the Lutheran Church

CHAPTER 14

When Pastor Doug Kuhl resigned his call to St Stephens, including his work at Jakes, at the end of 1974, the question of how Jacob's Ladder fitted into the Lutheran Church of Australia (LCA) became urgent. Doug was a pastor without a call, and after a period of time would be removed from the roll of pastors of the LCA. Only constituted congregations or parishes, and other approved bodies such as the SA District of the LCA, could issue calls. Jacob's Ladder would only be able to call Doug to be its pastor if it were constituted as a Lutheran congregation and the District approved its constitution and accepted it into membership.

The frustrations we experienced in dealing with up to three controlling committees were described in chapter 7. After Jakes was able to run its own affairs, it adopted a constitution so it could become incorporated and be legally responsible for its own affairs. I registered *Jacob's Ladder Christian Community Inc*, as an incorporated body in the State of South Australia on 11 May 1976. We had adopted a constitution that had not been approved by the SA District Church Council. We had to become incorporated, since we were applying for government grants and entering into legal arrangements such as leases on property.

The President's Committee for Pastoral Consultation

In April 1975, President Clem Koch of the LCA SA District called together a Committee for Pastoral Consultation with the Pastor of Jacob's Ladder. There are minutes of nine such meetings held in 1975 and six in 1976.[88] Apart from the president and Doug, the committee comprised another two pastors and three seminary lecturers.[89] The first meeting was held on 29 April. Not sure what to expect, Doug asked me to accompany him as a support person. I was not meant to be there but the minutes record that "it was agreed that he be allowed to sit in for the remainder of the meeting". I wasn't invited back! However, we eventually prevailed with the view that the issues involved more than the Pastor, and the Elders of Jacob's Ladder were included from the fifth meeting, which was held on 11 August 1975, and the title of the committee amended to *The President's Committee for Pastoral Consultation with the Pastor and Elders of Jacob's Ladder*. Karl Brettig, Stephen Haar, Steen

---

[88] 1975: 29/4, 15/5, 9/6, 21/7, 11/8, 22/9, 1/12, 10/12, 18/12 and 1976: 5/2, 11/3, 18/3, 6/5, 22/7, 22/10

[89] Pastors Artie Schirmer and Everard Leske and Drs Siegfried Hebart, Henry Hamann and Elwin Janetzki. Dr Daniel Overduin was appointed from the first meeting in March 1976.

Olsen, Doug Vogelsang and Ian Wade were therefore members of the committee from that point on.

After years of frustration in dealing with administrative committees, it was great to be able to talk about the underlying issues. After noting that frustration, I wrote:

> The President's Committee for Pastoral Consultation, on the other hand, was the best thing that happened in the long string of committees we dealt with. At last "whose fault is it that we are in the mess we're in" was a thing of the past and real issues could be dealt with. Our theological orthodoxy was challenged and we felt a bit defensive, but real progress was made. We had also received wise counsel to be very careful about what we put down on paper. A slip can be used against you. Combined with our general lack of time to write reports, let alone theological treatises, that led to much frustration for the patient men who met with us. After our orthodoxy received general acceptance, the issues were still complex.[90]

---

90 Steen Olsen, *The Growth of Jacob's Ladder Christian Community as a part of the Lutheran Church of Australia, South Australian District*, Forum 69 (May 1976), 8.

JACOB'S LADDER CHRISTIAN COMMUNITY 1975–1976

CHAPTER 14

Looking back, in spite of my positive comments above, I remember the earlier meetings the Elders attended as being difficult and unequal battles. We were a young relatively inexperienced pastor, two seminary students and three lay people, faced with the District President, two experienced and respected pastors and three seminary professors. We were there to debate theology! Still, there was a good discussion, but I am not sure we were always heard. I want to be both careful and respectful here, both because I counted all those on the other side of the table as personal friends, both at the time and in the years that followed, and because they have all long since received the call to heavenly theological discussions. (If there is such a thing—perhaps not!) However, I do remember at one meeting holding up a couple of pages of minutes and making the point that while we had had a good to and fro discussion, our comments only accounted for one and a half lines. In my youthful arrogance, I waved them around, with our bit highlighted, and suggested they were not minutes, but an instrument of propaganda. [blush] The minutes did improve after that. In fact, I think Doug Vogelsang was asked to take them. There was goodwill around the table, and the spirit was good, but we frustrated our teachers, pushing issues that they probably had not confronted before, and brought into question some of the narratives the church had constructed up to that point about things charismatic.

The appointment of Dr Daniel Overduin to the committee brought significant change. Daniel was pastor of a suburban parish in Adelaide and had already had some involvement with us, including providing workshops and seminars. When we were out of our depth in trying to explain something Daniel would rephrase what we were trying to say, and then often comment that it seemed OK to him. That usually brought nods around the table.

Constitutional Agreement

In May 1976, I was able to report that the Constitutions Committee of the LCA SA District had approved our constitution. However, my celebrations were a bit premature when I wrote:

> Another major breakthrough! After two years of "constitutional constipation" [pardon?] and many hassles in sorting out our relationship with the rest of the Lutheran Church of Australia, agreement has been reached.
>
> Jacob's Ladder has constituted itself and applied to the South Australian District of the LCA for admission to the District as a community (or congregation) of the District. At the time of writing we have met with representatives of the Constitutions Committee of the District and have

reached agreement with them, so we just wait the completion of the final procedures. We have also applied for incorporation as an Association so that we may have legal status as a community.

We praise God that this point has been reached and that our status as "church" in the New Testament sense has been recognised. For the past two years we have been saying that this is what we, in fact, are. This also means that the position of our pastor, Doug Kuhl, can now be put in order as far as the LCA is concerned. … We will soon be in a position to issue an official call to him and so end this abnormality.[91]

In a similar vein, President Clem Koch had issued a statement on 18 March 1976 that said:

In giving a very brief review of the activities connected with Jacob's Ladder of the past two years, I am deeply grateful to God that it appears that what seemed a complete impasse has now seemingly been resolved. … However, it has now become possible for Jacob's Ladder to adopt a constitution which accepts the Confessions of the Lutheran Church and the constitutional oversight of the Lutheran Church in regard to their activities. The Jacob's Ladder community adopted the proposed constitution on 16 March 1976. The constitution proposes that Jacob's Ladder will become a congregation of the SA District and will proceed to call its own pastor. It is a matter of gratitude that this position has been reached. However, we will all continue to need God's richest grace and blessing, so that the outreach with the Gospel might continue also in this aspect of work for the Lord.

Alas no. In spite of the recommendation of their Constitutions Committee and the statement of the President, it seems that the Church Council of the SA District never approved our constitution, and so we never became a 'congregation' of the LCA and we were never able formally to call our pastor. I do not remember that we were ever told why approval was not given.

LCA Statement on Charismatic Renewal

During this period, the LCA's Commission on Theology and Inter-Church Relations was working on a statement called The Lutheran Church of Australia and Lutheran Charismatic Renewal. It was finally adopted by the LCA General Church Council in

---

[91] Steen Olsen, **Constitutional Agreement has been Reached**, Jacob's Letter (May 1976), 26.

JACOB'S LADDER CHRISTIAN COMMUNITY 1975–1976

February 1977.[92] The process involved some consultation, and from the viewpoint of Lutheran Charismatic Renewal in Australia, it was a far better outcome than, for example, those produced by the Lutheran Church Missouri Synod in the United States in 1972 and 1977.[93]

The LCA statement runs to five pages, so a brief summary is difficult, but I will try. Early in the document there are positive statements about spiritual renewal:

> The Church thanks God and his Spirit for all signs of spiritual life. …
> Our purpose is not to question the sincerity or the conviction of those who believe that they have been filled with the Spirit in a special way. The Church praises God for all evidence of evangelical zeal, of a renewed desire to hear and study God's Word, and to use the gifts of the Spirit in the service of the Lord.
>
> The formation of charismatic groups could be a reminder to the Church as a whole of besetting weaknesses which may be found from time to time in our congregations: a lack of community life and rich spiritual fellowship, a cold profession of faith without the warmth of a glowing love, a lack of participation in worship and in the front-line of the Church's mission, and a lack of sincere striving for personal sanctification and piety—in short a quenching of the Spirit. All Lutherans will surely agree that the Church continually needs the renewing power of the Holy Spirit if it is to be the Church that the Lord wants it to be.

The statement then says that with all positive features of Lutheran charismatic renewal there are a number of things that give cause for deep concern. It lists four:

1. The influence of non-Lutheran theology.

2. The formation of sectional groups that run across the congregational life of the Church. "Lutheran charismatics should seek spiritual renewal first and foremost within their own congregations."

3. The denial of the Lutheran character of charismatic renewal through the rejection of infant baptism and the practice of rebaptising adults and celebrating 'open' communion. "Lutheran charismatic leaders should clearly reject such teaching and practice and do all in their power to see that these things do not happen."

---

92 The document can be accessed at https://www.lca.org.au/departments/commissions/cticr/ **Volume 1, G. Interdenominational-Cooperation—Church Movements**.

93 These can be accessed at https://www.lcms.org/about/leadership/commission-on-theology-and-church-relations/documents/lutheran-doctrine-and-practice

Fitting into the Lutheran Church // 113

4. Everything must conform to the truth of Scripture. "The Spirit today does not work counter to the inspired Word which he gave in the past." Specifically, treating stories from the Gospels and Acts as precedents which must be followed today. The Gospel description of what happened in NT times must not be turned into a Law prescription of what must be done and must happen today.

A long section then describes the central issues, including such things as any filling of the Spirit is always God's unmerited gift, that being filled with the Holy Spirit should be the earnest desire of every Christian and "is part of the growth in Christ which begins in baptism." The Spirit works through the means of grace, there is only one Christian baptism, and subjective experiences should not be relied on

as the foundation of Christian faith and life. "The Spirit is still the giver of every gift to believers today. Christians are not to reject these gifts and so quench the Spirit." But the validity and relative importance of every gift is to be tested against Scripture. Gifts are not a sign of Christian maturity and are to be used for the good of others. "Holiness is not a precondition for the filling of the Holy Spirit, but a result of that filling, as the Spirit fights against the flesh." There can be no theology of glory, which ignores the need for daily contrition and repentance. "The Spirit still gives special gifts today. However, it is by no means easy to understand clearly the function and operation of all the special gifts outlined." Finally, "we need to remember that God cannot be coerced by our prayer or piety, or dictated to in the name of faith. In the realm of sickness there remains the mystery of his permissive will…"

The final section of the statement deals with pastoral advice, in two sections, the first addressed to Lutheran charismatics; the second to all members of the LCA. Charismatics should not allow themselves to be controlled by undisciplined enthusiasm, avoid judgmentalism, and give a good account of their faith, which begins with God's Word. They should try to appreciate the rich heritage of the Lutheran Church, learn to live under the cross, respect the relationship between pastor and people, and "finally, and above all … to let Christ, his cross and bitter death, together with his glorious resurrection, remain the centre of their life, so that their spiritual life is one of continual union also with the Father and the Spirit."

Secondly, the statement then pleads with all members of the LCA to be prepared to listen to the concerns of charismatics, even when they are critical of present

JACOB'S LADDER
CHRISTIAN COMMUNITY 1975–1976

church life. They should not prejudge or condemn in ignorance, but they should listen with loving concern and avoid antagonising others with immediate rejection. When rejecting error, that should be done with a loving pastoral attitude that tries to understand "the psychology that lies behind and attends a powerful spiritual experience." All should use the Spirit's gifts while preserving the unity of the Spirit in the bond of peace. The very last paragraph of the statement reads:

> All members of the LCA should continually pray for the outpouring of the Holy Spirit in their own lives so that the old life of sin may more and more be overcome by the new life of the Spirit in Christ. They should also continually pray that the whole Church, its leaders, pastors, teachers, and people may be filled with the Spirit, and that his gifts may be poured out richly on all. Thus the Church, empowered by the Spirit, will increasingly reflect the glory of our Lord Jesus Christ and glorify the Father.

I have not included the many biblical references scattered throughout the text. I was obviously not a part of the Commission on Theology at that time, but later I did sit at that table for twelve years and can testify to the depth, thoroughness and pastoral concern of its discussions. I would suggest that for a document from the 1970s this is remarkable in its balance and wisdom. [94]

However, adopting a balanced document is one thing, living by it is quite another. Sadly, it appears that this document did not have the desired influence. Polarisations grew and many people ended up leaving the LCA.

---

[94] For a recent Australian Lutheran contribution to our understanding of the Holy Spirit, see Noel Due and Steen Olsen. **Spirit-filled: Normal Christian Living.** LCA, 2019. It can be bought from the usual suppliers or downloaded for free from www.lca.org.au/spirit-filled

CHAPTER 15: A New Direction

On 29 April 1977, our name was legally changed to "Servants of Christ Community Inc".

The average age of community members increased. As more and more of the singles married and had children, the nature of Jakes also began to change. For some, the emphasis on outreach changed to a desire to prioritise the forming community. *Jacob's Letter* became *Servant* magazine. Jan and Steve Haar, and Ruth and I with six week old Kirsten, headed to Queensland for our one-year internship that was part of our seminary training. The Haars went to Mt Gravatt in Brisbane, and worked with Pastor David Stolz, and Ruth and I to Redeemer / Good Shepherd in Toowoomba to work with Pastor Peter Wiebusch. Meanwhile more and more of the community relocated to the Brompton-Croydon area, in the inner west of Adelaide. A workshop led by Ian Wade was established that was to be part rehabilitation, part business. Closely related to this, Maurie May was the mechanic in charge of *Macroni, Kraut and Son*, which repaired motor vehicles—especially motorbikes—and other associated work such as painting and electrical stuff. The Co-op continued distributing food and other domestic essentials. *Servant Media* was serving through its extensive tape ministry, library and *Servant* magazine. But the most fundamental change was towards a primary focus on forming Christian Community and becoming what was then referred to as a 'Covenant Community'. We will therefore begin this section with a consideration of the journey of the community at this time and the content of the covenant. We will then return to various features of the life and ministry of the community during these years.

The beginnings of a change in emphasis

Commenting on the 1977–1978 period in the life of the community, Noel Hartwig writes:

> One of the almost unbelievable facts about Jacob's Ladder, at this point of time, [probably late 1978 / early 1979—though he still calls the community 'Jacob's Ladder'] is the turnaround in emphasis. In the past, much attention has been given to outreach ministry. In the schools, universities, McNally Training Centre, on the streets or wherever. Yes, practically wherever it was

SERVANTS OF CHRIST COMMUNITY 1977–1979

CHAPTER 15

possible for Jacob's Ladder Community to reach out and touch people with God's salvation message, they have done it. Not that there wasn't a healthy teaching and building up of community members in the past. But over the last two years and today, the emphasis swings heavily toward building and training the community… For by design, the street ministry … has slackened off, and in the words of Pastor Doug Kuhl, "We are getting our house in order; our community in order." Amongst other things, he says that society is up the creek. When you are able to help people, it's not the lack of people to rehabilitate that is the problem, rather it is how you handle the rush. At Jacob's Ladder the ministry relied on a few. Now we are maturing the whole community, so that they are ready to minister. Then away you go, you're into multiplication.[95]

A Key Explanation of the Change

Pastor Doug Kuhl's report to the 1978 AGM was a five-page document titled *An Overview*. It is, in effect, both the rationale for the change to focus on building the life of the community, and also a pathway to the adoption of the covenant. The document begins:

> We have moved! From Jacob's Ladder to Servants of Christ Community. We have also moved from the Jesus Movement mentality in our way of seeing ourselves and our mission, to a more mature, more broad self-understanding and vision of life and service.[96]

We were then given a number of examples. There had been movement from the Coffee House, ministering basically to troubled youth, to a broader base of outreach among various age groups and various sections of society; from being a group of people held together by ministry goals, to forming a community based on a common commitment to one another in the Lord; and from a ministry focused around the Coffee House location, to forming a people who would minister across Adelaide. Fourthly, the community had moved from thinking denominationally to a broader vision of the body of Christ. Finally, the movement had been from being a loose-knit gathering of people with different levels of commitment and calls to ministry to the point where the community was now able to contemplate being formed by "one call, one commitment, one direction, one mission [and] one ministry."[97]

---

95 Noel Hartwig, *The Story of Jacob's Ladder*, unpublished Thesis (1978), 41. Accessed at Lutheran Archives.
96 Douglas Kuhl, *An Overview (Pastor's Report)*, AGM (held on 22 February 1978), 1.
    This and the following quotations—Douglas Kuhl, *Pastor's Report*, AGM (held on 9 March 1979), 11–15.
97 ibid., 1.

The structure and membership criteria still needed to change and new premises needed to be found. "It may be helpful to some if they picture in their minds a disbandment of Jacob's Ladder and a calling together of something new." Then the natural question to ask would be, "What is the new thing Jesus is calling us to?"[98] Doug believed that the call was to community with one level of commitment. "Jesus does not call one to total dedication and another to slackness." He then warns against any understanding of a call by Jesus that is not total, final and all encompassing.

The next section of Doug's report considered priorities. What and who came first in our lives? Then there were some comments about lifestyle. "Inasmuch as these things are not in accordance with God's Word—they are questionable in some areas and damnable in other areas."[99] Doug then listed six areas where "we as a group of people constantly run into trouble:"

- *Negative speaking about life, ourselves, others, even God.*
- *Gossip.*
- *Debate that is mainly about 'baiting' others.*
- *Faithless thought patterns.*
- *Reactions of the flesh, the world and* Satan.
- *Organising and planning which has not bothered to consult God.*

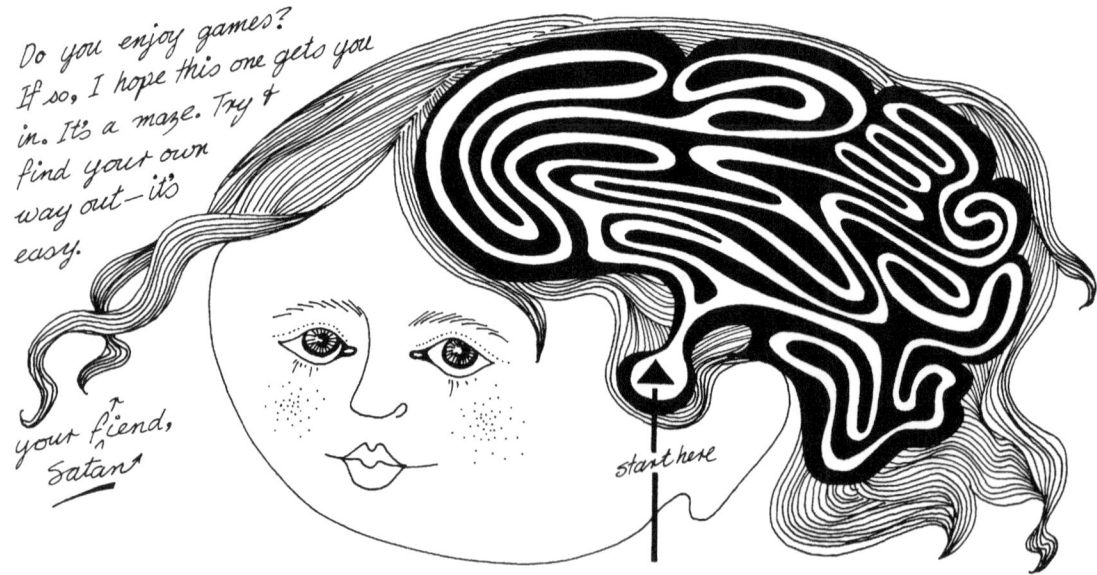

---

98 Douglas Kuhl, **An Overview (Pastor's Report)**, AGM (held on 22 February 1978), 1.
 This and the following quotations—Douglas Kuhl, **Pastor's Report**, AGM (held on 9 March 1979), 1.

99 ibid., 3.

SERVANTS OF CHRIST COMMUNITY 1977–1979

The next section spoke of the need to develop Christ-like forms of communication, with no hotheads, baiting, jumping to conclusions, waffling and fleshly responses. Finally, the pastor commended the community for their spiritual development. "Keep it up brothers and sisters, for your growth into Christ by the Spirit's power is beauteous to trace."[100]

The next section deals with leadership and community formation, which the Elders had focused on for the past four months.

> The complexities of pastoring a group of people pilgrimaging from 'old world life-style' into life within 'the kingdom of God' are so many and so great that unless we spend all of our energies, give all of our dedication, share all of our love, apply all of our lives, we simply won't make it.[101]

The final page of the document summarised what had gone before: It was necessary to detach ourselves from the world before we could attach ourselves to this new lifestyle. He concluded by saying there were a number of things he knew for sure, including that Jesus' call is sovereign and our response must be to surrender all, which is the norm and rule for every Christian person. The charismatic movement was God's visitation for that time, and God's plan and will is that his church be one, so we must work for unity.

Looking back on the Report

The minutes of the AGM simply record that the pastor read his report and that it was accepted by the meeting. It was a very long meeting, beginning at 7.30pm and only concluding at 12.20am. The final decision of the AGM was to form a covenanted community, and that a formation program for entry into the community be established.[102] The minutes record that I was present at the AGM, but I have no memory of it. While Steve Haar and I had not functioned as elders of the community during 1977 when we were in Queensland, as is noted in the report of the Elders, the minutes also recorded that the elections were postponed until Easter to allow for the formation of the covenant community. The present Elders and Council were to continue to serve until then. However, those who wanted to stand down could do so. The minutes tell us that, "Steen, Doug V and Steve announced their retirement as of tonight." Steve and I would be leaving at the end of 1978 in any case, when

---

100 ibid., 4.

101 ibid., 4.

102 **Minutes of AGM of Servants of Christ Community Inc**, held at 102 Gawler Place, Adelaide (Wednesday 22 February 1978).

we graduated from Seminary, and Doug Vogelsang remembers that since he had been in leadership roles since the very early days of the Coffee Lounge he felt that it was time for 'new blood' and for younger leaders to step up.

In written form, Pastor Doug's report sounded like he was passionate, but also in many respects, frustrated. Looking back on it after all these years, the view of community it presented was pretty idealistic and the solutions offered sound quite legalistic. In speaking of our priorities, there is no recognition that we also serve God by serving those he has put into our lives and those he brings across our path. The idea of priorities is therefore flawed. When I love my wife and care for our children, I am still putting God first, because those responsibilities are part of what God calls me to do. It could be argued that neglecting one's spouse and family in favour of other commitments, is in fact, disobedience to the call of God. It is therefore a question of balancing the various aspects of God's call and there are obviously seasons of life that also play into that. The old monastic idea of withdrawing from the world to spend all of one's time in prayer and meditation, is not Christian discipleship.

Secondly, while we live on this earth, we are always going to be broken flawed vessels, failing one another and needing to forgive each other. To quote a more recent understanding, the idea that we can be 'fully devoted followers of Jesus', leads to either despair, or an unjustified sense of pride. Perfection will have to wait for heaven. In one of our key resources from that time, Dietrich Bonhoeffer insisted that Christian community was not an ideal but a Divine reality:

Innumerable times the whole Christian community has broken down because it had sprung from a wish dream. The serious Christian, set down for the first time in a Christian community, is likely to bring with him a very definite idea of what Christian life together should be, and try to realise it. But God's grace speedily shatters such dreams. Just as surely God desires to lead us to a knowledge of genuine Christian fellowship, so surely must we be overwhelmed by a general disillusionment with others, with Christians in general, and, if we are fortunate, with ourselves.

By sheer grace God will not permit us to live even for a brief period in a dream world. He does not abandon us to those rapturous experiences and lofty

SERVANTS OF CHRIST COMMUNITY 1977–1979

SECTION iv

CHAPTER 15

moods that come over us like a dream. God is not a God of the emotions but the God of truth. Only that fellowship which faces such disillusionment, with all its unhappy and ugly aspects, begins to be what it should be in God's sight, begins to grasp in faith the promise given to it. The sooner this shock of disillusionment comes to an individual and to a community the better for both. A community, which cannot bear and cannot survive such a crisis, which insists on keeping its illusion when it should be shattered, permanently loses in that moment the promise of Christian community. Sooner or later it will collapse.[103]

Grappling with the Lord's call

While the Haars and the Olsens were in Queensland, the LCA leadership was grappling with what it was hearing from the Jakes community. At the time we left Adelaide in late January 1977, it was my intention to work for a time after graduation with the Servants of Christ Community as a layperson. I had communicated this to the acting principal of Luther Seminary and was then asked to clarify my decision in a letter in March. I replied, restating my intention and saying this was not a rejection on my part of parish ministry, nor did it exclude the possibility of a future call and ordination. That was still my intention when I met with the principal at a pastors conference in early August.

Sometime between the conference and the end of September, our intentions changed. Ruth remembers my saying something about it, and obviously, we talked, but neither of us can recall our reasons. Sadly, I had not informed the Seminary.

From 5–13 September 1977 we received a visit from representatives of Jakes. Karl recalls:

> Brian Proeve, Ruth & I were asked to take a trip to Queensland to connect with Steen & Ruth and Steve & Jan regarding their commitment to the community beyond 1977. Steen doesn't remember anything about this visit so we can't have been too heavy on the pressure.

Steve and I subsequently both received letters dated 22 September 1977 calling us to separate meetings in the Queensland District office on 3 October, with the principal of the Seminary and the president of the LCA. Apparently, various conversations had led them to the conclusion we had signed up to a covenant with the community. (The covenant had not even been formally adopted at this point.) Dr Hebart's letter to me said in part:

---

103 Dietrich Bonhoeffer, **Life Together**. SCM Press Ltd: London (1949), 15.

> [This commitment has an] entirely unevangelical character and … the way you have bound your conscience is a return to subjection to the Law. … [It is] no different from the vows against which Luther made such heavy attacks in his writings, because he recognised their anti-evangelical character. As I see it, your commitment or vow is entirely against the very meaning of the Gospel (cf John 8:36; Gal 5:13–18; Rom 7:1–17) and therefore is not a commitment prompted by the Spirit of Christ, but by the spirit of Anti-Christ.

It was clear that rather than wait until my graduation to decide what I was going to do, they wanted an answer before I returned to the Seminary. The implication was that otherwise I would not be allowed to complete my studies. The Seminary Council had resolved to request an undertaking in writing that upon graduation I would be available for assignment, and I would accept the constitution of the LCA and agree to teach, preach and practice in accord with its doctrinal position. Every pastor promises those things at his ordination, so there was nothing particularly unusual about that. They added that since the Church did not accept my commitment to Jakes was binding, it should be my own personal decision.

The letter to Steve Haar dated 28 March 1977 also raised the issue of his assisting with the distribution of 'open communion' on the occasion of the wedding of Ruth and Karl Brettig, which

> has resulted in heavy censure from the leadership of the Church, and quite rightly so. We know that at this communion Roman Catholics, members of the Assembly of God, a Presbyterian and even young unconfirmed children were communed. As vicar you are well aware of the fact that the rules of the Church laid down in its constitution is that Lutheran altars are for Lutherans only and whether you like it or not you are obliged to conform to this principle. Your action naturally reflects on the Seminary and its teaching and we have had to assure our Church leaders that no where in the Seminary have you ever been given to believe that you are free to break the rule of the Church. The fact that Pastor Kuhl was the responsible minister and you merely his assistant, in no way absolves you from the action in which you were involved. Please do not let this happen again.

Since we had been summonsed without further enquiry about our intentions, we decided to simply turn up at the meetings. My supervising pastor, Peter Wiebusch, had also been invited and had received a copy of the letter sent to me. He simply asked me if it was true I didn't intend to be ordained. I said no, that was not our current intention. Peter chuckled and said I was big enough and ugly enough to look after myself, so he wouldn't attend the meeting. Steve's pastor David Stolz

SERVANTS OF CHRIST COMMUNITY 1977–1979

heard about Peter's decision and decided to invite himself to my meeting as well, because he didn't consider it fair a student meet with those two 'heavies' without a support person present. Fair enough. (Dave and I became very good friends later in life when we both served as bishops of our districts. Since we had quite different opinions about a number of things, as Dave said when he retired, our friendship confused both of our respective sets of supporters.)

My meeting was first. They started by attacking Jakes, so I responded and defended it. After about half an hour, Dr Hebart, who genuinely liked me, sighed, slumped in his chair and said, "So Steen, it seems we are going to lose you." Until then, no one had actually asked me if it was true I had made this covenant, and in my youthful arrogance, I had not actually seen any need to put them out of their misery. So now, I said, "Oh no, Dr Hebart, it is my intention to graduate and then be assigned to a parish."

He of course immediately realised they hadn't actually asked me what Ruth and I intended to do, and so asked me to put things in writing and state that when I graduated I would go where I was assigned. More youthful arrogance followed, I am afraid. I replied I couldn't possibly do so because he had just been explaining to me that doing such a thing would mean I would not be open to the Spirit's leading at the time, and so it would be an unevangelical covenant. He smiled slightly, adjusted his glasses, and said, "Well Steen, I think a letter stating your intention will suffice."

I told them I valued my relationship with the Servants of Christ Community and since Ruth's and my intentions had changed, I wanted to make a trip to Adelaide to talk with the Pastor and Elders face-to-face before announcing we no longer planned to continue working with them after graduation. I did that. On 13 October, I sent my reply clarifying my intentions.

Steve replied to his letter on 18 October, saying in part:

> You will remember that I informed you at the above mentioned meeting, that my commitment to Servants of Christ Community does not preclude an individual (indeed, personal) decision on my part, either for or against ordination and assignment in the Lutheran Church of Australia. As such, I do not consider my commitment to be either unevangelical or a binding of my conscience (and as such a return to subjection to the Law), or prompted by the spirit of Anti-Christ. You will remember also that I informed both you and Dr Grope that at this point of time I did not consider myself ready to commit myself by writing an undertaking that on graduation I will be available for assignment and ordination in the Lutheran Church of Australia, even though that may ultimately be my intention.

A New Direction // 123

In the event both Steve and I were ordained after we graduated towards the end of 1978 and each accepted our assignment: Steve to Gladstone Qld, and me to the Hunter Valley NSW. At the time of writing, we have each served as LCA pastors for more than forty years. Steve has served as a lecturer at the Seminary (now Australian Lutheran College) since 2007 and is presently the Academic Dean and Vice Principal.

Summary

The community had moved into a new phase. Rather than being scattered across Central Adelaide suburbs it was increasing located in one area. The community was fundamentally changing how it understood itself, and had shifted its focus to engage in a season of community building. The community was also growing older. More were married. More had children. There is no question in my mind that the intention was still to reach out with the Gospel that is Jesus, to those who do not yet know him. That was etched in the DNA of Jakes. However, that had become more of a long-term plan. In the short to medium term, the community needed to mature and grow, so that others could be helped, without burning out the workers. Individuals and couples therefore also needed to consider God's call on their lives. Would they join the covenant or was God calling them elsewhere? What was God up to, as the community continued to evolve?

SERVANTS OF CHRIST COMMUNITY 1977–1979

A Covenant for the Community

David Skeat and Peter Muller had been asked to draft the covenant, which they had already done by September 1976. They then presented their draft to the Elders. However, as already reported, it was only at the AGM held on 22 February 1978 that it was resolved to form a covenanted community and establish a formation program for entrance into this community. We have no record of when or how the particular wording of the covenant was approved. In this chapter, we will have a more detailed look at the actual covenant and then consider the steps taken to form the covenanted community.

The Community Covenant Concept

The idea of being a covenanted community was of course not new. It owed something to monastic orders, past and present. At the time, there was a growth of Catholic-based covenant communities and books were written, outlining the efforts of various groups to build Christian community. Many of those did not involve a formal written covenant. A covenant can also be seen as an expansion on the *duties of members* section in many constitutions. It may include things that today might be in a code of conduct or ethics, or for example, the covenants included in a letter of call to a pastor that lists the responsibilities of both pastor and congregation. We also have the covenant of marriage, where a man and a woman commit themselves to each other 'until death do them part.' However, when such a covenant is drawn up for a community that is, in effect, a church, there are some pitfalls to be avoided. It is interesting that the first draft of the covenant we have (dated 28 September 1976) raises some of these dangers in a note at the end:

1. In considering a covenant, there is a real danger of us falling back under the letter of the law. That is, instead of being freed from the law by the Gospel, we set up another law or another ten commandments that we then have to obey. A covenant is only right if we covenant ourselves together in freedom, because what we are covenanting ourselves to is what God is already doing in our lives. It is his will. See Galatians 5.

2. This means that we're only making explicit what is already implicit in our Baptism.

3. We need to discuss this and study it in regard to a covenant.

We also have a copy of the covenant dated 1 March 1978, which appears to be identical to the draft version. We will now look at what this covenant actually said. I will quote it in full. It has three parts…

The Servants of Christ Community Covenant

Our Covenant to God: By God's grace we have been called in his love to be his sons and daughters through Jesus Christ, into whose death and resurrection we have been baptised and thus have been made free from the slavery of sin. Now we are no longer slaves of sin but slaves of righteousness, alive to God in Christ Jesus. Once we were nothing, but now we are sons and daughters of God, God's own people. Now we are a holy people, a consecrated nation. We have been called out of the darkness of not knowing God and of being dead in sin into God's marvellous light. Now as God's sons and daughters, we have been called to declare his wonderful deeds and to be his ambassadors of reconciliation.

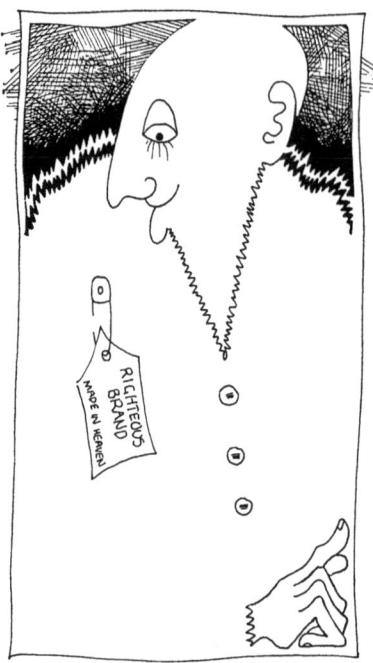

Having received all this as a free gift, we can do no other than to recognise Jesus as our sovereign Lord, whose sacrifice and service reconciled us to the Father who created and daily preserves us, who by the power of the Holy Spirit converted us and called us into the light of his grace by baptism and now sustains and preserves us through Word and Sacrament. It is through this grace that we are now able to covenant ourselves together in freedom, to serve each other in a new and spiritual way, even as we are already covenanted together in one baptism.

The Covenant to each other in the context of community: We believe that Christian Community can only be a true community in and through Christ Jesus, and that we only belong to one another in and through him.

We recognise that it is only because God himself has made us his children and is now at work in us, conforming us to the image of his Son through the power of the Holy Spirit, that we can come together and covenant ourselves

SERVANTS OF CHRIST COMMUNITY 1977–1979

to each other. The Lord himself binds us together and makes us one, and it is this oneness and the calling and ordaining by God through the Word and Sacraments that constitutes Christian community. This is what we have been called to, and this is our covenant to it.

Christ is Lord of our life; therefore, we can and do promise before God and each other, that: we will serve one another even as our Lord served us, even if it costs us our life, and that we will forgive one another just as we have been forgiven. We know that we remain in God and that he is in us because he has given us his Spirit. So then we know and believe the love God has for us that we may have confidence before him because God first loved us. Therefore, we will love one another because his love abides in us. We will be sensitive and honest with each other at all times.

We believe that God our Father is our only true Father, who cares and provides for all our needs. Therefore, as his children and heirs to all that he has promised, we call on his help as we now promise that we will share our lives with one another and work together as one Body, so that as one Body we may glorify God. We will live our lives under the authority of God's Word and in obedience to him. We recognise the authority of the Eldership that God has raised up in this community. We will exhort one another in the Word and pray for one another at all times. We will strive to encourage and admonish one another in the times when this is necessary. We will use our time, talents, and possessions, in the service of God. Indeed all that which God has given us we give back to him, for his service and the benefit of the whole Body.

Our Covenant to the World: We recognise that we are ambassadors of reconciliation to the world; we are the light of the world, the salt and the yeast. To this end, we openly dedicate ourselves to be light, salt and yeast and to be ambassadors of reconciliation for God to the world.

The process of becoming a covenant community

So when was the wording of the covenant adopted and how was the covenanted community initially established? Peter Muller remembers:

> For some reason, the Elders group decided during a retreat to immediately covenant themselves. This was before the community had the opportunity to review the document. ... I thought that this decision of the elders group was the most unwise and ill thought out that they had ever made. ... That initial premature covenanting predictably fractured the community into those on

the inside and those not. It had a knock-on effect that stymied the life of the community from then on. Subsequent intakes of most of the voting members did not solve the problem. In fact quite the opposite. The community never ever actually had a period of discernment and deep and honest discussion as to what sort of community we aspired to be and why. Such discussions over a period of six months or so would have informed the content of the covenant document and therefore individual decisions about how deeply people wanted to be involved. As it was, the *ad hoc* nature of the process simply unleashed a large number of competing and often incompatible visions of community. ... Working on the covenant document itself with David Skeat was a joy, but the chaotic process of the covenanting and its aftermath, has been one of my greatest regrets from community life.

How did others join the covenant?

We have an undated document, which includes the covenant and appears to be a guide for those who were involved with the community and who now wished to become full covenant members. Since it establishes a process asked for at the February 1978 AGM, it is safe to say that it was prepared after that in 1978 at the earliest. This document explained the process as follows:

> Servants of Christ Community currently consists of some 100 members. There are three levels through which persons progress as they desire to become part of the community. Initial contacts fellowship with the community and take part in the Sunday evening worship and prayers. They are invited to take part in a seminar on the role of the Holy Spirit in the midst of life related areas. Some may attend a course in Christian growth and maturity. Those interested in joining the community are invited to an orientation time (usually a weekend camp), in which they are informed about various aspects of community life. They are then invited to become 'Servants on the Way'.
>
> Becoming a 'Servant on the Way' involves making a commitment to attend community formation and training times, normally conducted weekly. The community is divided into several households (geographical areas), and new members would then begin to integrate into the life of a particular household. Hence there is both teaching and practical involvement in the community. 'Servants on the Way' enter into a time of discipling under the Lord and in relationship to their brothers and sisters. [The teaching program is then outlined.]

SERVANTS OF CHRIST COMMUNITY 1977–1979

SECTION iv
CHAPTER 16

Having experienced a time of being discipled into the life of the Christian community, intending members are then invited to become full covenant members of Servants of Christ. A person's call to and readiness for membership is mutually discerned by the person and the covenant members themselves. Once this has been established, members are invited to make a covenant commitment to the community.[104]

Everyone is in Community

The document included a preamble that explained the rationale for the covenant.[105] Rather than quote it in full, I will provide a summary. It explained that we were a part of many different communities, large and small, long term or fleeting, shallow or deep. Christians, however, are called to live in specific kinds of relationships that are modelled on the relationship of the Trinity, Father, Son and Holy Spirit. "The New Testament, without using the term 'community', nevertheless constantly refers to the life which our modern word 'community' describes." The document then cited a number of biblical examples.

It is then clearly stated that it is not possible to establish Christian Community by making laws about it. Rather, Christian community is one that is experienced as freedom in love. It has to flow from what is inside, not from external controls. Christian community is unattainable unless people want to love in freedom. We don't have the power to do that; it is only possible in the power and presence of the Holy Spirit.

The church had often adopted worldly structures and processes to bind its people together, but has found that in spite of its good intentions it had still become caught up in merely maintaining an institution or an organisation. Rather it is Christ's life and the power of his love, which binds and keeps us together in our relationships. That life is described in much detail by Paul, Peter and John, who tell us how this life can be lived in Christ.

The document states, "We believe that the 'institutional' approach to the Christian life has put the cart before the horse, as had the 'programmatic' approach where people

---

104 *A Look at the Servants of Christ Community* (undated document), 6–7.

105 ibid., 2.

revolve around programs." Instead, we have begun by establishing relationships under the umbrella of a supportive environment. In the current age individuals and family units have become isolated and so cannot stand, let alone grow and mature.

Finally, the preamble also briefly outlined how the covenant operated and cared for its members. It is noteworthy that the community was described as ecumenical in nature and that it was seeking to establish its link into the body of Christ through becoming a congregation of the Lutheran Church. Outreach was described in the second last point as being conducted "through interaction of community members with other people, through the praise meeting on Sunday nights, street concerts, evangelism, etc." Lastly, the community was a service body to Lutheran Charismatic Renewal.

The first covenanted members

There was a proposed constitutional change on the agenda of the February 1978 AGM, but according to the minutes, after nearly five hours the meeting adjourned without considering the proposal. The proposal would have allowed all Core members to decide whether they wished to become covenant members or remain core members for a time. At the end of that time core membership would cease and only covenant members would have voting rights. Apart from this proposal, I have not found any detailed written description of how the first group of full covenant members joined the Elders in covenanting themselves, but it was reported that at one point they numbered 19, with 35 Disciples on the Way, out of a community of about 100 people.[106]

Looking back on the Covenant

Most larger groups of people have an inner, or core, membership, but that is usually an informal arrangement. In effect, the arrangement described above has one category of membership and one level of commitment. Others could associate with the community, or be in the process of becoming covenanted members. Children are not dealt with specifically but other documents suggest that at an appropriate age they would be invited to go through a course, perhaps paralleling confirmation, after which they would become covenanted members. There is nothing that said that this was a life-long commitment, as in unevangelical monastic vows. It had been the previous practice of the community to commend people elsewhere when they discerned that God was calling them out. So for example, the minutes of the Core Meeting held on 16 October 1977 report that concerning Bikie Dave Tee:

---

[106] Noel Hartwig, *The Story of Jacob's Ladder*, unpublished Thesis (1978), 42. Accessed at Lutheran Archives.

SERVANTS OF CHRIST COMMUNITY 1977-1979

CHAPTER 16

The discernment of the Core was that Dave should be released to join Bethesda Fellowship, after Peter Muller shared that this had been worked through in their house and that the household feels at peace about Dave's decision. Doug Kuhl suggested that we write to the pastors and congregation of Bethesda Fellowship, asking that they receive our brother in the Lord Jesus, Dave Tee, in love and that we commend him to their loving care and nurture in the Lord.

The section on eldership talks about pastoral care and concern for the welfare of each member of the community and does not speak about obedience to elders or of anyone having inappropriate authority over someone else's life. Regarding finances, there is no edict concerning a compulsory common purse, rather one of the explanatory notes says:

> The community is supported by the contribution of its members. Members are expected to hold the attitude of the believers described in the book of Acts. "The group of believers was one in heart and mind. No one said that any of his belongings was his own, but they all shared with one another everything they had." (Acts 4:32) Sharing of resources takes place at household, district [suburban area] and community levels, according to what we believe to be the New Testament pattern.[107]

Summary

This community covenant, therefore, sought to stay within the parameters of a New Testament understanding of a particular Christian community,

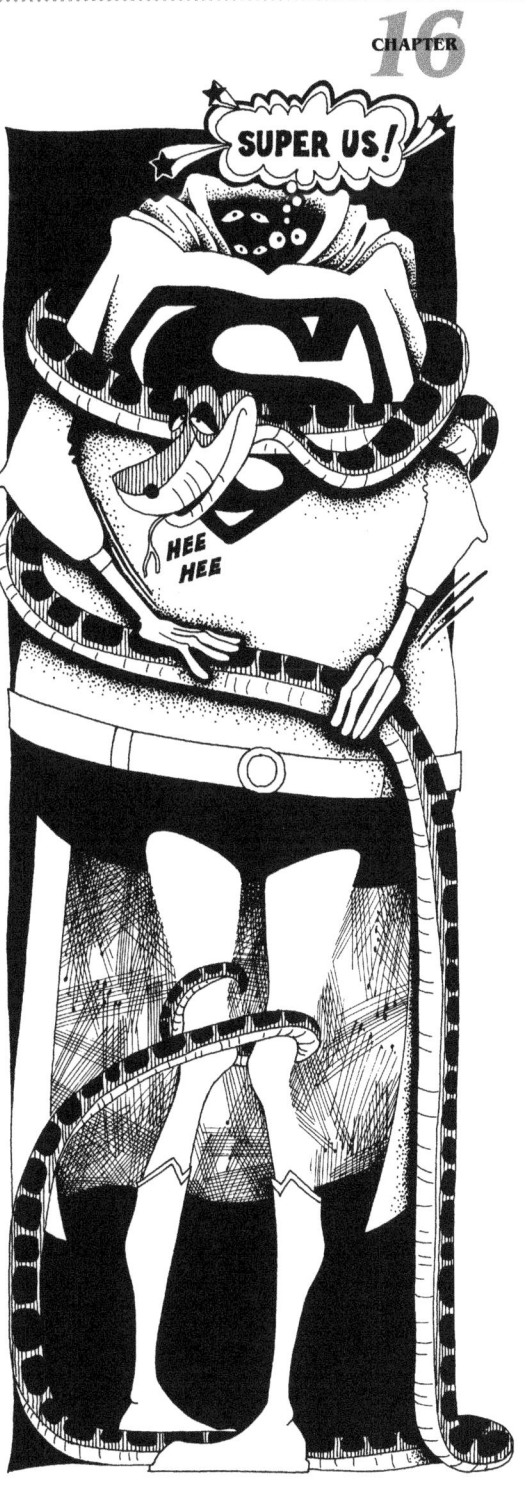

---

107 *A Look at the Servants of Christ Community* (undated document), 5.

A Covenant for the Community // 131

or church. Some of the things said and written in the process leading up to it, and following its adoption, may have gone further, but the actual document itself sought to unpack and make explicit a biblical understanding of Christian discipleship. In regard to issues such as authority and submission, the Lord's freedom to call members to other things, and financial or property matters, it only repeats biblical exhortations.

How this was understood at the time is of course another matter. What is written down and what is practiced may differ. It seems that the way the covenant was initially formed by the elders did not help. While the draft document had been in existence for well over a year, it seems that it hadn't been discussed, owned and adopted.

A number of people have expressed the thought to me that, when looking back, they think that the Covenant was the beginning of the end of the community. Others have said that we didn't need another covenant, since we are already included in the New Covenant (or New Testament) which is God's gift to us in Jesus Christ. That may be true, but it has also been the practice of the church to summarise such things as in the duties of members found in congregational constitutions and in the mutual covenants of pastor and people, in the LCA Letter of Call and other denominational call documents.

We will now take a step back to look at developments in various areas of the life of the community during this period.

SERVANTS OF CHRIST COMMUNITY 1977-1979

Servant Enterprises and Nurture

During this time, the Servants of Christ established a number of new enterprises, and continued others, that were designed to provide employment and/or work experience as part of their rehabilitation for members of the community, as well as producing goods and services for others in society. Community finances were strained. The nurture of the children of the community developed, there now being more children to nurture, but the rehabilitation of those grappling with addiction and other issues struggled.

Kingdom Workshops

On Sunday 27 November 1976, *Jakes' Epistle* reported a development it described as 'quite significant for our community industry'. It is not clear who is writing:

> On Wednesday morning, Ian Wade and I met to discuss the concept of "Industry" and to begin to take some concrete steps towards getting a workshop and tools together. We had some discussions about tools and shared some ideas about the kind of things we could make, for example toys, tables, chairs etc. Ian had been given $50 and another member of the community had donated $200 for the purchase of tools.
>
> Ian has for some time had a vision for a workshop and has already committed his extensive range of equipment for the Lord's purposes in creating a community industry. We decided that several basic items like an electric saw and planer would bring our workshop to the point where we could begin to work economically. We purchased these and got a discount so we were also able to get a sharpening kit for the planer and a drill, which was needed to complete the tables being made for the coffee house.
>
> We agreed to commit ourselves to spending every Wednesday morning working in the 'Industry' and to welcome each member of the community to become involved in one way or another. Ian Wade is the leader of the work and is well equipped to help the willing to learn new skills. It is, after all, the same kind of work that Jesus did in Nazareth some years ago.

By early the following year the workshop was up and running. The desire was to make it self-supporting so that it could provide meaningful employment as part of the rehabilitation and nurture process. They had already produced a dolls' house,

Chinese checkers and chess tables, a toy box and flower boxes. Making furniture and gates were being planned.[108]

A year later, at the 1978 AGM, Ian Wade reported that the operation had become too extensive for their house in Dartmouth Street, necessitating a move to a house at 98 Frederick Street, Welland, which had a large shed. Tools and other equipment were only bought when finances were available. Nothing was obtained on credit. The items that had been made now included beds, cupboards, picture frames and new tables and other fittings for the Coffee House / Drop-in-Centre at Gawler Place. There were plans to build more furniture and make more toys necessitating the purchase of more machinery. Geoff Turner had established another aspect of the workshops, "Ichthys Signs", manufacturing, painting and effecting all types of signage.

Macroni, Kraut & Son

Macroni, Kraut and Son was initially focused on repairing, servicing and maintaining Italian and German motorcycles. Sometimes it was referred to under the general umbrella of the workshops, at other times it was listed as a separate enterprise. Maurie May was the mechanic. They also did painting and electrical work. Once again, it started as a 'backyard' operation before moving into one of a group of factories on the corner of Coglin and First Streets, Brompton.

> As from January 1978 under Macroni, Kraut and Son, a spray painting section has opened, specialising in motorcycle custom work, but also looking to do larger work on cars. Some very interesting work has been done in this area, both in paint jobs and in personal contact with 'outlaw' bikers.[109]

The minutes of the 1978 AGM also record the following discussion and decision:

> Maurie asked that Macroni, Kraut and Son have permission to take up a bank overdraft of $10,000 to set up the business. Steen moved that Maurie be given permission to seek a bank overdraft and/or private loan up to $10,000, and the Servants of Christ Community Inc take responsibility for the repayment of this loan. Seconded David Southern. Carried.

By the end of March, the community was in a difficult financial position. Pastor Doug Kuhl wrote a letter to members stating that Jakes had been unable to pay all its bills that month. Doug mentions that the two workshops involved two salaries and rent on two premises, as well as other costs. In addition, there were three

---

108 **Servants of Christ Workshop**, *Servant* (February–March 1977), 21.

109 Ian Wade, **Report for Servants of Christ Community Workshops**, AGM (held on 22 February 1978).

SERVANTS OF CHRIST COMMUNITY 1977–1979

loans requiring repayment totalling $8,900. On 21 April 1978, a meeting was held to deal with unfinished business from the AGM. We have a detailed agenda, but no minutes. The agenda explains that "the motion concerning $10,000 was not carried through." The reason being that the community and Macroni, Kraut and Son were not able to service the current debts, including bills owed from January–March totalling approximately $2,900. The total owed by the Community was now in excess of $12,403.

By the time of the 1979 AGM, Ian Wade reported that:

> Much time was spent on the business side of our community, as we worked through the ways of coming to grips with the problems of our two workshops. With prayer and counselling from various sources, the woodworking shop was closed and the premises at 98 Frederick Street, Welland was taken over by Macroni, Kraut and Son, which we have now also had to close as a community venture. This business has now been taken over privately by Maurie May. However, we learnt much that will always be of value, in setting up these workshops and developing ideas.[110]

The treasurer's report to the 1979 AGM includes more detail:

> At a Covenant meeting on 9 February 1979, it was decided that Maurie May would immediately cease employment with Servants of Christ Community, and that the following should happen with Macroni, Kraut and Son:
>
> 1. The Covenant Group is to bear the responsibility for the private internal loans. Should any of those who loaned money decide to surrender their loan as a gift, then that loan should be specifically set aside for a special fund, like repaying the loan on the bus.
>
> 2. We pay back the internal loan out of what would normally be paid to Maurie May each week. This is after 98 Frederick Street is re-leased, since what would have been Maurie's salary will have to go into paying this until someone else takes up the lease on the property.[111]

Finances

The Financial Reports for 1977 and 1978 were presented to the AGMs by the respective treasurers Christine Schubert and Marty Rosenberg. Income increased

---

110 Ian Wade, **Elders' Report**, AGM (held on 9 March 1979).

111 Marty Rosenberg, **Treasurer's Report**, AGM (held on 9 March 1979).

slightly from $40,407 in 1977 to $41,615 in 1978, and offerings rose significantly from $18,108 to $24,481. Donations however were down from $8,262 to $5,504. In each year, an $11,000 government grant for salaries was received.

On the expenditure side salaries went up from $18,484 to $22,814, as did rents: from $2,290 to $4,537 for 102 Gawler Place, and towards the end of 1978, 122 Torrens Road; and from $2,290 to $2,511 for 98 Frederick Street. All told, this indicated that the community was in a stable and sound financial position. However, that is only part of the story. In his written treasurer's report, Marty informed the community that staff had only been paid their full salaries for half the year, with partial pay for four months and with no pay for nine weeks.

The community was also carrying significant debt of $4,720 for Macroni, Kraut and Son and $6,800 for the bus. All the loans are described as loans from members of the community. During 1978, fulltime paid staff were reduced from five to three and part-time from four to one. Marty concluded, "We are trying to plug up all the big black bottomless holes that money has been poured into in the past." The budget for 1979 required an increase in offerings to $600 per week, up from $470 per week in 1978. $120 per week, or nearly all of the increase, is for repayment of the loans.

Mustard Seed

The Mustard Seed Christian Bookshop was established around October 1977 and managed by Anne Sellers. Trade accounts were established with major Christian and Music suppliers, both in Australia and overseas. Some would not deal with the Mustard Seed because it wasn't open on Mondays and Saturdays, nor for late night shopping. Sales averaged $100 per month for the first four months. By the end of the year, they had $2,478 worth of stock. The Mustard Seed was located at 102 Gawler Place and was open 9am–5pm, Tuesdays through Fridays.

Servant Media

Servants of Christ Community, in association with Lutheran Charismatic Renewal, Australia, established Servant Media in November 1977. It was a continuation and expansion of the Media Resource Centre begun at Gawler Place after the doubling of the floor area in 1974. As well as publishing *Servant* magazine, Servant Media produced cassette tapes of various speakers, as well as music. Karl Brettig was its fulltime staff member, working with various other volunteers. The 1978 AGM Minutes record that *Servant* magazine had 142 subscriptions and a total circulation of 350–400. By the end of 1978, subscribers numbered 220. The tape ministry

SERVANTS OF CHRIST COMMUNITY 1977-1979

expanded and served two major conferences in 1978, and the Mustard Seed had provided a good supply of material. Looking ahead, Karl wrote:

> Since the end of 1978, we have needed to re-examine the financial viability of Servant Media. It has been felt that *Servant* magazine should continue to be subsidised by the community and Lutheran Charismatic Renewal, however Mustard Seed need not operate on a fulltime basis. The tape ministry continues to be self-supporting.[112]

During 1978, Tape sales totalled $3,688 and the Mustard Seed sold $5,406 worth of materials. *Servant* magazine brought in $240 in subscriptions and cost $460 to print. Lutheran Charismatic Renewal contributed $800 to overall costs. Blank tapes cost $1,514 to buy and labels cost $151 to print. $776 was paid in sales tax. A high speed tape duplicator had been purchased. Renting it out raised $113 in 1978.

The community magazine *Jacob's Letter* had become *Servant* from the first issue in 1977. Gradually the emphasis changed from the Servants of Christ Community to Lutheran Charismatic Renewal. Obviously, there was considerable overlap between the two, but over time there were less stories about what was happening in the community. There were still teaching articles by Pastor Doug Kuhl and other community members, and reports on renewal conferences attended by Jakes people, but they were aimed at the Lutheran Renewal audience. It is also noticeable that gradually there were more and more reprints of articles from other sources and less original material. That is especially the case from the first issue in 1978 onwards.

Co-op

The first item of business at the 'Core' Meeting on 11 September 1977 was John Grimwade's employment by the community. The minutes note that 'John has a knack with gardens'. The proposition was that John should be the community market gardener, and that therefore the community members should buy their vegetables from him. There was garden space in community houses that was not being used to full advantage and so John could take over some of the gardens, with any excess being sold to the markets. It was resolved that "in line with his call to be Co-op director, John become Community Garden Co-ordinator Director."

Sunday School / Ministry with Children

David Skeat presented the Sunday School Report to the 1978 AGM. There were five other teachers: Erna Kuhl, Chris George (Wills), Sue Jasprizza (Stopp), and

---

112 Karl Brettig, **Servant Media Report**. AGM (held on 9 March 1979).

Chris and Peter Schubert. There was one class of children aged three to eleven. At the beginning of 1978 the children were divided into age-based classes, and more members of the community became involved teaching lessons prepared by the teachers. The AGM Minutes record that the teachers felt that the children should be more involved in worship.

In the 1979 AGM report David Skeat mentioned that early in 1978 a children's *Life in the Spirit* Seminar was run, with many of the children receiving a deepened awareness of the presence of the Holy Spirit in their lives. Marie Skeat and Marg May joined the team of teachers, with Peter Schubert and Erna Kuhl withdrawing late in the year due to other commitments. Chris Tierney-Smith and Naomi Rosenberg joined the teachers at the beginning of 1979.

One of the major issues facing the Children's ministry was the need to establish a confirmation or discipleship course for the senior students. A separate class was established for two to three year olds. There was a need for members of the community to spend time with the children:

> Our children need to know that grownups are interested in them as people; they need to know that grownups are also people. So try to spend time with our kids and get to know them. There is a treasure in them that we really need to see and latch onto.[113]

Nurture Houses

Marty Rosenberg remembers:

> Somewhere in 1975–76, a decision was made to consolidate our homes into one area of Adelaide. The Bowden-Brompton neighbourhood was a needy area in the Adelaide inner suburbs, so it was decided to slowly move into houses in this district in an attempt to make a difference there, and in the lives of those who lived with us. The Housing Trust of SA could see the benefit of what we were doing and provided two large houses in Chief St, Brompton.

---

113 David Skeat, *Children's Ministry Report*, AGM (held on 9 March 1979).

SERVANTS OF CHRIST COMMUNITY 1977–1979

SECTION iv
CHAPTER 17

More homes quickly opened up and soon there were about a dozen houses, all rented, in this area, most of them occupied by people very new in their faith.

By 1978, there were numerous community houses around the Croydon, Brompton area and word got out to the Department of Community Welfare (DCW) that we were taking in "boarders" to care for them. I (Marty) was employed as Social Worker for the Community to screen those referrals and to oversee/troubleshoot the Community Houses when issues arose—and they did—frequently. Most of the issues were related to those with middle class backgrounds, whose faith in God was shaped there. They were living with those who were just learning about their Christian faith and trying to make it fit into their working class backgrounds. Vastly different past lifestyles, faith matters, ideals, personalities and expectations were all in this mix and often these clashed. This created many challenges for the leadership of the houses. In addition, many of the house parents were only discovering how to run a house for the first time, after leaving their own mum and dad.

Those referred to us by DCW included the homeless, some with intellectual disabilities, an exotic dancer who had medical problems, drug addicts, alcoholics and an hermaphrodite. There were numerous others who we were ill-equipped to deal with, but we took them anyway and did our best to care for them.

Marty Rosenberg reported to the 1978 AGM that at the beginning of 1977 there were four houses around the community that were willing to take in people with problems:

> During the year, one by one, each house said, "No more!" until finally there were no vacancies left for more people to come in. Only those people that we committed ourselves to stayed on, and slowly, they too have been leaving.
> … The primary reasons why these houses could not keep functioning in this capacity are two-fold:
>
> 3. There was no proper assessment of the people going into the houses, that is, there were people allowed in that should not have been allowed in because we were not equipped as a community or as houses to cope with them.
>
> 4. The commitment of the people in the houses (in many cases, although not all) was not primarily to the house and the people there. There were many other "ministries" that people were involved in, which took them away from the house, very often at very crucial times.

Servant Enterprises and Nurture // 139

Around September, it was decided to begin a special training program, to equip specially called people, to a greater degree, to be able to cope with people with problems. This team was to specialise in this ministry of living with people with problems, to help them to grow out of those problems and into the kingdom of God. After a number of weeks interest waned due to things like the Christmas break and holidays, and some pulled out due to other commitments. We discovered that there were not enough capable, single people left to head up a venture like this, so training ceased.[114]

Marty concluded by saying that he looked forward to a time when the community would again be able to offer a secure family environment for people needing this support in order to blossom. He reported that in the previous six months, 27 people had wanted such help, but he had needed to say "No" each time.

Conclusion

Big changes continued to happen in the community. New ventures began with much prayer and expectation. A number thrived for a while, and then folded. Some, like the Co-op, seemed to struggle along, without ever reaching a stage where it was operating in a sustainable manner. In one sense that is as it should be. If nothing fails, then we are not trying hard enough. Jakes / Servants of Christ was never a community that 'played it safe'. Not from the very beginning. It pushed the boundaries and went out boldly with its focus on the Lord and his call. Risks were taken, but not wild irresponsible risks. Dreams were dreamt, as they should be, but during this time there were still checks and balances. Mistakes were made, but the community moved on.

Secondly, the motivation, commitment and plain old-fashioned hard work of those involved cannot be questioned. There was a sense of being on a journey with others who shared the same faith and desire to serve the Lord and see others come into his kingdom. These mainly younger people were not too concerned about getting ahead in the world or achieving personal financial security. They weren't living for the next party. Personal fulfilment and chasing happiness was not what motivated them. They followed the beat of a different drum, because they knew a different Drummer.

In a personal email recently, a community member said, "We don't need another Jakes. But we need something like it." That is important to remember as we consider the decline and ultimate closure of this work that Jesus raised up in the 1970s.

---

[114] Marty Rosenberg, **Report on Nurture**, AGM (held on 22 February 1978).

SERVANTS OF CHRIST COMMUNITY 1977-1979

Lutheran Charismatic Renewal and Manoah

The Servants of Christ Community worked together with a growing Lutheran Renewal movement across Australia. Seminars, Workshops and Conferences were organised, teaching tapes distributed and publications produced. There were meetings with Church officials and overseas speakers. As the Servants of Christ Community was coming to an end, the renewal movement grew and spread. The story of Lutheran Charismatic Renewal after Jakes folded, is for someone else to tell. Here we are only concerned with the overlap between the two.

Manoah Christian Community

Three couples—Judith and Glen Heidenreich, Sue and Hugh Walla, and Karma and Con Heyer—combined their resources to buy a burnt-out mansion at Upper Sturt in the Adelaide Hills. It had been built in the 19th Century by Sir Josiah Henry Symon, a lawyer, politician and co-framer of the Australian Constitution. He lavished time and money on it, hiring Hans Heysen to decorate the ceilings and establishing a significant private library. By the mid-1970s, it largely lay in ruins having been ravaged by fire some years earlier, but it still had lots of potential. The three couples saw the potential for it to become "a place where God was glorified and where people would come to meet him in a life-changing way."[115] It was dedicated on 13 November 1977 with Revd Doug Kuhl giving the address, Revd Bill Bennett offering the prayers of dedication and Revd A Wilson the final prayer and blessing, thus representing the various denominations of the founders.

Glen Heidenreich wrote a long letter (ten foolscap pages) to the Manoah community on 30 March 1981. It fills in some of the background. The Heidenreichs and Heyers moved in on 19 August 1977 with the Wallas following around Christmas time, after their house sale was finalised. Until some renovations were done, there was a shortage of liveable space, so the Heyers lived in the swimming pool (I remember seeing their 'family bedroom'), the Wallas downstairs in the servant quarters and the Heidenreichs upstairs. John and Di Grimwade, of the Servants of Christ Community moved in during January 1978 and lived upstairs in the so-called Doll's House.

---

115 **Notes & News**, *Servant* (January 1978), 18.

Judy and Glen joined Servants of Christ for a while and Glen served as an Elder for some of the time. Manoah functioned with the three initial men as elders. Glen recalls:

> No one was seen to be in authority among these three, but rather the three were jointly in leadership. Probably this was unwise, but we were loath to change it as no one wanted to submit to the other. We would make decisions on the running of the community in a whole variety of areas and then tell the others of our decisions. This was pretty much a copy of what was happening at Servants of Christ. No thought of submitting our decisions to the body, but rather telling them afterwards. Some tension arose over this.

The last comment was telling, especially, for our purposes. Decision-making processes are partly related to size. For example, very small congregations tend to make all decisions over coffee after the service, whereas in very large congregations the board makes nearly all decisions. However, it also reflects an understanding of headship, leadership, anointing and discernment that we will return to in a few chapters time. Glen continues:

> During the first two years or so we had regular meetings with the Elders of "Servants". At one stage we nearly joined forces with them. We had wonderful times of fellowship and worship at these meetings. ...
>
> Gradually the honeymoon period that we were enjoying at Manoah began to wear thin. The Heyer family became increasingly discontented with the lifestyle. ... One of the significant lessons for me in this whole business was that instead of judging your sisters and brothers, you should intercede for them. You intercede for your brother with whom you are having a battle, and still try to judge him at the same time, and you will discover that the two (intercession and judging) are most uncomfortable bedfellows. The good in intercession far outweighs the evils of judging.

Karma and Con Heyer then took time out, renting a house in Hahndorf, while they discerned their future involvement in Manoah. They never returned to live there. John and Di also decided to leave. Glen comments, "They were no doubt rather disillusioned with us here. Unfortunately for them, they were caught up with our growing problems and lack of unity." Then Sandy and Rob McCarthy joined Manoah. Others followed. At the time Glen wrote his letter, Sue and Hugh Waller were also elsewhere, a separation which Glen says could easily last a year. The context suggests they were called to minister somewhere else for a time.

Finally, we go back to the start of Glen's letter, where he talks about Judy's and his desire for Manoah to be part of the Servants of Christ Community. This is before

SERVANTS OF CHRIST COMMUNITY 1977-1979

they met the Heyers and the Wallers. Jakes relationship with the Heidenreichs goes back to the time when they were farming near Padthaway in the State's South East. I remember one Easter camp was held on their property. Glen writes:

> Initially we thought that the Servants of Christ Community was to be part of the work here. Judy and I approached them and invited them to be partners with us. However, they did not seem to have God's peace about it. Thinking back, it was probably because we would have been providing most of the finance, which would have placed them in a difficult position regarding leadership. Judith and I didn't see it that way, as we were happy to be part of a team with Doug Kuhl as leader of the work. However, after the initial shock of "Servants" deciding not to be part of it, we thought maybe the timing was wrong, or perhaps God had something else in mind.

Eventually the Manoah Community also folded and the property was sold, but that takes us beyond the scope of this story of Jakes. Many Servants of Christ and then Lutheran Renewal events were held at Manoah, which was rebuilt into a lovely facility.

Glen's Testimony

How did the dream of Manoah begin? Glen's testimony was published in the July 1977 edition of *Servant*:

> It's not the first time it has happened in a marriage. My wife, Judith, received the infilling of the Holy Spirit twelve months before I did—why? Because she asked for it and didn't reject it when God gave it to her, unlike most of us who say, "If God wants to bless me in a special way, he will—but please God, no tongues." Life was uncomfortable during those twelve months. My wife was growing spiritually through this beautiful release of the Holy Spirit in her life, and I was resentful and confused. [Aside: I remember Glen telling me during that time that he would gladly swap a few Bible readings and prayers for a well-cooked meal.] "Why should the Lord bless her and not me?" I complained. "After all we are married." I made life difficult by doubting this newfound "experience" in her life. ...
>
> My wife and I had been good churchgoers for 18 years and I held many offices and had been on committees in our congregation and in the LCA SA District. Although we received a real blessing from our Sunday services and serving in the Sunday School, we always knew something was missing in our lives. We found our joy in worldly pleasures (tennis, golf, parties, fishing trips

etc). ... Then it happened! My wife became "Charismatic". All she wanted to talk about was Jesus and the Holy Spirit. ... Subsequently, I too was blessed by the Lord with this beautiful infilling. After praying to him for the gift of the Holy Spirit, he filled me with a love for him and for others that I had never known before. ...

The rest of the story is a fairly familiar one. Some people didn't understand what had happened and were doubtful whether it was really the Holy Spirit we had received. Our opportunities to serve in the congregation became less and less and we were generally considered a bad influence on the others within the body. However, we were led to join a very precious group of believers at Jacob's Ladder, called 'The Servants of Christ'. Here the Lord is very precious and real, leading his people into a ministry to the poor and lonely. It's a hard ministry, but one that gives a great joy to those who serve. Many are being led to the Lord, and under the capable leadership of Pastor Doug Kuhl, are nurtured and given homes, and above all, love—God's love.[116]

Glen was called home in 2018. Judy in 1996. Their legacy lives on!

Larry Christenson Visit

Well-known author and speaker, Pastor Larry Christenson was the leader of the Lutheran Charismatic Renewal Movement in the United States. He was brought to Australia by the Temple Trust to speak at the National Charismatic Conference in Melbourne on 23–28 January 1978. Lutheran Renewal then arranged for him to speak at a number of mini-conferences during the first week of February in Horsham Victoria, Naracoorte and Adelaide in South Australia, and Perth Western Australia. As well as his involvement in renewal, Larry had also written a great deal about relationships and family life. David Trudinger writes:

> It was with anticipation and expectation that over two thousand people assembled in the Dallas Brooks Hall, East Melbourne for the opening session, Monday evening 23 January 1978.

---

116 Glen Heidenreich, **Filled with the Spirit**, Servant (July 1977), 11–12.

SERVANTS OF CHRIST COMMUNITY 1977–1979

CHAPTER 18

And they were not disappointed. Pastor Larry Christenson's opening address set the spiritual tone for the whole conference. He spoke of the work of God's grace in every aspect of our Christian lives, saying that human work and effort has no part. Pastor Christenson was the leading speaker at the conference and for the first session each day he gave the Bible study. These were an outstanding series of studies on the book of Hebrews.

Pastor Christenson gave the conference's concluding address at the final rally on the Friday night. The Dallas Brooks Hall was filled to capacity. The program was long and Pastor Christenson was only able to commence his address at 8.45pm. However, it was worth waiting for, and had a tremendous impact on those present. Within his address he listed the manifestations and fruit that accompany the life and community that is experiencing a genuine renewal in the Holy Spirit.

During the conference, the Lutherans present had an opportunity to gather with Pastor Larry for a brief time of sharing and mutual encouragement. Pastor Christenson was also able to have an afternoon with a number of Victorian Lutheran pastors and we praise God for opening the way for this to take place.[117]

In Horsham and Naracoorte Larry spoke on the role of husbands and wives in pastoring their families in a world that runs against the grain of Christian truth.

In Adelaide, Pastor Christenson was the guest of Lutheran Charismatic Renewal Australia at their regular monthly conference, which was held in Way Hall, Franklin Street. Here he spoke of the effects of the charismatic renewal throughout the body of Christ, and its implications for Lutherans here in Australia. A lively question time followed and Pastor Larry was able to give much sound advice from his 13 years of experience in the charismatic dimension. Also while in Adelaide, Pastor Larry was the key speaker at an ecumenical rally ... Maughan Church, which holds 1,400 people, was filled to overflowing for the occasion. Pastor Christenson gave some guidelines for those involved in the renewal, as well as those who are not able to be involved directly, but desire to adopt a pastoral concern for renewal. The meeting was a joyous occasion and ended with a powerful time of ministry. Before he left for Perth, Pastor Larry also spoke at a meeting in Adelaide Uni's Union Hall, on the subject of leadership, drawing on the experience of the Israelites as they crossed the Jordan River and entered the promised land. In Perth Pastor Larry spoke to over 500 people ... in what proved to be a lively rally for those who attended.[118]

---

117 David Trudinger, **Conference Reports**, Servant (April 1978), 14.

118 ibid., 15.

Servant magazine ran a series of three articles by Larry in its first three issues in 1978. They were titled, 'The House we live in' and dealt with the Christian life and its place in the modern world. He described becoming a Christian as something like moving into a new house with many doors. The doors represent different ways or places that Jesus seeks to open to gain fresh access to our lives. We experience renewal as we respond to his knocking.[119]

Members of the Community attended many other conferences, both in Australia and overseas. Here are a couple more examples.

Kansas Conference July 1977

Doug Vogelsang and Doug Kuhl attended the five-day 1977 Conference on Charismatic Renewal in the Christian Churches, together with Neil Lehmann from Victoria. There were nearly 50,000 registered delegates from many different countries and denominations. More attended the rallies. The Catholic group numbered some 10,000 people, who were especially vocal in the worship times. At their closing denominational gathering, some 300 priests concelebrated the Mass.

Christianity Today reported that:

> For four nights Arrowhead Stadium, the sparkling 79,000-seat home of the Kansas City Chiefs football team in the south-eastern section of the city, reverberated with their singing and jubilant praises to Jesus. Cardinal Leon Joseph Suenens of Belgium, a leading figure at Vatican Council II and in the Catholic charismatic movement, spoke gently but powerfully. "The world is dying because it doesn't know the name of its Saviour, Jesus Christ," said Suenens. This name, he stated, is one "no one can pronounce without the power and the grace of the Holy Spirit."[120]

Lutheran Pastor Larry Christenson spoke on the Thursday evening about the many doors the Lord was knocking on, stressing the need of the church to hear what the Lord is saying to his church today, while not forgetting what he has said in the past. Doug (Vogelsang?) reported:

> The sight of more than 50,000 people from many parts of the globe, including representatives from all the major denominations, praising and worshipping

---

[119] The last occasion I spent time with Larry was in June 2015, when we met together with Paul Anderson at Paul's place in Minneapolis MN, USA. In spite of his age, Larry drove himself an hour each way from his home and was as sprightly as ever. Larry was called home, after a fall when out on his daily six-kilometre prayer walk, in December 2017, at the age of 89.

[120] **Charismatic Unity in Kansas City**, *Christianity Today* (12 August 1977).

SERVANTS OF CHRIST COMMUNITY 1977–1979

the Lord, as the giant electronic scoreboard ... flashed "Jesus is Lord" across the arena, was an historic event for the Christian Church. ... They gathered for a purpose. The message came loud and clear that God is calling together his people from all corners of the world, encouraging us to hear his voice. ... All churches are being called of the Lord to repentance, obedience, and to hear what the Spirit is saying to the churches in these days of Western decadence. There is an urgency. All Christians must be about their Father's business and live under his lordship.[121]

Emmanuel Covenant Community Conference in Brisbane July 1978

Marty Rosenberg attended this conference sponsored by the 700-member ecumenical Emmanuel community. He wrote a brief report:

> The various workshops covered a large range of areas including leadership, family life, children's ministry, introduction to the life of the Spirit and youth outreach in cities. ... It seems that the Lord is drawing people closer to himself, sorting out our lives into various areas of responsibility and generally ordering our lives and the group life of Christians. ... One of the results of this reordering or renewing process is a closer and more committed working relationship between groups within different denominations. The God-given emphasis of each denomination is then able to be used in a powerful way. As an example of this during the conference a Pentecostal brother led in times of praise, while much of the teaching in relation to authority and family came from Catholics, and the call to spreading the Gospel came from Lutherans.[122]

There is much more that could be said about the conferences organised or attended by members of Jakes, but this sample gives an indication of the extent of the involvement of the community with the wider body of Christ. Many more conferences, regional gatherings and overseas speakers were also organised by Lutheran Renewal in the following years. But that is another story.

---

121 Doug Vogelsang and Doug Kuhl, **Report from the Kansas Conference**, Servant (October 1977), 17.

122 Marty Rosenberg, **Growing Together in Christ**, Servant (October 1978), 13.

CHAPTER 19: From Gawler Place to Torrens Road

The Jacob's Ladder Coffee House and Drop-in Centre was established at 102 Gawler Place in the CBD. At various times other options were explored. In the mid-70s there was a desire to be closer to the action in Hindley Street, but either the idea never gained sufficient momentum or suitable premises were never found. In September 1977, an offer was made to lease premises on Light Square in the CBD for $18,000pa. The owners made a counter offer of $19,500 + rates and taxes, but the Core Meeting decided to leave the initial offer stand, without increasing it. At the same time there was discussion of buying the McNally Building and leasing it to the existing tenants.[123]

A little over a month later, the Core Meeting again considered relocation. This time the minutes record the following comment from Pastor Doug Kuhl suggesting that there was a need to consolidate operations:

> Ought we not give up 102 Gawler Place and move operations to the Brompton area, therefore needing to find an alternative worship centre (Sunday morning and night) and a venue for the Spirit in Life seminars on Tuesday nights?
> It was noted that such a move would also impact the Mustard Seed, and the music, dance and drama ministries and music hall. Karl shared that he feels a too hasty move would not be wise and therefore we would need to give at least 2–3 months warning to the wider body of Christ.[124]

Further discussion continued around the idea of consolidating the community's activities to the area in which more community members were now living. It was pointed out that this would allow more time to do work through the community houses, and the workshops, Mustard Seed and Publications. The bikie ministry could be based out of the workshops, rather than on the street. It was also said that many had been living in the Brompton area for almost two years with very little impact on the area. Some suggested that the overall community outreach should be examined if outreach was to flow out of that life. Finally, the minutes record, "Doug K. shared that we should make community activities a priority over any outside activities."[125]

---

123 **Core Meeting Minutes** (11 September 1977), 1.
124 **Core Meeting Minutes** (16 October 1977), 1.
125 ibid., 2.

SERVANTS OF CHRIST COMMUNITY 1977–1979

By October 1978 *Servant* was able to report:

> For some time Servants of Christ Community have contemplated the possibility of moving the 102 Gawler Place centre out into the suburbs. It seems the time has arrived and negotiations are currently taking place for the lease of a former Salvation Army premises at Torrens Road, Renown Park. Further news soon…[126]

The January 1979 edition of *Servant* had pictures of the final worship in the City and the first in the new centre. It reported:

> THE OLD—The old Jacob's Ladder worship centre. Once the scene of many struggles and victories, it will live in many of our hearts as the place where God answered so many of our needs in reaching out to people on the streets of our city.

> THE NEW—The opening of the new Servants of Christ Community worship centre at 122 Torrens Road, Renown Park, marks the transition of the old Jacob's Ladder ministry into the new concept of a Christian Community in the midst of a post-Christian City.[127]

It seems that the final worship service in Gawler Place was on Sunday 19 November 1978. The Community Newsletter sets out the process for the move, beginning

---

126 ***Servants of Christ Move***, *Servant* (October 1978), 21.
127 ***New Centre for Servants of Christ***, *Servant* (January 1979), 24.

From Gawler Place to Torrens Road // 149

Monday 20 November at 95a Chief Street, Brompton (the Kuhl residence), with a time of prayer and then assignment of tasks. People were needed to clean both the new and old centres, and to pack, move and unpack all the community's belongings. Others were required to prepare food and drink, and to mind children. Finally, a team was needed to erect equipment in the new centre. Donors were sought for more chairs and a piano.

The Newsletter also floated two suggestions for the celebration of communion. The Elders thought it should be midweek, while Sunday mornings be a time for community gathering and formation. Others proposed the opposite, namely Sunday morning communion service and Thursday evening community gathering and formation. The final note was a personal one:

> Steve, Jan and Nathan Haar and Steen, Ruth and Kirsten Olsen will be leaving us the first week in December for their respective destinations of call within the Lutheran Church. [the Haars to Gladstone, Qld and us to the Hunter Valley, NSW] As a community, we bless them—and will always hold them dear.

Establishment of a new Office

The Kuhls had moved from the house in Sheffield Street, Malvern to a specially prepared and renovated Housing Trust place at 95a Chief Street, Brompton. A separate bungalow was then added, which functioned as Doug's and the community office. On 6 August 1978 the Community Secretary, Marty Rosenberg reported that:

> The Bungalow at 95A Chief Street, Brompton is near completion now and should be moved into this coming week. This will certainly streamline the office work considerably and enable life to flow more smoothly throughout the community. This is one of the many steps being taken to get the community functioning in a more orderly manner. We are expecting an account to come in for over $1,000 for all the final trimmings that have been needed to complete the office. So far, $1,400 has been spent on the initial materials. This was donated for this project.

Consolidation into two Households

The various community houses were now organised into two households, one based in Croydon, Ridleyton and Renown Park and one in Brompton. By early 1979, the former included 29 adults and 10 children, while the Brompton Household had 10 residences, housing 29 adults and 15 children. A year earlier the Brompton

SERVANTS OF CHRIST COMMUNITY 1977-1979

household had four residences with nine adults and seven children, while the Croydon one was the result of combining two previous groups in November 1978.

The 1979 AGM report lists those living in each of the Brompton houses:

Chief Street	95A	Doug, Erna, Heidi, Ingrid, Kurt Kuhl, Ruth Bennett
	101	Jo Milford, Kay Jackson (de Vries), Chris George (Wills)
	89	Sue, Erika Antal (Anear), Liz Bennett
	Fl 1	Marty Jaeschke, Peter Bennett
	Fl 2	Marcia and Kevin Lieschke
	Fl 4	Hamish Anear, Phil Jefferis
	Fl 6	David, Marie, Ben, Jemimah Skeat
	79	Marty, Naomi, Luke Rosenberg
	84	Faith, Darryl, Douglas Martin
	92	Ian, Helen, Kym, Martin Wade Anne Sellers, Tiffany, Olivia Bolton
Coglin Street	107	Maurie, Marg, Carolyn, Lindy, Steven May Dave, Angela, Virginia Southern Mal Turnbull

The nature of the community had obviously changed from a group who were mainly singles, with a few older married couples, to a community where families with children were becoming the norm.

Helen and Ian Wade remember that their house at 92 Chief Street had bedrooms added at the back. Ian made a beautiful native garden out the front and a very large shed was erected in the back yard, where the activities of the workshops continued. Ruth and I shared a house with Jan and Steve Haar in 34 Second Street, Brompton through 1978, which was our final year of seminary. It had previously been occupied by Di and John Grimwade. I still remember the landlord saying to us when we moved in that John had left the garden in very good shape. Then he added, "Not many do that, you know." He was also learning about Christian community!

The Brompton Household

The writer of the Brompton Household 1979 AGM report wrote:

> One of the main reasons for the dramatic increase in numbers is the God-given call for consolidation of community in our midst. We believe God wants to call us to a common life together that will glorify him and shine light into

the world, but as you can imagine, to do this with such a large and increasing number of people is a very difficult task. However, we have ploughed on and attempted to do this in our Monday night meetings. We met together and shared together and got blessed together. We made Monday night a special night in which we emphasised and grappled with the whole concept of being a family together.

In July, we began the 'Oblate New Testament Way to Community' course and we completed it at the end of October. What a blessing this course was! I don't think there was anyone who didn't come away from the course challenged and edified by the whole concept of sharing common life together.

Of late God has said to us that we must use our time together to edify and build up one another in practical ways, consequently we have spent family nights helping with house renovations and sewing curtains, or doing each other's ironing, and this has proved itself to be a real blessing. The coordinators are feeling that it is right that as these needs come up, we should do something about them corporately.

Chris George (Wills) remembers:

When we moved into the house at 95A Chief Street, it had been renovated extensively but with poor quality, ill thought out, fittings. Who puts a light background linoleum in a high traffic area like a kitchen & dining room? It was a constant challenge to keep clean & there were Saturday afternoons when Doug had gone off to Jakes that Erna and I would be on hands and knees discussing the cares of the world and the community, while we scrubbed and polished. Often with great mirth!

Erna's organisational skills & ability to stretch the finances would put a professional housekeeper to shame. Then in her abundant (joke) 'me time', she managed to forge relationships with the families living either side. These were an interesting diverse group of Italians, Greeks, Indigenous Australians of different generations. Part of Erna's appeal was that she too knew what it was like to be a refugee/immigrant. She shared the gospel with all and sundry without apology and they shared the abundance of their high density backyard farms. Erna's love and care of Mrs Mac(allister) across the road was a blessing to both of them and there were many discussions about tele-evangelists over the preparation of the evening meal.

Erna has had a profound effect on my life, as the big sister in the Lord that I needed at a formative time of my life. I'm so pleased that we have been able

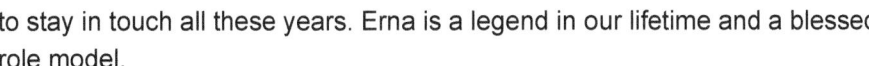

to stay in touch all these years. Erna is a legend in our lifetime and a blessed role model.

The Croydon, Ridleyton and Renown Park Household

Peter Jasprizza reports on behalf of the other household:

> Due to the changes in the household structure, new relationships were formed, and there was a noticeable change in the way we met together. In the previous household structure, a more intimate relationship existed between all the members. While in the present form, there are several groups who seem to relate on the basis of similar need. To this point there has been no organised life sharing, apart from a 'household tea' and 'fellowship' evening, where we attempted to follow the 'New Testament Way to Community' program. At this point it appears there needs to be authoritative teaching that would establish realistic expectations of community and at the same time, develop a sharing and caring lifestyle.

Lindsay Webb remembers:

> It was 1976 and the Jesus movement was in full swing. Aged 17, I attended a National Christian Youth Convention and befriended members of a Christian Motorcycle club "Christ's Crusaders" These people were different, they were real, genuine. It was the first time I knew true Christian love and acceptance. They were special people, who were pivotal to my Christian awakening. Through them, I came to know Jakes and attended the coffee shop and Sunday night services. At the same time, I attended presentations by John Hirt (House of the New World), John Smith (God's Squad) and Athol Gill (House of the Gentle Bunyip). They were charismatic preachers, who gave powerful addresses and spoke against 'respectable analgesic' Christianity and the call to radical discipleship. It resonated deeply with me and I longed to live out the Christian call.

> At 21, I left home and lived in a Jakes community house. This produced a great rift between my parents and I, whom I still loved, but who never really understood me. My experience with Jakes community life lasted only twelve months, as I was living in a community that was falling apart. From there my life fragmented for a time.

Family Worship

We turn the clock back slightly now, to consider worship in a community house. In the February–March 1977 *Servant* magazine, Peter Muller described the patterns of life in the house he shared with others. The day started at 7am as they gathered for breakfast. Late risers were roused. They read and studied a chapter of the Bible each day. Then they prayed, as some needed to go to work. At lunchtime those who could gathered to eat together. Helen was dieting so she read to the others as they ate. They prayed, praised and then returned to work. The evening meal could last well over two hours. This was their greatest opportunity for fellowship. Peter comments:

> This sort of daily routine was completely foreign to my 'normal' way of life, but now I cannot recommend it too highly. Why? I want to copy Jesus, and I live with a family who wants to copy Jesus too. Jesus spent hours in prayer and meditation and teaching. In following his example, we proclaim him as Lord. … Our family is a nurture family. That is, we build young Christians (and each other) up in the stature of Jesus. … A consistent life means we are always calling upon God to renew us, refresh us and lead us deeper into his life and power.

Their late evening devotion times were usually spontaneous times of song and sharing the Word. Because of differing work schedules, early mornings were the only time the whole family could gather. Therefore, if anyone consistently lay in bed then it was Peter's responsibility to get them up—by any means necessary. "We need to daily immerse ourselves in his Word, together crucifying the old self and daily allowing the new self to rise up to proclaim Jesus as Lord by serving one another in truth and Spirit."[128]

Conclusion

The Servants of Christ Community was now mostly living in close physical proximity, having organised itself into two extended households. They no longer gathered and worked from 102 Gawler Place in the City, but met at 122 Torrens Road in Renown Park, which was only 6km or 10 minutes' drive away, but the change was significant. The focus was now on forming a Christian covenant community. There was still the old evangelistic concern, but with less emphasis on street ministry and other forms of outreach. In the next chapter, we will look at the content of the devotional life of the community and consider a few testimonies of those who wrote down the impact it had on their lives.

---

128 Peter Muller, **Family Worship**, Servant (February–March 1977), 11–12.

SERVANTS OF CHRIST COMMUNITY 1977-1979

Devotional Articles and Testimonies

This chapter is a bit different from others. It doesn't deal so much with the story, but with some of the things that lie behind the story. We have reported elsewhere regarding preaching and teaching, and in Chapter 27 will deal with the theology being taught and some of the conflict that resulted. As I read through the materials that have come to light I found many examples of what might be called 'devotional' writing and of course testimonies. I don't mean someone writing a series of devotions to be used by individuals or small groups, but someone writing to encourage us in our Christian walk, to help and support us when we are down, to assist us to think through a particular issue or just to share an insight that has 'blown their minds', as we would say back in the 1970s.

Difficult people in our lives

So, for example, Helen Wade wrote in the 10 October 1976 *Jakes' Epistle*. It is in the form of a letter and begins "Dear friends and loved ones". She talked about meeting our needs and how God does that by putting us in situations with other people. Some of our real needs may not be things we are aware of, or that we would ask for. He meets deep needs in us by bringing all sorts of people into our lives. Helen continues:

> Does that mean the person living in our house who I just can't seem to get on with is absolutely necessary for my growth? Yes. Absolutely! As Basilea Schlink says on the tape "But have not love", we should pay $1,000 to bring someone to us, whom we cannot get on with. We talk a lot about being bombed out spiritually, mentally and physically through ministry, but this is all to be accepted as part of the Lord's working in us. So what do we do when we are under terrific pressure and feel like a rubber band stretched to its extreme limit? Rejoice always! Be strong in the Lord! ... May, we each one, realise our Father's promises in our own lives.

The following week Helen took this further by asking how we responded when we tried to avoid having such needs met. First, we might rebel. Secondly, we might be outwardly compliant but inwardly resentful. Thirdly, we might try to do it our way, to somehow make this our achievement, rather than the Lord's work. That reminds me that the battle is with our will, not just our mind. For example, Martin Luther of Reformation times, wrote on the "Bondage of the Will." A lack of knowledge is fixed reasonably easily. Our will represents a much greater obstacle.

Growing in Prayer

Steve Haar wrote on personal prayer in the first *Servant* magazine in 1977. He recognised that many of us struggled with our prayer life. Too often, it became a chore we needed to fulfil, rather than an engagement with God from which the rest of our life flowed. Contrast that with what we read of Jesus' prayer life. He stressed that all relationships needed both times just spent hanging out together, as well as times of deliberate intimate communication. We also share such times with others, just as we engage in communal prayer. We can say that our whole lives are prayer, but that doesn't come about simply by saying so. Nor, said Steve, should we view worship together with others in the church as the only thing that matters in the Christian life. Rather, as Jesus said, "When you pray, go into your room and shut the door … and your Father who sees in secret will reward you." (Matt 6:5)

> Many of the problems we experience and burdens we bear in prayer stem from our not knowing the full promise of God for us. Jesus not only commands us to pray, he provides us with the means to pray. By his death we have been made God's children, who can now stand before God's presence in Jesus' name. We have received the Spirit of adoption, of Sonship… Prayer is indeed a "spiritual" gift. Prayer would be impossible without the indwelling of the Holy Spirit.[129]

Steve advised us to find a time and a place that worked for us for a regular prayer time. He warned against trying to overdo it at first, perhaps starting with just 10–15 minutes and then building up the time. Finally, Steve suggested a simple structure for our personal prayer time. He suggested that we start with a Scripture reading, allowing God to speak, and then letting God release us into a time of praise of him, both for who he is and what he has done. He encouraged us to be free and flexible in this, letting the Spirit lead us, using different ways, verbal and silent, as well as physical actions such as clapping or dancing. Confession of sin and bringing our needs to God are also part of personal prayer. "God may clearly reveal to us something in our life in particular, that he wishes to remove. It may be something I hold against a brother or sister that I must make right." Finally Steve wrote, "The Spirit will lead you in your prayer time to pray for the needs of others and sometimes your whole quiet time may be a time of intercession."[130]

---

129 Stephen Haar, **Personal Prayer**, Servant (February–March 1977), 8–9.

130 ibid., 10.

SERVANTS OF CHRIST COMMUNITY 1977–1979

Help with Discernment

In the 30 October 1977 Newsletter, Marty Rosenberg wrote, 'A letter of concern on finding God's will.' He had seen that some people appeared to be seeking God's will for their lives in a potentially dangerous way, seeking guidance from others and then simply acting on that advice without testing it. At other times someone may say, "That is not God's will for you" and then expect that the other person will unquestioningly take that as God's truth for them, again without testing it. Marty continued:

> Whose job is it to decide finally, whether something a person is planning to do, is God's will? ... How can a person grow if he is not encouraged to make decisions for himself? How dare anyone make a decision for another person, or (to get closer to the truth of what actually happens), how dare anyone come across so strongly to another person, so that that person feels guilty for going against what his brother has said?

Marty then encouraged everyone to first seek help in discernment from those who lived in the same house. That way the family would grow closer together and in their ability to minister, not just to each other, but also to others. If more experienced, wiser counsel is needed then the family could bring it to others, especially those in leadership. Marty concluded:

> So if anyone does say to you, or imply, "Thus saith the Lord," then take this to your family and ask for their discernment, because all prophecy is imperfect and what the person sees is only "like a dim image in a mirror" (1 Cor 13:12), so it needs confirming. And who better to confirm something like this than one's own family?

It doesn't happen much these days, but I remember over the years people coming to me with a highly directive prophecy concerning what I should or should not be doing. I would always thank people for their love in bringing it to me, and then ask them to pray that the Lord would also reveal the prophecy to me, if it was his will, because it was neither safe, nor right, for me to take someone else's word for what the Lord wanted me to do. I needed to hear from the Lord myself.

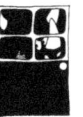

Healing from a life-long affliction

Judith Heidenreich testified to the Lord's healing in a brief article in *Servant* magazine:

> Since I was a child, I had constantly been plagued with bronchitis and head colds. It caused me to miss quite a lot of school and even as I grew into my teens and was married, the trouble kept recurring. The doctors discovered that I was allergic to quite a few things. An antihistamine tablet was prescribed and I was supposed to take them to stop the effects and symptoms. The drug tended to make me more than usually tired and lethargic, and this combined with blocked antrums slowed down my Christian service quite often to a halt.
>
> Finally, after asking the Lord to help me with no apparent results, I threw myself across the bed one day and cried out to God with tears of almost despair. "Lord, how can I serve you when I even fall asleep when I am praying and lose my concentration while reading my Bible? How do you want to heal me, Lord? I don't want to take these tablets any longer."
>
> I fell asleep and had a dream. In the dream I was busy looking through drawers and cupboards for something. It was a bottle of oil. I took it to a Christian brother I recognised, who was outside the house. When I woke up I pondered the dream, wondering what it was about. I understood it to be a direction to me, and an answer to prayer. So I found the bottle of oil and took it to the man I knew from the dream and asked him to anoint me with oil according to the James 5:13–16 passage. We did this in accordance with the guidance of the Lord and I was healed as the Scripture says. I haven't needed antihistamines since. What a wonderful relief to be freed from this bondage.[131]

She is precious to me

When Helen and Ian Wade came to the community they had already experienced the Lord working through them in caring for those society had rejected. When their sons were just a baby and a toddler, they had been led, in no uncertain manner, into a residential care home for troubled children, many of whom, as Helen said, knew every four-letter word in the book and often behaved aggressively. From there they were led into running a halfway house for newly released prisoners. Then after 18 months they moved again when they began their work with Jakes. They moved into a house in an ordinary suburban street, just their family. Helen remembers how good it was to be able to lock the door, go out and then return to a tidy house without fear

---

131 Judith Heidenreich, ***Anointed with Oil***, *Servant* (April 1978), 6.

SERVANTS OF CHRIST COMMUNITY 1977-1979

of what might have happened in their absence. She looked back on the previous three years and felt that at times they had barely been hanging on, stretched like a rubber band almost to breaking point. They had been there a month, when one Friday evening Helen was enjoying a quiet night at home while Ian was at Jacob's Ladder in Gawler Place. Helen takes up the story:

> The telephone rang. It was Ian, and he had a proposition to make. My heart sank. Here it came. Yes, he had a girl there who was only just coming off drugs. No, she didn't have anywhere else to go. Yes, she's with me in the office now. (I thought that was most unfair!) Yes, you may think about it, but please don't be long. So we hung up, me fuming and fighting, crying and praying, feeling guilty and rebelling, all at the same time. Then, as a little quietness settled on me, as I leant my head on my hands on the table and sought the Lord, a word dropped into my mind, "She is precious to me."
>
> We took in, that same night, a girl who, at seventeen, had tasted most things of the world, and had found them bitter in her mouth. Yet Jesus was near to her, and she gave herself to him. Even before this time, the Lord constantly reminded us (and still does), that he died for every person we laid eyes upon, and that God is no respecter of persons. He who created all things has no favourites.[132]

He stood at the door about to knock

Peter Schubert remembered growing up in the country, where he played football for Wunkar, in a league renowned for being tough. However, it wasn't the opponents that he needed to watch out for, it was the rabbit holes and mallee stumps on the oval. Most of the people out there in the Riverland of South Australia were God-fearing folk, including Bert's parents. (We tend to call Peter, "Bert".) Hardly a Sunday went by when they didn't find their way to St John's Lutheran Church, Myrla, which is near Loxton. He remembered his childhood as a time when he received sound Bible teaching and when he was doing confirmation class. He also

---

[132] Helen Wade, **She Is Precious to Me**, Servant (July 1977), 18.

Devotional Articles and Testimonies // 159

remembered the difficulty he had memorising Martin Luther's Small Catechism. Bert takes up the story:

> But the thing I will always remember is this. It was a hot, dry day on the farm and I'd been outside playing alone. As I approached the back door of our farmhouse, a picture of Jesus standing at our farmhouse door just about to knock, came into my mind. Just before he did, I raced to the door and calmly opened it. (You've always got to be calm before the King.) With a welcoming gesture of the hand, I bade Jesus to enter. At that moment a flood of warmth and peace pervaded my being, and I vowed that I would serve the Lord all the days of my life.
>
> Little did I realise that the opening of the back door of a farmhouse could be so significant. I had experienced something that I really didn't have words to describe, and so kept it a secret for many years. I wanted to share it but didn't know how. I was afraid people would mock me. What I didn't understand was that for the next few days, peace reigned in our house. You see, I didn't know Revelation 3:20 back then, but I believe now that Jesus, the Prince of Peace, was eating and fellowshipping in our house. …
>
> Those days of service, which I promised Jesus, have been many now, and I must confess that I failed on many of them, and that often, I wouldn't have been "calm before the King." But, praise God for his gift of forgiveness, and praise God for the gift of his Spirit. For the Spirit has called me by the Gospel, with the saving grace of Jesus and enlightened me with his gifts.[133]

Bert related how, after a time in a spiritual wilderness, the Scriptures came alive, and his understanding grew. He continued, "I'm involved in a Christian motorcycle group, which consists of a number of people who believe they are called to witness to the outlaw bikie scene in Adelaide." As the risen Lord Jesus said, "Behold I stand at the door and knock; if you hear my voice and open the door, I will come in and eat with you and you with me." (Rev 3:20)

From the United Kingdom to Australia and a new life

Sheila and Stan Whittam had made a decision. They were going to leave family and friends in their home town of "coal mines, smoke stacks, terraced houses and rain" in the UK, for a land of "sunshine, opportunity, a home and garden and space for children to grow" in Australia. Their wider family did not understand, but off they went and before too long they had a lovely home and garden—everything they wanted, yet it seemed something was wrong. Something was missing.

---

133 Peter Schubert, **He Stood at the Door (and I calmly flung it open)** Servant (January 1978), 8.

SERVANTS OF CHRIST COMMUNITY 1977-1979

CHAPTER 20

Sundays were purposeless. Go for a drive or stay at home and deal with salesmen and Jehovah's Witnesses? They had no Christian background but eventually they agreed to do a course with the JWs. The pressure was put on them to join and so be among "the only saved people in the world." They rejected that, but still there was something missing. Maybe they should move out into the country, but all the properties they looked at were either really run down or too expensive, and they didn't seem to be able to sell their home.

Then one weekend they took a drive into the Riverland of South Australia. They made enquiries at Waikerie and were directed to a property that was an old stone house, a bit run down, but not too bad inside, sitting on ten acres of scrub land overlooking the river. In a former life it had been the Lutheran Manse and was only five miles out of town. They paid a deposit and within two days, their house had sold. They moved in and had lots of work to do. The JWs no longer bothered them and Stan had to choose between the three jobs that he had been offered. This was amazing in itself, and something they had never experienced before. Sheila continues:

> The people in the community of Lowbank were incredibly kind and we seemed to be inundated with neighbours from everywhere, wishing us well and welcoming us to the district. Never before had we experienced such a wonderful feeling of belonging... Before long, a neighbour invited our children to Sunday School and personally called to take them each Sunday morning. Stan and I took advantage of this, and played tennis on the church's courts, to the background sound of hymns. Now and then we went to church as a thank-you gesture to our community. They cared for us, and we so wanted to fit in. We didn't understand any part of the liturgy that everyone knew by heart, and the sermons seemed to be addressed to 'angels' and not to people... I recall feeling very much like a second-class citizen, dominated by the men. I noted that the ladies didn't have much to say in meetings. It was very much a man's affair.[134]

In spite of that, they took a new members course, joined the congregation and had their youngest daughter baptised. They still hated Sundays. Things continued that way for two years. Sheila's parents (who must have also emigrated) heard about this and decided to check out a local church for themselves. Soon they were talking about being baptised with the Spirit, and so the Whittams went to check out that church. They observed how close God seemed to be to people, who had a joy they had never seen before, and seemed to love one another. Sheila explains what happened next:

---

[134] Sheila Whittam, *Search for a New Life*, Servant (October 1978), 18–19.

A minister laid hands on our heads and in the next few days, for the first time, I met Jesus. I knew I had been missing something. That had been Jesus. No one had told us that we could know him, that we must be 'born again'. Both of us now had Jesus in our lives in a living real way. Oh how eager we were to share this in our congregation, and how the Lord showed us in his Word how to begin living this abundant life—we even began to understand the liturgy!

Oh, what happy days. We were assured of Jesus' presence in our lives, it overflowed as we freely expressed these things in our congregation— we couldn't understand why some looked rather shocked. We thought they would rejoice with us. We were a very misunderstood family, and yet with some, we were led into deeper relationships and sharing—with those who had like minds and convictions. We had a deep longing for Bible study with others and prayer.

It was exciting to attend the first Lutheran Spiritual Renewal meeting early in 1976, and to be with others who had heard the Lord call their names to be his disciples in the Kingdom. Praise God we no longer have to rely on self but on Jesus who strengthens us. Praise him who led us heathens to a home and congregation in which we have been blessed so much. Praise him for those who have shown us the ongoing Christian life! And incidentally, we now love Sundays.[135]

Conclusion

When you read stories such as these, like the stories you read in the Bible, they are not about exceptional people; they are about the faithfulness of God. Ordinary people and an extraordinary God. God is good. All the time!

---

135 Sheila Whittam, **Search for a New Life**, Servant (October 1978), 19.

SERVANTS OF CHRIST COMMUNITY 1977-1979

The 1979 AGM

CHAPTER 21

On 9 March 1979, Servants of Christ Community Inc held what turned out to be its final Annual General Meeting. Within three months, the community was being wound up. That makes this meeting important in understanding what led to the end of Jakes. Apart from the previous AGM which was held on 22 February 1978 at Gawler Place, this is the only AGM for which we have found what appears to be a full set of reports and at least some of the minutes.[136]

We have already looked at most of the reports presented to the 1979 AGM. They paint a picture of business as usual. Some things were going well; some things needed work. There were some financial pressures, but then that was true most of the time. The commercial ventures, such as the workshops, had not developed as had been hoped. 'Sisterhood', the Ladies prayer meeting, which had started in 1978, reported having participated in a number of significant studies. Colin Smith reported that the music group was about to meet for a day of prayer, sharing and planning. David Skeat reported that the Sunday School had been blessed with more teachers and 1979 looked like being a good year for children's ministry. The community had relocated into what was considered to be more suitable premises, and most of the community now lived within a fairly compact area. In short, there were positives and negatives, but nothing that indicated the rapid demise of the community that was soon to come.

I remind you, that I was no longer part of the Servants of Christ Community by this stage. Ruth, Kirsten and I had left late in 1978 for our first parish. When I began the project of writing this book (thanks Marty!), it was something that immediately puzzled me. What had happened? Therefore, I began to ask people and received a variety of answers. Later, documents emerged, and I began looking for clues. Why did Jakes collapse? That was my question.

The Elders' Report

So let's delve a little deeper, beginning with the Elders report to the 1979 AGM. It was written by Ian Wade on behalf of the remaining elders: himself, Karl Brettig and of course Pastor Doug Kuhl. They had been joined by Anton Hochwald, who was described as an 'interim elder'. The report began by stating that they had been

---

[136] With thanks to the late Julie Anne McBride for keeping these and many other important documents.

"continually faced with the central concern of oneness and unity." Early in 1978 the elders put together a series of Bible studies called 'Foundations'. However, that didn't achieve what they had hoped, "due to the different stages of community development, which the various groups and individuals were experiencing." They then set out to unify these different levels of understanding of community life by producing four series of studies, which were led by the elders and other leaders in four different locations, taking the place of the Sunday morning services for at least some of those weeks. The topics covered were:

1. Commitment to the Lord—knowing Jesus and discipleship.
2. Release in the Spirit—being freed from besetting sin and released into love.
3. Personal Order in Life—the individual's walk with God, priorities and routines of daily life.
4. Relationships in Order—family and old friends in the world, forgiveness and priorities in relationships.

The elders report also listed a number of areas of concern they were dealing with, including:

- Formation of covenant life among covenant members, into a single integrated body sharing all of life together.
- Definite households and the fleshing out of relationships there.
- Authority and submission, and the beauty of this in Jesus and how to see it in its practical out-workings.

The elders were also dealing with issues such as the shape and form of worship services, relationships in community, rehabilitation and nurture, the personal needs of the community and its friends, and ladies and men's fellowships. Overall, the report has a business as usual flavour, but there are hints that unity was a growing issue, and that the attempts to address that had so far not been successful. They continued, however, to look to the future with confidence and trust in God.

The Pastor's Report

Pastor Doug Kuhl's final AGM report runs to five foolscap pages. The frustration that he expressed in his report a year earlier had not lessened.[137] He began his

---

[137] See chapter 15.

SERVANTS OF CHRIST COMMUNITY 1977–1979

1979 report by saying that it would take a book to adequately cover the topic of "community formation and its facility to share a Gospel-centred life with the world around us."[138] He then spoke of confusion in the community:

> I have listened to the stream of various advisors who have come like Job's friends to my study to assist me in establishing "what in the blazes is going on around the place". I have been aware for some time that most people haven't got a great clue as to "what in the blazes has been going on around the place". [Emphasis here and elsewhere in the original.] That is not their fault. … So often, I have witnessed blocks of people and certain strong-minded individuals, reacting to various kinds of non-information, mis-information and mini-information, and have sadly pondered the fact that a better informed person would more likely not react at all in such a way. Or better still, they might have reacted a little more wisely and constructively, had they really understood what was really going on around them. I do hope that the following notes taken from an overview of last year will enable us to begin a more constructive analysis of "where in the blazes we've come from."
>
> First of all, I want to make this pointedly clear—WE ARE NOT JACOB'S LADDER ANY MORE! It is pointless trying to dress up the present in the clothes of the Great Gatsby of Gawler Place. Looking at our present situation, ie Brompton, Croydon, Renown Park, I believe that instead of Levis, Indian skirts and incense being our present cultural badge, macaroni, spaghetti, blue singlets and blue stubbie shorts with thongs might be a more appropriate form. Seriously though, we do have to take stock of our memories and future expectations and begin to gear them to where God has placed us in the now, whatever that means. In Jacob's Ladder we were a group of "young, single, enthusiastic, do or die, JESUS freaks", desiring to tell the whole world that JESUS lives today. Today, we are primarily a group of young married families, caught up in this problem of being a Christian man, woman, husband, wife, mother and father in today's world. The tendency of some, who are unable to perceive the forces at work among us through all of this, is to do the following: REACT!

Pastor Doug then stated that this could be explained by the lack of models to follow in establishing community. Therefore, all faced the tendency "to copy the models of marriage, family, home and security forms which we have experienced as children." It was understandable that many would want to build their lives on middle class suburban values and then try to tailor a community lifestyle to fit that. Single young

---

138 This and the following quotations—Douglas Kuhl, *Pastor's Report*, AGM (held on 9 March 1979), 11–15.

people in the community were also bewildered. When Jacob's Ladder changed to Servants of Christ, a disappointment grew among them.

Many of the young, single persons felt that their original search in Jacob's Ladder, for a true Christian alternative life, had been abandoned by the married couples for Fletcher Jones and poodle dogs, safari suits and comfortable secluded ease of one couple per house, per suburb, in the now Servants of Christ Community. Not without reason, these single persons felt more than a hint of betrayal at all these new turn of events.

Then there were those who had arrived in the meantime, searching for community. Pastor Doug said that he believed that "many of these persons possess an objectivity over and against 'community', which many of the rest of us would do well to listen to and consider carefully." They understood that the key question was, "Are we doing an efficient job of completing what we set out to achieve, when we decided to try to form community?" They questioned why the community was fighting each other, rather than dealing with the things that blocked and hindered the formation of community life. They were, in effect, saying:

> Why don't we go ALL OUT to form a MODEL of community in operation, actually functioning, instead of trying to protect what we have and trying to justify why we should continue to keep it? [Pastor Doug explains] I believe I have heard these people saying over and over, "Why don't you show us community, so we can join it, instead of always talking about it?"

That is the end of the introduction to the report. Pastor Doug then stated that these were some of the factors involved, which illustrated the point that "many or all of us are only seeing a small portion of all that is involved in community formation." He then says that some cling desperately to individual entrenched positions, and recite "the stubborn reply given by the pigs to the big bad wolf, that, 'By the hairs of my chinny, chin, chin, I will not let you in.'" Pastor Doug then wrote that over and against these negative forces, it was absolutely essential to understand community structure in positive loving terms: "I appeal for us to be able to see a great God of love surrounding us—his Spirit of love is amongst us. He is at work to call forth his loving outcomes to his purposes of love for us."

The remainder of the report then deals in note form with five areas of the life and work of the community, namely pastoral care, community formation, our life together, headship, and Servants of Christ and the whole body of Christ. I will only provide the briefest of summaries.

Pastoral care requires the formation of God's order in the structure of the lives of individuals and households. Facilitating this in each person is the primary objective of pastoral care. *Community formation* requires the covenant group to say 'do as you see me do', not 'do as I say'. If you can answer, "Yes! My life is an exemplary one of how community life should function, then you are ready for a covenant commitment." The others should be lovingly patient with the covenant group that already existed, until they reach that point of maturity. The report then addresses confirmation of young persons into the faith, and whether a slow (8–10 years) or quick (3–5 years) approach to community formation be used. Servants of Christ would need to decide which approach to take. If it were the quick road then personal goals would not be getting one's own house, car and furniture. Rather we would have done other things such as joining together in extended families with daily worship, regular community work projects, common recreational activities, common housing, coordinating timetables and limiting (so-called) personal freedom of space, time and possessions.

Life together still needed to be established by the covenant group and so the acceptance of the then current number of 'disciples on the way' was a little premature. When life together had been achieved, then the community would be able to engage in various forms of outreach. *Headship* was difficult in a community that had very young members, so maybe some outside counsel was needed. It was most urgent to understand what was meant by 'submission and authority in JESUS', and the authority of Jesus' control and Lordship needed to be established in the community's life. Secondly, all must be 'submitted to JESUS in the body with the issues of our lives.' *Servants of Christ and the body of Christ* raises the question of the relationship with the Lutheran Church of Australia and being submitted to them, or if not them, then submitted to whom.

Finally:

> I warned you that all this could amount to a book. However the above areas of concern are the concerns I as pastor in your midst, am battling through every day. I'm never sure you understand what is involved. I do hope this very brief summary has helped to outline these areas. A servant in Jesus. DOUG KUHL.

There is no record in the minutes of the meeting to suggest that this pastor's report was discussed on that evening. After four hours, the meeting was adjourned at 11.34pm and was to be reconvened a week later on 16 March 1979, again at 7.30pm. Minutes of the reconvened meeting have not come to light.

Records of what happened in the weeks following the 1979 AGM are sketchy to non-existent. We are largely reliant on the memories of those involved.

There is trouble brewing

It is clear from this report that all was not well. There was quite a lot of emotive language. Those who had a different point of view were now like 'Job's friends'; well-intentioned, but sadly out of step with how God viewed the situation.

I imagine that if I were a newly married person, listening to the report at the time, I might have felt condemned for being reactionary and not constructive. It seems that there was only one valid form of Christian community. As has been reflected on previously, there is wisdom in newly married couples having time to establish their relationship, and those who have young children have a God-given responsibility to prioritise their family for that season. That doesn't mean that they can't have others living with them, if that works out. It does mean that they should not be accused of choosing "Fletcher Jones and poodle dogs, safari suits and comfortable secluded ease", over serious Christian discipleship.

It is true that the report at times says this situation of confusion is not people's fault, and that the community should see itself as being surrounded by the great love of God who is at work bringing forth the outcome his love has for us. Yet it is also clear that many, if not most, in the community do not measure up. While I am sure it was not intended, the report has features of an unbiblical perfectionism. Which of us, even after all these years of living as a Christian, can say that, "My life is an exemplary one, of how community life should function?" Yes, St Paul said, "Be imitators of me, as I am of Christ" (1 Cor 11.1), and we can also say that, but that is not claiming to have an exemplary life. It is recognising that even in the midst of our brokenness and failings, Jesus through his Spirit is really at work in and through me. As we mature as Christians, we become more aware of our weaknesses and sin, as Mother Basilea Schlink so eloquently points out in her book, 'Repentance, the joy filled life'. It was one of our favourite books from that time.

It seems like the community had come to a point where it was no longer able to wrestle with issues together. Having made the decision to form a covenant community, the implications of what that meant were obviously not clear to people. A number of long-term members have expressed the view that they suddenly found themselves on the outer. Having not 'signed up' to the covenant, they felt disenfranchised. The process the community used is not entirely clear. Secondly, the actual written covenant says nothing of how this was actually to work out in practice, especially in regard to issues like having all property in common, a shared purse in each household, and the authority of leaders.

We will pick up some of these underlying issues in the next two chapters.

The End of Jakes

The August 1979 *Servant* magazine reported:

> During the past months, the Servants of Christ Community had been considering the possibility of becoming a congregation. However, members have decided to join with the sacramental life of local congregations, after much prayer and discussion with church leaders. Pastor Doug Kuhl has made himself available for a call within the LCA. Currently a fellowship involving an evangelical outreach meeting on Sunday evenings and Servant Media is in operation, as well as the existing household fellowship groups. A new name for this ministry is being considered in the light of these developments. Please pray for the Lord's continuing guidance and support during this time.[139]

That was for public consumption, and so, perhaps glossed over some of the issues involved. It doesn't really answer the question: Why did this happen?

In this final chapter, then, we consider the issues that brought about the end of the Servants of Christ Community. As is usually the case when a Christian work comes to an end, there is not one issue that explains everything. What's more, especially after forty years, different people will have different ideas about what was most important. We begin by noting that there were divergent views about the focus and direction of the community. We then look at some of the issues behind the different views, and then at the final steps of bringing to an end the work of a decade through Jakes. In the most important respect, this was of course not the end, for the participants in this story went on to other service in the Kingdom of God. Some had already done that before the end came.

So what were some of these different views and issues, where the children of God in this community had differing opinions about what they were called to do?

Different Visions of Covenant Community

As we noted in the last chapter, Pastor Doug Kuhl's 1979 AGM report indicated that there were competing visions of what Servants of Christ Community should be. He was clearly of the view that it should have a particular form, but it seemed that a significant number of the community had different ideas. Peter Muller picked that up:

---

139 **Notes**, *Servant* (August 1979), 17.

> Instead of being empowering, covenanting into a formal community seeded Jakes' demise by becoming a means of keeping the world out. The community split three ways: the covenant group, the 'core' community and the rest. Rapid efforts to include as much of the community as possibly ultimately failed, as the community began fracturing, with energies pulling in contrary directions. Expectations of what was meant by community and what it could provide, differed enormously.
>
> Some people wanted a security blanket. Others wanted a platform from which to launch into the world. Should we live the same lifestyle with the same amenities and the same type of toilet paper (bleached or pastel, eco-sensitive or merely convenient and efficient)? Some people had the expectation that being a real community meant subsistence agriculture and self-sufficiency. To others it meant L'Arche-style service to the disadvantaged. To others it meant an almost closed devotional community. Combining all the competing visions of the church universal, was far beyond one community to fulfil![140]

Anne Sellers looked back at this time and remembered:

> For years I, and many others, joked about the idea of "don't trust anyone over the age of 30". This was a theme in the youth culture at that time. By 1979, we were getting closer to 30, and realised that we would have to find ways to live in the world, and not be overly influenced by all the bad ideas and bad habits. We were not called to be a monastic community, but rather to enter into the spheres of influence where God was placing us.

The Covenant Issue of shared ownership

What did it mean to form a covenant community as understood by Servants of Christ Community at that time? What was understood by sharing possessions and assets? Clearly people still had bank accounts, because members were able to make loans to the community at times and some lived off their savings. At least one couple bought a house. Some owned cars, motorbikes and bicycles. All had various things like tools, kitchen appliances and utensils, clothes, toys for their children, books, musical instruments and much more. What did that mean? Was the aim that eventually each household would have only one bank account and all assets would be owned by the community? Karl Brettig reflects:

> In the lead up to the covenant, I remember talk about such things as what would happen when furniture wore out, with Doug Kuhl writing our name on

---

140 Peter Muller. *Jacob's Ladder Retrospective: The Community*, The Messenger, St Stephens Lutheran Church, Wakefield Street, Adelaide, vol. 60 no. 6 (November–December 1998), 6.

SERVANTS OF CHRIST COMMUNITY 1977–1979

a hammer and saying it was still ours, even though anyone in the community could use it. (I still have the hammer with my name on it!) When I expressed concern about the level of insecurity that seemed to be behind the covenant, I received an unsolicited visit from another community member, who handed me a copy of a book by the Bruderhof about their way of community life. Sure, there were plenty of covenant communities around at the time and the Servants of Christ covenant was being modelled more on the Catholic covenant communities, than anything, but these were much larger communities, more connected with the wider Body of Christ than we were. We often used to talk about a siege mentality in the institutional churches, but we were pretty close to developing the same thing. One of my enduring memories of that period, after it was all over, was going to a football match for the first time in years and thinking how great it was that you could leave whenever you wanted to!

Anne Sellers remembers:

We made promises about how we would relate to one another, in commitment, selflessness, sharing life in common. This included living in "common purse" with others in one's household. I lived in this way for about two years and learned to be a good steward of my finances. I saw funds released for Christian workers because the people in my household shared things in common, and didn't need to have multiples of everyday items because we shared lawn mowers, household equipment, etc. I remember community meals, and sharing life. Sometimes the community activities seemed "mechanical"; doing the activity because it was listed on the calendar, rather than whether we felt like participating. I see now that this is an essential skill for a mature adult.

The aim of living simply and sharing resources for the sake of the work of the kingdom of God is of course both admirable and Christian. When it becomes a lifelong commitment to live as one economic unit with a particular group of people that raises other questions. Firstly, the overwhelming evidence is that in this sinful, broken world, it often turns out badly. Even in the apostolic church, there is no evidence that the situation described in Acts 2:44–45—"All who believed were together and held all things in common; they would sell their possessions and goods and distribute the proceeds, as any had need" was a law for the Christian life or an experiment that failed. It clearly did not become the only model for the church going forward. In any case, it sounds more like a community welfare system, where those who had the means, helped those that didn't. If they simply had one purse, there would be no need to distribute anything.

The End of Jakes // 171

The Anointed Leader Issue

The issue of headship, leadership and authority in a covenant community is a complex one. In reviewing the covenant, we have already noted that it didn't give leaders authority over the lives of others in an unhealthy way. What, then, does it mean to submit to leaders? When is a line crossed, where submission means no longer taking responsibility for one's own life, but rather a simple obedience to someone else's discernment? In regard to Jakes, it is worth asking what the end game was. What would this have looked like, if the community had ever reached the point of being 'fully formed'? We will never know, because Jakes never reached that stage, but the issue had been identified. Peter Muller wrote:

> The flirtations with Pentecostal and charismatic ideas had a profound influence. The effect of a prophetic word on a close community could be very powerful. When a significantly large percentage had tendencies towards creating a closed community, it could be dramatic or downright dangerous. One of the less appealing doctrines to emerge from the Pentecostals was the doctrine of "The Lord's anointed"—a particular person, a Moses-like leader in a community, with special prophetic gifts. To argue against this idea of the designated person was almost equal to sacrilege. Unfortunately, even some of the more mature members gave credence to this bit of mumbo jumbo. Asking Doug to resign the ministry and come in as an ordinary member was an attempt to create a circuit breaker, to diffuse the impasse with the LCA and neuter the unhealthy "Lord's anointed" nonsense. It failed. The rest, as they say, is history.[141]

Pastor Doug was a gifted, charismatic leader and a captivating teacher with an obvious ability to 'hold an audience without a rope.' So often, the strengths of a given situation are also its weaknesses. We all benefitted greatly from Doug's ability to unpack the Word of God and hold it all together, so that we heard a unified, consistent and coherent message. For a community with one outstanding leader to be sustainable for the long term, it needs to develop into a 'foremost among equals' situation where there is a team approach to leadership, with checks and balances. This team approach was developing in the middle years of Jacob's Ladder, but appears not to have continued to the end. Maybe this is just my bias, but I have come to the same conclusion in comparing the elders and pastor's reports for the final two AGMs. While there are obvious overlaps, the vision of the pastor does not seem to be owned to the same extent by the elders.

---

141 Peter Muller. *Jacob's Ladder Retrospective: The Community*, The Messenger, St Stephens Lutheran Church, Wakefield Street, Adelaide, vol. 60 no. 6 (November–December 1998), 6.

SERVANTS OF CHRIST COMMUNITY 1977-1979

The Outreach vs Nurture Issue and the desire for a Country Location

Jakes, as Doug Kuhl correctly notes in his final AGM report, was born on the street as a very effective outreach ministry, bringing Jesus to many whom society, and even the church, had largely given up on. Of course, out-reach also needs in-reach. There needs to be training, mentoring and oversight. Maturity does not happen overnight, and since even baby-Christians can exercise spiritual gifts, it was easy to come to the conclusion that we were further down the road, than we actually were. During the final days of Jakes, it seems there were those who wanted to stay out on the street, doing what the community had always done. Others wanted to withdraw, at least for a season, to focus on building community and growing in discipleship. In spite of the number of houses that the community lived in, it became increasingly difficult to find accommodation for those who needed nurture and support.

It is difficult to find the right balance here. It is our engagement with the world, as well as with our fellow Christians, which brings personal growth and maturity. We grow as we go in ministry. The Spirit sends us out, pushing us into situations we can't control, and we learn to depend on the Spirit's work. We also learn where we need to be better equipped, where we need more training and the help of others. We need to withdraw from time to time, but if we withdraw too far, or for too long, the growth eventually stops and we become insular.

Into this context came the suggestion that Servants of Christ should establish itself in a country location in order to focus on building up the covenant community. A property named *Anlaby* near Kapunda, north of the Barossa Valley in South Australia, was investigated and steps taken towards purchasing it. Nothing came of it in the end, but the possibility again raises interesting questions about the ultimate vision for the covenant community. There were potential dangers here, as has been seen in many other situations during that time and since. Sometimes there is a fine line between community and cult. At the time, some in the Jakes community were concerned about that.

Pastor Doug Kuhl Resigns

There seems to be a consensus that Doug Kuhl resigned as the pastor of Servants of Christ Community sometime in the second quarter of 1979. The community then needed to decide whether to accept the resignation. Anne Sellers recalls:

> I remember hearing that something had happened at a leadership meeting, where Doug's leadership / decision making was questioned. I don't know who, or when exactly. I believe it was early 1979. I remember that it was

> quite serious, and somehow, information was shared among the community and a "vote of confidence" was taken. The community did not support Doug enough to continue. The tone was "sober". Things were not right, but I didn't know what. I remember thinking long and hard about that vote. I lived in a community house, was part of the Covenant Community, worked as a staff member with the Mustard Seed bookstore, and coordinated the tape ministry for the Lutheran Charismatic Renewal meetings. I was living off my savings from previous employment. I knew that a vote of no confidence in Doug meant the end of SOCC in its current format. It's as if the wind went out of the sails. SOCC had become confused or lost direction. ... In hindsight, the end of SOCC felt like a divorce for me. Our community life shattered.

It has been suggested that the vote was a way of testing the resolve of the 'dissenters'. Whatever the case, the support for Doug to continue was not strong enough, and so it was time for him to move on. Pastor Doug Kuhl, Erna and family, together with the Lieschkes, Skeats, Jasprizzas and some singles relocated to Redfern in Sydney, where they established a ministry that was called the Coolibah Community before becoming Elijah Task Ministries. They worked with other groups and made a number of mission trips to Japan.

Pastor Doug also resigned as a pastor of the LCA at the request of President Clem Koch. There is evidence that the president had concerns that went beyond the doctrinal issues that he raised publicly. I therefore want to be fair to the President and to how we remember him. I only became aware of this during the process of researching and writing this book.

At some stage, Doug was told that if he resigned it would be easier for him to be reinstated at a later date, than if he was removed from the Roll of Pastors by the action of General Church Council. I supported his application for reinstatement in February 1989 and wrote a proposal to the NSW District for him to serve in inner Sydney. The LCA told him to join a Lutheran Congregation for a year and then to reapply. The Kuhls joined Trinity Lutheran Church in Chinatown in the Sydney CBD. However, in the end that application was not successful.

The End of the Community

We have a letter dated 22 July 1979 that was signed by Peter Jasprizza, Marty Rosenberg and Anne Sellers as the 'Winding up committee, Servants of Christ Community Inc.' The letter states:

> For various reasons Servants of Christ Community Inc has taken the decision to dissolve the organisation under the Associations Incorporation Act. Various

SERVANTS OF CHRIST COMMUNITY 1977–1979

ministries and outreach ventures are continuing and personal relationships amongst us are formed in Jesus Christ himself, not in the legal structure we use to relate to the State.

The committee had therefore been given the task of disposing of the assets of the organisation and meeting its liabilities. Therefore, everyone who had loaned items of equipment to the community needed to claim them before 31 August 1979. Likewise, those who had borrowed items needed to return them to their owners. Marty and Anne remember that the sale of assets only just covered the liabilities of the community. Some established churches, like Ridgehaven AoG, were very pleased to receive many resources for their children's ministry.

A worshipping community, which included former members of Jakes, continued for a number of years at the 122 Torrens Road, Renown Park. It came to be known as *Truth and Light*. However, that is another story!

CHAPTER 23 *Epilogue*

As we look back from the vantage point of forty years, what do we see? Much more was done than we will ever know, in this lifetime at least. There were mistakes and plenty of them. We were young and enthusiastic. God did remarkable things. We learned a lot about the world, the church and ourselves. Here are a few of the comments I have collected over the last few months leading up to the writing of this book.

Karl Brettig took the time to write down his reflections over twenty years ago:

> It wouldn't be too difficult to write a book of reflections on lessons learned at Jacob's Ladder.[142] Here are a few that stand out:
>
> ▶ The importance of mission teams and teamwork as means of proclaiming the gospel.
>
> ▶ The need for accountability through designated shepherds, rather than through hierarchical structures.
>
> ▶ The need for teams to operate within agreed mission plans and core values.
>
> ▶ The tendency to see your own particular group as one of the few taking the gospel seriously.
>
> ▶ The need for confessional cohesion while refraining from sectarianism.
>
> ▶ The reality that we can't live out the gospel in our own strength.
>
> ▶ The need to 'get real' with God and each other.
>
> ▶ The reality that we are saints and sinners at the same time.
>
> ▶ The reality of spiritual warfare.
>
> ▶ The necessity of prayer and intercession.
>
> ▶ The significance of the gifts of the Spirit as equipment for ministry.
>
> ▶ The need for a holistic approach to spiritual, rational and social growth of new Christians.

---

142 I am not sure you got that bit 100% right Karl!

SERVANTS OF CHRIST COMMUNITY 1977–1979

- The need to anchor new Christians in the Word of God and to teach spiritual disciplines over an extended period of time.
- The importance of cultural relevance in communicating eternal truths.
- The significance of indigenous, Spirit-filled worship styles.
- The need to maintain unity in the cause of the gospel (Phil 4:2–3).
- The need for teamwork between people with apostolic, prophetic, evangelistic, pastoral and teaching gifts.
- The effectiveness of coffee lounge / café style relational evangelism ministry.
- The need to maintain balance in reaching the unchurched, rather than being overwhelmed by attempting too much too quickly and without appropriate planning.
- The need for a healthy parent body to support outreach with prayer and pastoral support.

> Those of us involved with Jacob's Ladder went through many highs and lows, joys, tears and moments of sheer exhaustion in the process of wrestling with these issues. ... It was a steep learning curve which I have always valued.[143]

There is no question in my mind that the rapid expansion of Jakes during the first few months of 1974 in many ways contributed to the ultimate decline of the community. We were always playing 'catch up' and there simply was never time to build proper foundations. Everyone was stretched to breaking point most of the time. Looking back, we were continually presented with the needs of people and opportunities for ministry, which were obviously beyond our expertise and even our capacity to meet.

In that regard, the constant battles on that other front, the Lutheran Church, was also a distraction that we didn't need. The official support from the wider church was good in the period up to the end of 1973. During 1974 that turned, and Jakes suffered badly from not having a sense of the encouraging, supporting, affirming, resourcing and guidance in what we were doing from our Church Leaders. That is not all together the Church's fault, as has already been noted. We were combative at times and didn't make it easy. However, the Church's obsession with procedure, "good order" and precise theological formulation was not helpful. Cutting us a bit of slack and walking alongside us would have been better. Having said that, it is

---

143 Karl Brettig, **Reflections on Lessons Learned at Jacob's Ladder**, *The Messenger*, St Stephens Lutheran Church, Wakefield Street, Adelaide, vol. 60 no. 4 (July–August 1998), 8.

important also to mention that we had a lot of support from individuals, including pastors, in our Church, and also ecumenically.

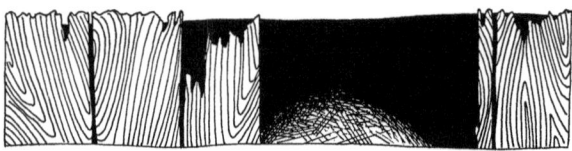

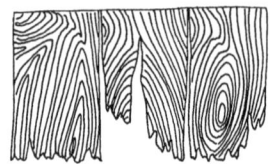
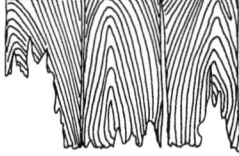

A Prophetic Dream

David Skeat remembers the end:

There are lots of memories. The Jesus celebrations, the prophetic words, the weddings and the kids that came along nine months later. The people who were drawn to the idea of Christian Community and the life that it gave, the pain of its demise. I remember at the time we disbanded and the incorporation was dissolved, I had a dream of a large campfire with huge logs burning and giving off a lot of heat. In the dream, the devil came along with a steel bar and started rolling off logs and beating them with his bar—sparks were flying everywhere as each heavy blow came down on each of the logs. Soon the fire was out and logs cooling as they lacked the heat to burn. In the dream, the devil threw away his steel bar and brushed his hands and began to walk away. As he looked up a hundred fires were now burning around him all lit from the sparks that had been beaten out of the logs. The campfire was out but the bush fire had just begun. As I look at the people who came out of Jakes and what they have accomplished over the years I wonder if this dream was not a prophetic explanation of God's purposes for those who made up the Jakes community. Over the years, we had many words about going to the nations and affecting the world with the Gospel. In the book of Acts, it took persecution to get the Gospel out of Jerusalem. I wonder if it took a demonic temper tantrum to get

SERVANTS OF CHRIST COMMUNITY 1977–1979

those who made up the Jakes community (and later Servants of Christ), to walk outside of their comfort zones and into their destinies!

That is an apt picture of what happened in the aftermath of the community. We were scattered but the fire continued to burn within us and therefore around us.

Pastor Doug looks back

At the time we began working on this book, Pastor Doug sent a letter to the Jakes community. He speaks of himself in the third person. This is part of what he said:

> This Pastor wounded, broken, untrained in the ways of counter culture street cred, was now faced with the task of being a Pastor of the Good News of Jesus in the middle of a mess. He was a mess! He didn't realize how much he was until much, much later. But he knew that the task was way, way beyond him. He was out of his depth with only his very basic understanding of Jesus to cling to. So here was 'Pastor brokenness' attempting to repair broken people, a 'Pastor who was deeply wounded' attempting to bring healing to the wounded.
>
> This might have been a recipe for complete disaster, but for the pillar that stood in the middle of the Jacob's Ladder Camp. The Pillar was Jesus. He, Jesus, was actually there in the midst of Jacob's Ladder. But why would he choose to come into the middle of a mess like Jakes? I don't know, but only to say that Jesus is really real, and that just as the Scriptures describe him, he really does love the lost and lonely—even if it should kill him in doing so. As the Gospel's picture him, he came and comes among the broken and wounded to bring his healing. Healing of hearts, minds, souls, spirits, bodies and of past, of present and future. Healing of relationships of families and broken friends, just as the Bible says he would do. Therefore, at the very heart of it all, Jesus now, here among us, is the story of Jakes.

It is truly all about Jesus. It comes down to that. Jesus is at work, in spite of our failings and betrayals. That doesn't justify us, or excuse the wrong we have done, but the Spirit was still bringing the kingdom of God into the lives of people. I am amazed that God is able to use me, even though I sin against him and hurt others with the things I say and do. The gift of repentance is an amazing thing. God can heal and restore. Nothing is too difficult for him. He sets us free from both guilt and bitterness. There is freedom to live in forgiveness. Broken relationships are restored and healed. Many people met Jesus at Jakes, and we who already knew him, got to know him even better. That has been a lifelong journey.

Another reflection from a community member and leader

Anne Sellers reflects:

> Towards the end of Servants of Christ Community (SOCC), I remember thinking and feeling that Doug Kuhl was moving away from the central purposes and calling of SOCC. He talked about finding land in the Barossa Valley and retreating from the city to form a better community. He was going in many different directions. He felt a strong calling to minister among counter-culture people, and develop apologetics as well as relationships with them. Doug had regular battles with the Lutheran Church leadership. Doug had vision, knowledge, and zeal for God and concern for people. He was a big personality. He also had some character flaws (as do we all). He needed and sought approval, and I think he struggled to allow others to "temper" him, to bring balance and correction. He loved being in the middle of things. He didn't manage his time/calendar well and so priorities became confused. I saw a man who was driven and didn't know how to rest. This was not a good example for me.
>
> One of the problems with SOCC was no strategy (or not well implemented) to disciple younger people and mentor them into their gifts and calling. I know that was one draw-card for me to go to a Discipleship Training School at *Youth With A Mission*. I saw a foundation being laid with common topics and experiences that the community could build upon. We had some pieces like this at SOCC but it seemed pretty loose. Of course, SOCC grew quickly, we were young, and there were a lot of things going on in just a few years: charismatic renewal, emphasis on community living around the world, struggles with the Lutheran Church.
>
> We lost sight of evangelism. Another factor was that many in the community had married and borne children and this changed how people wanted or needed to organize their lives, housing, finances, and even their hopes and dreams for the future.
>
> God's purposes are often difficult to understand when we are in the midst of an upheaval, yet God is still at work. God remains faithful. God continues working all things together for good for those who love him and are called according to his purpose. There is often pain and disappointment, but God opens new doors and he continues to work in us and through us. God is good.

Many married and had children

Trish Brice wrote:

> Doug's idealism drove people to joy, praise, faith, commitment. I think there was more idealism than sense, which was probably reflected in the marriages within the community. We had lots of street kids coming in and marrying each other. They had come from troubled family backgrounds and still had lots of issues to sort through, so once children came along the pressures started to take their toll. A friend estimated that there was a 50% breakdown in marriages within the community.[144]

I remember someone saying that there had been about twenty-five weddings at Jakes. And yes, many of them did not last. That is sad, and yet more brokenness, but even then most moved on, dealt with the situation, re-established their lives and continued to serve.

The final word

Marty Rosenberg initiated the project of writing this book, so it is only fair that he should have the last word in this the last chapter in the main sections of the book:

> Despite all the naivety, the exuberance of our youth won out on many occasions. There were numerous individuals who lived in the community houses that came to faith in Christ and there were many who never found that faith but were helped during a difficult time in their lives. Each of them joined in with the household community and experienced an alternative lifestyle to the way they had been living. Not everyone had a positive experience. Some can only remember the difficulties and cannot speak positively of their time in community. This was always going to happen (so we have realised in hindsight). All of them were exposed to God's Word in one form or other, be it through discussions, Bible studies, acts of kindness, music or preaching, and only God knows how many lives were impacted positively from those experiences.

---

144 Trish Brice, *Jacob's Ladder Retrospective*, The Messenger, St Stephens Lutheran Church, Wakefield Street, Adelaide, vol. 60 no. 4 (July–August 1998), 7.

CHAPTER 24  The Dorian Society
Geoff Strelan

The Dorian Society was established in 1970 to foster the use of gifts and talents in communicating the Gospel in a contemporary and relevant way. (The name comes from a Greek word for 'gift').

Right from the start there was a concern to help Lutherans to find ways of reaching the unchurched, which helped to pave the way for the ministry of Jacob's Ladder. Initially five groups were set up to work on mission, worship, drama, TV spots/films, and a coffee lounge.

Worship

While the Dorian Society supported the existing cultural aspects of church life, there was a great desire to provide worship settings that would be more accessible to someone coming from a completely non-church background. For example, a Reformation Day recital by various church choirs was held. But also music and service orders which used guitars and drums (unheard of in those days!), drama, photography and contemporary forms of liturgy were prepared. This helped to enable Jacob's Ladder to develop more informal worship styles and settings.

Drama

Reaching non-churched young people meant re-evaluating the theological terminology common in church culture and finding relevant ways of expressing the same truths. A play presented to the SA Synod was called 'Cain doesn't understand'. That is, typical church language (salvation, sin, etc) needed to be reworked for the young people off the street. For example, the concept of God as Father was often threatening because of their relationship with their human fathers.

Coffee Lounge

Several of the leaders of the Dorian Society were also heavily involved in the establishment of Jacob's Ladder. That is described elsewhere in this book.

FURTHER BACKGROUND TO OUR STORY

SECTION V

CHAPTER 24

SingOut

This was a group ranging from 20–120 young people who presented programs combining contemporary music and drama with a message. This was often in church settings but also included for example a public high school and a Festival of Light (Mary Whitehouse) program.

Challenge Evenings

Again, these were a combination of music and drama to get a message across to young people at LYSA conventions or churches.

Eventually the establishment of Jacob's Ladder and SingOut as separate organisations, and probably the leaders' marriages and interstate moves led to the disbanding of the Society.

Chapter 25

Kerux Apostles Motorcycle Club
Marty Rosenberg

In 1974, the forms of outreach from Jacobs Ladder (Jakes) in Gawler Place, Adelaide were many and varied, as has been described in other chapters. In response to the many different forms of outreach, many were drawn to Jakes, where they experienced acceptance and love in ways they had not expected from a bunch of Christians. Among those drawn to Jakes were a number of bikers and since some members of Jakes already rode motorbikes (Japanese bikes mostly) the possibility of forming a Christian motorcycle club was raised. It would be an outreach arm of Jakes to the outlaw motorcycle clubs in Adelaide.

There were already two other small Christian motorcycle groups in Adelaide, one being God's Disciples MC. Eventually these two groups amalgamated and those in Jakes who rode bikes also joined and so Kerux Apostles MC came into being. While a design for the "colours" was being discussed, we agreed that no one should wear any colours until we had grown through the ranks of "Nominee," to eventually earn the right, proudly to wear full "colours" on our backs.

At the same time, Harry, a member of an outlaw motorcycle club had found his way into the shed at the Kuhl residence, where he was cared for by the family and others who lived nearby. Genghis, another outlaw biker, joined that shed community soon after.

On a run with the outlaws

We learned a lot about the world of outlaw motorcycle clubs, their language and culture. Some of us were from middle class backgrounds, so had a lot to learn. The steepest learning curve came when Harry, who acted as the intermediary between some outlaw clubs and Kerux Apostles, arranged for Kerux to go on a "run" with the Mandamas and the Undertakers—two outlaw motorcycle clubs around Adelaide. After a quick briefing about what we should not do, we joined the run of about 70 bikes that took us to a remote quarry outside of Burra in the mid-north of South Australia. Soon after we arrived, the other campers who were there quickly packed up, so we had the place to ourselves. They didn't have to leave.

FURTHER BACKGROUND TO OUR STORY

There was much drinking and plenty of drugs going around. Police arrived to check out the party, but soon left after they realised that we were not a risk to the public. A high mound of dirt provided some antics for those bikers who could still ride. A large PA was set up so there was music. A campfire was lit and some of us were politely asked to go and collect firewood. We camped there overnight and awoke to the alarm bells of "Time" by Pink Floyd at full volume. That is now my most memorable Pink Floyd song.

The Kerux Apostles Pub

Kerux Apostles had their own pub, like other motorcycle clubs. It was called the Land of Promise Hotel on Port Rd, Hindmarsh, and we affectionately renamed it "the Land of Milk and Honey". It was a place where we could congregate on a Friday or Saturday evening, and it was a place any biker would feel at home to visit. We were learning what it was to be "all things to all people," a principle taken directly from 1 Cor 9:19–23. "To the weak I became weak, so that I might win the weak. I have become all things to all people, that I might by all means save some." vs 22.

We were trying to understand the culture of the biker's world, while maintaining our faith-centred lifestyles. In that pub there were many conversations with other bikers about why we followed Jesus and what made us different, while we heard from them why they had chosen their lifestyles.

We made many mistakes, especially in the early days of the club. When we went to the Land of Milk and Honey, we always arranged for one person to be look-out for the bikes, to keep them safe, but one evening we were too slow to make those arrangements and by the time our cockatoo got into place, Scrooge's (Geoff Turner) Kawasaki 900 was gone. It had been stolen from just outside the hotel and we learned later that there was a roaring trade happening with interstate bike groups—stealing bikes and shipping them interstate to be rebirthed.

Ian Wade // Maurie May

Being a part of the Bikie Scene

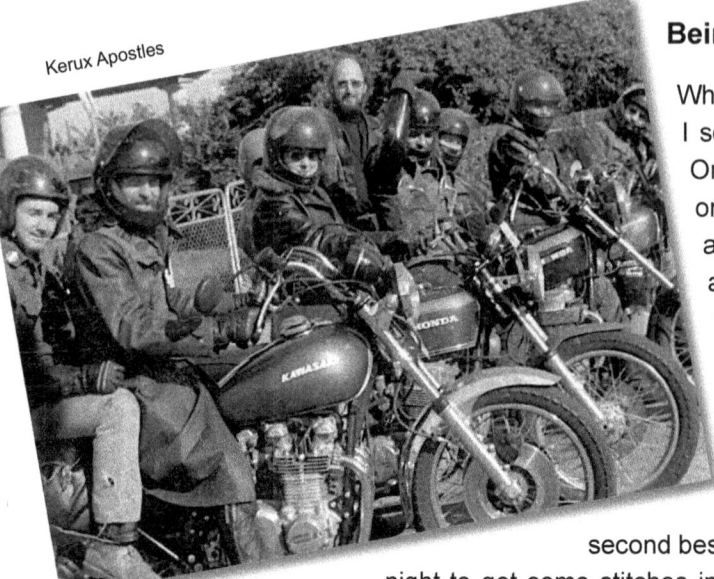

Kerux Apostles

While my bike was being modified, I sometimes rode pillion with Scrooge. One evening we were headed home on his bike from the Land of Milk and Honey, and we came up behind a small group of outlaw bikers travelling very slowly along South Road. Scrooge made the mistake of overtaking them and then he turned off into the back streets of Croydon. They followed, caught up with us and pulled us over. We came off second best and I ended up visiting hospital that night to get some stitches in my upper lip. Violence is a normal part of their culture and we broke one of their rules, so …

The fact that we were a Christian Bike group attracted a number of other Christians who rode bikes. They came to see if we were the real deal and to see if they wanted to join with us. Some were on the wild side, while others were trying to make a statement about how cool they were. In due course, some were accepted as "Nominees" or apprentice members. This was the structure of the outlaw bike clubs and the nominees who passed the various tests and proved their integrity and loyalty to the club, were "initiated" into full membership, but in a different way from the outlaw groups. I remember one evening, while we were at a gathering of outlaws, we witnessed one of their initiation ceremonies, but I can't describe what was done as the classification rating on this book would have to be increased significantly.

Some of those who came to check us out, were eventually given full colours, but many kept their distance, unable or not willing to commit fully to the club.

Harry recently shared some memories of his involvement with Kerux Apostles:

> I joined the Kerux boys as their first outlaw. They had no flaming idea how to talk to my people. Some of the names of those I remember: Basil Brush, real name Gary Jupe, also big Bert Schubert who rode a Yamaha 650 I believe. Basil rode a 750 Laverda, backbone frame. There was also Geoff Turner (Scrooge), who married Ava Leitner at the cross on O'Halloran Hill, Ian Wade, and Maurie of course who keeps in touch often. Kuhl on his 750 Duke. Maurie also had one. Me, with my reworked Honda 750, which I still have.

FURTHER BACKGROUND TO OUR STORY

SECTION U
CHAPTER 25

Marty also had one. There was also Ghengis, who became a good friend. Nothing to do with motorcycles. Ghengis, Bob Lewis and myself lived in the shed at Klemzig.

We were often asked by the public if we were like the God Squad, a Christian motorcycle club in Melbourne, under the leadership of John Smith. God Squad was an arm of the community called "Truth and Liberation Concern." We did explore the possibility of becoming a chapter of the God Squad, and we rode to Portland, in Victoria (halfway between Adelaide and Melbourne) to meet with God Squad and discuss that possibility. The leaders met and I understand they could not agree on the principles under which to operate, so the amalgamation never happened. However, the respect for each other and acceptance of how the other operated, remained. We visited each other on a number of occasions to share and learn. Some of our more memorable long-distance runs were to Melbourne where we were hosted by the God Squad.

Marty Rosenberg wearing the first version of Kerux Colours

Ava Leitner // Geoff Turner (Scrooge)

Kerux Apostles Motorcycle Club // 187

CHAPTER 26 Music and Drama
Colin Smith

It was 1973 and the Jesus Revolution / Christian Counter Culture movement was in full swing.

I had just been to the Nimbin Aquarian festival with a Christian group of people sharing the good news of Jesus in the midst of hippies, Hare Krishna, Divine Light, witches and just about any spiritual and religious sect that you can think of.

A month or so before that I was involved in a large Christian event called Kairos that involved concerts and School visits throughout Canberra. We marched through the centre of Canberra before totally encircling parliament house and praying for the new Whitlam government. It was a time of actively declaring Christ as Lord.

I was then asked to work with John Smith and God Squad (Truth and Liberation), in Bayswater Melbourne.

It was on an outreach event in Swan Hill that I got to know Doug Kuhl, the Lutheran Pastor there. He told me he was moving to Adelaide at the end of the year to lead a drop in / outreach centre called Jacob's Ladder which was attached to the St Stephens Lutheran Church.

At the end of 1973 an evangelist called John Holberton (who had also been part of the team at God squad), asked me to accompany him on an outreach in Alice Springs. We had already done some ministry together in Brisbane the year before. It was while I was in Alice Springs that I received a message from Doug Kuhl about coming to Adelaide to work as music coordinator at Jacob's Ladder.

It was now early in 1974 and I had just completed a Queensland tour with the Christian band "Family" who had a number 1 hit song on the radio. I had been praying about moving to Adelaide and found out that "Family" was going to Sydney and then Adelaide. I told them I wanted to go to Adelaide, so even though the support acts were already sorted for those cities, they employed me as a roadie and I drove their truck.

I was impressed with the work they were doing at Jacob's Ladder, so the following month I moved down and became part of the team. As well as being a drop in centre during the weekdays we also had Christian bands, solo and duo artists performing at the centre on Saturday nights. We did outreach concerts virtually every weekend in the City Mall, Victoria Square and North Terrace by the Museum of SA. We also sometimes visited Schools and Universities. These concerts consisted of street theatre, our regular community musicians and guest artists performing original songs and theatre.

Henley Beach Outreach

We had a comedy duo called *Fool Phil* (Phil Jefferis) and *Tune Smith* (Colin Smith). I played the guitar and Phil played the toilet brush. We entertained people with funny songs like Chad Morgan's *The Fatal Wedding*, and an original song designed to remind people of the temporary nature of our existence here. This is the chorus of that song: "Don't you worry about money, don't you worry about sex, but where you're gonna go to in the life that's next."

The songs we did were seed sowing and provoked a questioning of the purpose of life. We also had teams mingling with the people passing by, ready to share God's good news. Here are a couple of my songs that we used during that time:

Solitaire
by Colin Smith

VERSE 1
I saw you walking from afar.
I called you by your name.
I wanted so to bring you home,
but you just turned away in your shame.

VERSE 2
I heard your voice I felt your pain.
Ah but in yourself you chose to remain.
What blind fears you chose to love,
are the only friends you wanted to have.

CHORUS
The only game you know is solitaire.
Why don't you let go and give God the cards,
and he'll direct you there.

VERSE 3
I saw you walking from afar.
Walking down that dingy street.
All alone beside your feelings,
and the memories that you meet.

CHORUS x 2

Whose Kingdom
by Colin Smith

VERSE 1
Whose kingdom do you live in?
Do you really want to be free?
So much hate, so many feelings,
in a world of death and greed.

CHORUS
Light has come into the world to stay.
Never, never, never,
Never leave me alone even if I stray.

VERSE 2
Life is love, love is giving
and in giving he gives us life.
For if you believe in the one who was slain,
He'll restore your sight.

BRIDGE
Colours, colours in his eyes
like I've never seen before.
New day, new day has begun,
in the light of the Son.

VERSE 1

CHORUS

BRIDGE

TAG
In the light of the Son.
In the light of God's Son

FURTHER BACKGROUND TO OUR STORY

A lot of street kids became Christians and so they needed to be discipled, but they couldn't relate to normal church-goers or the traditional church buildings. Therefore, we started having our own less formal celebration worship on a Sunday.

We had our own worship band comprising flute, bass guitar, acoustic guitar, electric piano and male and female vocals. We put together our own worship songbook initially and later used the "Songs of Praise" books from The Word of God Music, Ann Arbor, USA. We also did some of our own songs written by members of Jacob's Ladder. Here is an example:

Day of Days
by Colin Smith

VERSE 1
Well I, I'm looking forward,
to that day, that day of days.
When I, I'll be delivered from the evil
that plagues our world today.

CHORUS
No more fighting, no more war,
no more sin and no more pain.
No more wondering when all this strife
is going to end.

VERSE 2
So how are you gonna be able
to get there if you don't even know the way.
You gotta seek the one who loves you.
Turn to Jesus you can know him right away.

CHORUS

VERSE 3
Well you, you might be wondering why
I'm bothering to sing this song right now.
It's for you to get you thinking,
an amazing destiny we'll show you how.

CHORUS

CHAPTER 27 *Theology and Teaching*

This is a much longer chapter than the others in this book. It is probably also, in places, a little more technical, as we deal with complex issues. After some introductory comments, I deal with three sets of documents. In order to make for easier reading, I have identified each of these three sections with headings.

The theology taught at Jakes caused a lot of controversy at the time and was heavily criticised by some Church leaders. In order to keep the main story flowing, a more detailed analysis of what was taught at Jakes has been left to this section dealing with additional background to the Jakes story.

In chapter 14, I described the LCA's 1976 statement on Charismatic Renewal as a balanced, well thought out document. There were, however, many other approaches and opinions that helped shape the context in which we lived and worked. For example, one Adelaide-based LCA pastor, who had better remain nameless, wrote an evaluation of the Charismatic Movement in October 1978. He briefly listed four strengths, including prayer, joy and expectation in worship, community, and a consciousness that God is close at hand. Then under the heading *Their Weaknesses*, the first thing he wrote was:

> This a dangerous generalisation, but probably worth making: Many of the people involved in the Pentecostal and Charismatic Movements are people who tend to react emotionally, rather than rationally to situations (the kind of people, for example, who, in other contexts might, under stress, turn to drugs etc).

Really? Or, maybe this 'generalisation' was actually not worth making! I have been accused of many things during my life—some of them even true—but I don't think I have ever been accused of tending to react emotionally to situations. Over-thinking? Sure. Over-analysing? Definitely. Potential druggie? Well, you can draw your own conclusion about that one.

A more balanced understanding

That doesn't mean that the majority of those who didn't identify with charismatic renewal held such extreme views. In fact, there was quite an outcry when early in 1976 Pastor Doug wrote an article in which he used the example of an Adelaide Lutheran Fraternal meeting where a pastor said, "This Charismatic Movement is

FURTHER BACKGROUND TO OUR STORY

SECTION U
CHAPTER 27

making inroads into our church. Our church must immediately equip itself to fight this thing."[145] And a little later:

> This Charismatic Pastor, who is myself, sat in that meeting and heard so-called Charismatics referred to as the arch-heretics of Christendom, and wondered what God was thinking and what God saw as total truth at that moment. I wondered whether God, who sees all things for what they really are, wouldn't cringe at the sight of Christians accusing each other in blind prejudice and fleshly bias? Who of us is absolutely doctrinally pure?[146]

In the following issue of *Jacob's Letter*, we needed to print a clarification:

> The article on Lutheran Spiritual Renewal in the May 1976 edition of Jacob's Letter has caused some controversy. Pastor Doug Kuhl has written a letter of apology to the Adelaide Lutheran Fraternal for any inference that the opinion quoted represented the view of the Fraternal as a whole. ... No "blanket condemnation" is intended and we apologise for any misunderstanding we have caused.[147]

Things could get pretty heated at times. However, we didn't sit around judging others, because we had more than enough to deal with in what the Spirit revealed to us about ourselves. While not wanting to suggest that we who were part of Jakes and Lutheran Charismatic Renewal Australia got everything completely right all the time, I would suggest that we did not hold to the excesses of classic Pentecostalism. We did not teach a second baptism with the Holy Spirit, that the gift of tongues was the evidence of such a baptism having taken place, that everyone could be healed if only they had enough faith, that baptism of infants is unscriptural, and so on. In fact, in the same article, Pastor Doug wrote that baptism was often treated as some sort of white magic in line with society's 'instant' mentality. He continued:

> Whatever has happened to Christ's call to repentance, to faith in him as being the 'how' of salvation, to the clear statement of Scripture that baptism is being baptised in the Holy Spirit. There is only one baptism, and infant baptism is valid, but how do these factors and more fit into the whole biblical concept of baptism?[148]

---

145 Douglas Kuhl, **Lutheran Spiritual Renewal**, *Jacob's Letter* (May 1976), 13.

146 ibid., 13–14.

147 *Jacob's Letter* (September 1976), 22.

148 Douglas Kuhl, **Lutheran Spiritual Renewal**, *Jacob's Letter* (May 1976), 13.

Emotionalism and Ecstasy

Even though most didn't think that we were in danger of becoming drug addicts, many held a view of charismatics that focused on emotionalism and even the idea that such experiences led people to become ecstatic, or if you like, being under a spell, as it were, and so lose control of themselves. Pastor Doug dealt with that in a postscript to his article:

> I have read of people reacting against emotionalism, freaky conditions of ecstasy in association with the charismatic movement, and their case for the rejection of the charismatic renewal seems to be heavily based on this factor. I don't know what actually qualifies as being emotionalism, for my whole being is caught up in and involved in Christ's redemption. Not just my mind, but my whole being is made vulnerable to God's saving grace, to Jesus' redeeming love, to the Spirit's indwelling power, even my emotions!

> As for a state of ecstasy, it is a myth as far as I am concerned. Something a few people have read in the gossip columns of the local grapevine and theologians have subsequently stuck it into their papers and books, and so it has been propagated down to this day. Even if a few extremists have been carried away, there have been extremists with every kind of doctrine over the 2,000 years of Christendom and we do not therefore throw away baptism, the Lord's Supper, justification etc.[149]

In a letter addressed to the pastor and elders of Jacob's Ladder, dated 29 June 1976, President Clem Koch wrote: "This is surely no less than saying that I am lying and defaming, when I say that I have experienced worship where excessive ecstasy, emotionalism and freaky conditions were connected with a charismatic service!" It seems that the president was using the word 'ecstasy' to mean the same as an intense form of 'emotionalism', while we were using it in the sense of being in a state that is beyond rational thought and self-control. We wouldn't speak of 'excessive' ecstasy, because all ecstasy as we are using the word, is by definition, excessive. That illustrates a couple of points. Firstly, we need to be precise in our definition of words. Secondly, no one was accusing the president of anything. He may indeed have witnessed such a situation. Yet he feels accused. Why do people feel judged, when no judgment is intended, and a simple reading of the words used, say nothing that is judgmental? We all stand under the judgment of the Word of God.

Judgmentalism, of course cuts both ways. A little later in this chapter, I will refer to a debate on the Charismatic Movement, between LSF Chaplain John Sabel

---

149 Douglas Kuhl, **Lutheran Spiritual Renewal**, Jacob's Letter (May 1976),15.

FURTHER BACKGROUND TO OUR STORY

CHAPTER 27

and Pastor Doug Kuhl. Right now I just want to quote from the evaluation of the presentations by Eric Grace:

> The most prominent danger from either side is stereotyping. Doug admitted that Charismatics had labelled the church as cold, dead and traditional. But he also confessed that it was wrong to do this. And he also realised, as John pointed out, that God works with tremendous power in the ordinariness of old established Churches. But it seems that the church is now guilty of being prejudiced and unduly biased. Statements such as, "Don't get mixed up with that lot. It's demonic. Those nuts that speak in tongues, only emotionally unstable people go in for it. It won't last", have been spoken by Lutherans.[150]

Experience and Doctrine

Subjectivism was also a criticism that was often levelled against us. We were told that we understood spiritual gifts from our experience of them, not from Scripture, while our critics said they objectively looked at the Word of God and deduced doctrine, without distorting it by their subjective biases. I doubt you would hear that today. We now understand that even when we think we are being absolutely objective, all manner of subjective life experiences and prejudices still play a part in forming our conclusions. We are all very subjective in our 'objectivity'. God alone is objective; everyone else needs to acknowledge that past experiences play a part in everything we do.

So apparently, we believed that spiritual gifts are given by the Spirit today, because we thought that we had experienced them. However, the fact that our critics seemingly hadn't experienced such gifts, played no part in their rejection of them. They maintained that their reading of the Bible was 'objective'. So what, I wonder, do they make of the Acts of the Apostles? After all, Lutherans are not dispensationalists, who believe that spiritual gifts were only for the time before the New Testament was written and formed into an authoritative collection of documents.

Many modern Western Christians, especially since the Enlightenment, have tried to domesticate the Holy Spirit, and bring him under our control. Therefore, prophecy has come to be understood as preaching, demonic oppression as almost always being explained by mental illnesses, words of knowledge and wisdom as the result of intuition which we don't fully understand yet, and so on. In other words, for many Christians, practically speaking, God is only at work between the covers of the

---

[150] The copy I have does not include the name of the publication, but it is probably *Lutheran Student*. Date unknown.

Bible, and in the sacraments. The danger is that we may say that we believe a lot of things, but then live as though we were atheists. We know that God has promised to work through the Word and the sacraments, but it is not for us to tell the Holy Spirit what he may or may not do among the people of God, who dwell in the Word and come to his table. We pray for guidance that we won't directly find on the pages of our Bibles. We pray for healing for the sick and for the wisdom and discernment to deal with difficult situations. Besides that, we know that God is at work in and through creation, sustaining and supporting that which he has made. Therefore, to go back to the 1970s, we weren't saying that God must give such gifts today, merely that he does and that is consistent with how his Spirit worked in the early Church. As Pastor Doug wrote:

> When the Church says that she holds to the principle of "Sola Scriptura", does this mean that the Church stands in faith believing that God says what he means and means what he says in his holy Word to us? If so, then it becomes no little challenge to us, as to what a person is to do with whole slabs of the teaching of Jesus, of miracles, of spiritual gifts, of God's power over evil and sin, and yet remain standing where whole numbers of Christians are living out their lives today.[151]

Descriptions and Precedents

The argument goes something like this: If something is described in the Acts of the Apostles, that doesn't mean it is a precedent or prescription for all time. God may have done something then that he chooses not to repeat again. True. Though one would then wonder what the point is of including in the Bible incident after incident of the Spirit at work in various ways, if we are not to learn something from it. However, let's accept the statement that no precedent is being set. Clearly, in spite of what happened to Jonah, God has not made a regular thing of having people swallowed by big fish and regurgitated on distant shores. Likewise, Paul may have been unharmed when he picked up a poisonous snake (Acts 28:3–6), but that doesn't mean we should presume to be able to do the same.

However, if God's Spirit acted in particular ways in the early church, and this is recorded for us in Scripture, then at the very least, it is possible that the Spirit may choose to act in such ways, also in our time. Moreover, when something that is described in Acts is very much in line with the teaching of Jesus and the writings of the Apostles, then maybe we shouldn't be surprised when we hear of the Spirit doing similar things in our day.

---

151 Douglas Kuhl, **Lutheran Spiritual Renewal**, Jacob's Letter (May 1976), 13.

FURTHER BACKGROUND TO OUR STORY

1 Correspondence with the President

In March 1976, President Clem Koch issued a pastoral letter, *Concerning Special Gifts of the Spirit in Church Life*. In May of that year, Jacob's Ladder published the article on *Lutheran Spiritual Renewal*, referred to above. Following that, a number of letters were exchanged between the president and the pastor and elders of Jacob's Ladder. President Koch wrote to us on 29 June 1976. For our purposes here, I will just consider how the response to the president in the letter dated 22 July 1976 and the addendum dated 21 October 1976, clarifies the theology and teaching of Jacob's Ladder.

Firstly, we as the pastor and elders of Jakes, denied that we had been reluctant to answer specific questions or that we had made 'blanket condemnations' or accusations that the Church was guilty of falsehood. As to whether the May 1976 article on Spiritual Renewal, referenced above, was ethical and pastoral, we pointed out that the pastor attacking us was not named and that we had already apologised for any suggestion that his view was that of the whole fraternal. We were puzzled by the statement that nowhere in our article is there even the hint that the Pentecostal movement contains false doctrine, since we were not writing about Pentecostalism. Likewise, Pastor Doug was asked if, as a self-described charismatic pastor, he rejected any aspect of the charismatic movement. We replied that since the charismatic movement exists in each denomination, obviously there are things in the Catholic or Methodist charismatic movements that we would reject. We then addressed a number of specific theological issues that were raised in the President's letter.

Righteousness

We had stated that the church "generally had a bankrupt understanding of Christ's righteousness." Apart from the fact that the president's letter omitted the word 'generally' which qualified our statement, we stated that the church's teaching on righteousness had generally emphasised Christ's righteousness outside us, which is imputed to us for our salvation, but had largely ignored the righteousness that is a gift of the power of God at work in us. In support of that we included lengthy quotations from respected Luther Scholar Paul Althaus and from Luther's first lectures on Galatians. Ernst Käsemann sums it up with his comments on Paul's use of the term 'the righteous of God':

> We take the decisive step along the road to a proper understanding of Paul when, and only when, we grasp the indissoluble connection between power and gift within the conception of the divine righteousness … The key to this

whole Pauline viewpoint is that power is always seeking to realise itself in action and must indeed do so.[152]

In other words, we are not to confuse justification and sanctification, and thereby suggest that somehow we help to earn our salvation by what we do. However, we need to understand that God's righteousness, which is given to us as a gift so that we are declared righteous, is also at work in us renewing us in righteousness. The gifts of God are dynamic. They are declarations of altered circumstances, but they are not just that. They are also an ongoing power at work in us, bringing us toward the goal of maturity and remaking us in the image of Christ. This will of course only be complete when we stand before the Lord on the final day. There is no perfection in this life.

Baptism

Doug Kuhl baptises Amy Brooks at Henley Beach

We were challenged over our statement that baptism is sometimes made into a sort of 'white magic' that produces instant salvation. We explained that some seemed to understand baptism as though merely going through the act gives the person an automatic ticket to heaven. We quote the thirteenth article of the Augsburg Confession: "Our churches therefore condemn those who teach that the sacraments justify by the outward act, and they do not teach that faith, which believes that sins are forgiven, is required in the use of the sacraments." Baptism, therefore produces the "fruit of repentance, faith, new life and obedience—all of which require the power of the Holy Spirit to be at work in a person's heart, mind, soul and life." It is therefore significant that the baptism of Jesus, in contrast to the baptism of John, is with the Holy Spirit. Without

---

152 Ernst Käsemann, **New Testament Questions Today**, SCM Press Ltd, London (1969) 174–175.

FURTHER BACKGROUND TO OUR STORY

ongoing faith, there is no salvation, even if a person has gone through the rite of baptism.

The Kingdom of God

We said that there was a general dearth of understanding of the Kingdom of God in the Lutheran Church. This also relates to the article on the *Counterfeit Kingdom* in the May 1976 *Jacob's Letter*. We were asked to explain what we meant. In reply, we made three basic points:

a. Jesus brings the kingdom of God among us. It is a kingdom indeed, not a figment of the imagination. We enter it through faith and we go out as citizens of that kingdom to proclaim that Jesus, the King, lives and his kingdom has come into the world.

b. Satan has a counterfeit kingdom that blasphemously mimics the kingdom of God. This kingdom makes false promises that don't deliver, and is therefore a delusion and a lie. When Christians live in a worldly way, they are following the values and practices of this counterfeit kingdom.

c. The only possible way into the kingdom of God is through the death and resurrection of Jesus, which in turn means death to our 'old nature' and being born again through water and the Spirit, into a new life which is being created after the likeness of God in true holiness and righteousness. We therefore don't enter the kingdom by understanding and contemplating it, but by participating in it. This is a gift of the Spirit of God, working through Scripture, as Paul says in Romans 12:2, "Do not be conformed to this world, but be transformed by the renewing of your minds, so that you may discern what is the will of God—what is good and acceptable and perfect."

*Yours fatefully,
Satan*

Scripture Alone

We had said that it appeared to us that whole slabs of Scripture were often being ignored. That included what Scripture said about miracles, spiritual gifts, and God's power over evil and sin. We were challenged to justify that. In reply, we reiterated the importance of the Reformation emphasis on *Sola Scriptura*— Scripture alone. "Scripture and Scripture alone must be the basis and authority for our understanding of the kingdom, its life, its principles, and its distinction from the world." This brings into focus our understanding of miracles today, spiritual gifts, and the victory over all evil powers. Is Paul's Romans 15:18–19 description of how the Gospel was proclaimed just for the first Century, or does it apply today: "For I will not venture to speak of anything except what Christ has accomplished through me to win obedience from the Gentiles, by word and deed, by the power of signs and wonders, by the power of the Spirit of God." How do we understand Luther's statement that Scripture is basically clear and explicit in its meaning for us, rather than a labyrinth of problems that only theologians can hope to sort out. Finally:

> It seems to us that in many of the above matters the Church is often using a 20th Century worldview ... to judge the application of Scripture today, rather than allowing the Scriptural worldview to judge our 20th Century presuppositions. For this reason there seems to be a reluctance among many of our Church members to accept the fact that God can and does will to work among his people today in similar ways to those described in the New Testament. If indeed we worship a God who acts in history, then surely these divine events in history are not merely descriptions of never to be repeated occurrences, but represent a forth-telling of the kind of God we worship and serve, and how this God has revealed to us the way in which he desires to move among his people. Jesus Christ is the same yesterday, today and forever.

Accusations or not?

Our letter of 22 July 1976 then states that a lack of time prevented us from replying to the rest of the points in the President's letter. However, a final paragraph takes up the important point that whenever we questioned something that seemed to us to be a relevant and pertinent issue that was being discussed by other pastors and people in the Church, we were accused of being judgmental. It was a constant source of frustration at the time. Others could raise questions that were then discussed. When we did so, we were condemned. The letter continues:

> The tone of your letter seems to be one of a person who feels personally threatened by the fact that these questions are being asked within the arena

FURTHER BACKGROUND TO OUR STORY

of our Church. There is no other reason than this, we believe, for the fact that our questions are constantly being interpreted as accusations. As we have struggled to present the Gospel to people along the highways and by-ways of the city and State, we have experienced a whole host of these questions coming tumbling down upon us. We have struggled to provide Scriptural answers to these questions that the world around us is asking of us, of God's Word and of the Church of which we are a part. We believe that many of our answers, not only hold out exciting possibilities revealed to us for the people of the world, but also for the people of the church. We wish to share these possibilities with our brothers and sisters. They are not new possibilities; they are as old as the church is old. However, we feel like we have been treated as some freaky, way-out, clandestine group, whose only relevance was seen to be for other weirdos like ourselves.

Pastors and the Priesthood of all Believers

On 21 October 1976, we sent a supplementary letter addressing the four points in the president's letter that we had not covered in the previous correspondence. The first of those concerned our belief that the Church had emphasised the office and role of pastors at the expense of promoting the understanding of the priesthood of all believers. That would be fairly commonplace today, as we speak of the problem of having a pastor-centric Church. Back then it was "obviously an accusation", to quote the president's letter. We made it plain that we were not disagreeing with the Church's understanding of the office of Pastor, but wanted to see the priesthood of all believers receive greater emphasis, so that all the people of God may grow in exercising the gifts of the Spirit in the church and the world.

Christians attacking one another

The president's letter questions our assertion that Christians are attacking each other in blind prejudice and fleshly bias. He then asked, "Just who has been doing this? Who is making the fight, causing division, and giving reason for spiritual grief?" Our answer was brief. We admitted that we had been far from perfect, but also asserted that the opposition and in places the rejection that people involved in spiritual renewal had been experiencing, did not stem from a genuine knowledge of what had been happening, but from a lack of understanding and subsequent prejudging of the renewal. This sort of reaction leads to disunity.

Healing

The president then asked if we were saying that "God heals all migraines, drug addiction, influenza etc in answer to prayer?" Our answer was very brief:

> God can and does heal. When and how is his business. We can't manipulate God but he does invite us to bring to him in prayer, all our physical, emotional and other ills. Many people can testify that in many cases God did indeed heal them in response to such prayer. Indeed, it is our duty before God so to pray.

Ecstasy

Finally, the president raised the statement in the article that says that renewal involving a state of ecstasy is a myth. I have already referred to that earlier in this chapter. In our reply, we stated that of course somewhere, sometime, what can be described as ecstasy may have occurred in charismatic groups, but that has not been our experience. We then expressed a word of caution:

> As spectators, we would have to exercise care, however, in defining "excessive ecstasy" in someone else. What we are wanting to say is that this is nowhere near as common as some seem to imagine and is certainly not descriptive of the experience of Jacob's Ladder or Lutheran Spiritual Renewal. Further, the use of the words "ecstatic utterance" to describe the gift of tongues or prophecy is equally misleading in terms of common experience. We believe that such designations are also going to further polarise our church if they are used in such a way as to imply that this is the experience of Lutheran Spiritual Renewal. We dare not use an extreme example as the means of establishing what is normal.

FURTHER BACKGROUND TO OUR STORY

SECTION V

CHAPTER 27

II Three Servant Magazine Articles

The journey from new understandings to a new life

In the first three editions of *Servant* in 1977, Pastor Doug Kuhl wrote a series of articles, *Guided Together into Renewal*. In them, he outlines the journey the community took in its studies and reflections from early in 1974. They are long articles, but I shall try to give an overview. In doing so, I also hope to put to bed the idea that the only things we ever talked about were the Holy Spirit and spiritual gifts.

The first article began by saying that Thursday mornings were set aside as a prayer breakfast from 7am. They were also a time of in-depth Bible study, beginning with the Gospel according to Luke. On the day we began that study, we were still there at 1pm. Through Luke's account, we received a vision of the life of Jesus, as he taught and demonstrated a model of discipleship that captivated and claimed our lives. As the Word of God spoke to us, we heard a call to a life of disciplined submission under the authority of Jesus. We were warned against calling him 'Lord, Lord' yet not doing what he told us (Luke 6:46) and we heard the promise, "Do not be afraid little flock, for your Father is pleased to give you the kingdom" (Luke 12:32). This was not a call 'to put God first' and then order everything else under that, but to serve God in everything we did, and not divide our lives into the sacred and the secular. Doug continued:

> This was not seen as a life of legalism. Rather, the group plainly saw, through the Spirit's anointing, a vision of their worldly shackles falling off their lives because of the

Theology and Teaching // 203

gracious call to life in Jesus, of being released from the bondage of this world, into the perfect freedom of discipleship within the kingdom of God.

Thus, they prayed that day, some three years ago, that Jesus would show them how to do this. They were convicted against legalism on the one hand, and against the apathy of a ritualistic Christianity of formalism, on the other. They believed with their whole beings that Jesus would show them how his words could become literal truth for them in a Gospel-centred way, and how they could live out such a life of love for him—their beloved Lord.[153]

The studies continued through the rest of Luke, then John and Matthew, and the letters to the Ephesians, Colossians, and the book of Hebrews. We also looked into the letters of James, Peter and John, as well as the Old Testament prophets Isaiah, Jeremiah and Ezekiel, and the Psalms. Many questions were raised: Can we accept Jesus' words at face value? When it says he is our Saviour from sin and sets us free from its bondage, power and condemnation, is that claim realistic? Should we expect to experience that—after all, every one of us struggles with various sins? Does that begin now, or is it only something for heaven? Are the descriptions of these early Christian communities more than interesting historical curios—or are they the setting down of how God worked in history, and therefore reveal principles that speak to us in the present?

All this was happening in the midst of a fast-growing outreach mission, with many conversions, and new Christians needing to be nurtured. We were working long hours and struggling to keep up. This was no mere academic exercise, but something that was shaping both the mission and our community forming around this mission. What did we learn:

> We believed sin to be constantly present with us, in the world and in our flesh. What excited us though, was the discovery that Jesus has conquered sin, overcome sin's power, stripped sin of its mastery over us, and set us free from sin's slavery. We discovered

---

153 Douglas Kuhl, **Guided into Renewal**, *Servant* (February–March 1977), 3–4.

FURTHER BACKGROUND TO OUR STORY

that the Gospel was really good news. ... All this sounds like a heap of wonderful sounding theological jargon, and true, sitting by itself there on paper, it is. However, place these principles in the midst of life, and you have a transformation of human life of stupendous proportions. We believe that we were now beginning to understand the kind of living force which drove the early disciples into a pagan, corrupt world, with a message of victory![154]

The Spirit began to bring to the surface of our lives all kinds of sin, weakness, egotistical rebellions, and a glimpse of what a spiritually mature life in Christ might look like in practice. We received the opportunities to surrender such things to Christ's forgiveness, and to receive the gift of reconciliation to God again and again. A cleansing, transforming, renewing force was being unleashed in our lives at the cost of our egos, and bringing with it pain along the way as we experienced divine conviction and then the infilling of the spiritual power of a new life.

The 'street' kept us honest

In the second article, Pastor Doug wrote about the high expectations of what Christians ought to be that we found among people of the street. We were taunted and questioned. "If God exists and Jesus is real and alive today, then why are the Christians I know hypocrites?" "Satan is obviously more powerful than God. Look around you at who is winning?" "I tried church once. All I got out of it was a lot of guilty hang-ups and inhibitions." Street kids could smell a lack of authenticity a mile off. Pastor Doug concluded:

> Today's generation needs God's power for life generated among them. In this respect, people today are no better or worse than those of New Testament times. A sinner is a sinner, bondage is bondage, god-forsakenness is god-forsakenness, no matter in what time or culture it is found—New Testament times or now! All of us, people of yester-century or of tomorrow or of today, we all need God's powerful personal act of deliverance and rescue just as much now as then.[155]

Pastor Doug found help in JB Phillips' preface to his translation of the Acts of the Apostles. He quoted some of what Phillips said:

> It is impossible to spend several months in close study of ... the Acts of the Apostles, without being profoundly stirred, and to be honest, disturbed. The reader is stirred because he is seeing Christianity, the real thing, in action

---

[154] ibid., 5.

[155] Douglas Kuhl, **Guided Together into Renewal**, *Servant* (July 1977), 3.

for the first time in human history. The newborn Church, as vulnerable as any human child, having neither money nor influence, nor power in the ordinary sense, is setting forth joyfully and courageously to win the pagan world for God through Christ.[156]

Doug then shared something of his own journey of discovery. A few excerpts:

> I was thoroughly convicted of the obvious fact that I simply wasn't "open to the God-ward side" in my life. My life was largely closed to any real expectation of, or vulnerability to, God's Spirit working, changing, subtracting, adding, transforming the details of my character and life-style. Could it be that the problem of God not acting to rescue me from my weaknesses, which had led me to despair, was really not to be found in any unwillingness on God's part—but in stubborn, ignorant, unbelieving ol' me?
> … I prayed. God met that prayer with his promises and has continued to do so ever since.
> … But this was not without cost.
> … The Lord gave me the gift of speaking in tongues. It happened quietly in a Lutheran chapel one morning while at prayer. I felt utterly foolish… My immediate reaction was to refuse to pray out loud for four days. … Jesus became real for me in a way I had never known before—through the pages of Scripture, through the sacrament of the Lord's Supper, through prayer, and through the voice of the Holy Spirit, addressing my thoughts in and through various circumstances.[157]

Many others had similar experiences. Meanwhile, on the street, kids were coming to faith, many of them from a world of drug addiction, gangs, outlaw bikies, and alcohol abuse. "The story of this street outreach team, now grown into a community, is surely one which testifies to God's power at work today, within the lives of people—leading them from defeat to victory in Christ." Out of this, three basic things became clearer to us:

---

156 Douglas Kuhl, **Guided Together into Renewal**, Servant (July 1977), 3.

157 ibid., 5.

FURTHER BACKGROUND TO OUR STORY

1. The forgiveness of Jesus is a power at work within our lives and not just a formula we recite to make us feel better after we have sinned. It is God re-establishing fellowship with us through Jesus. All the barriers have been torn down and a whole new situation has come into being. We witnessed this happening in the lives of young converts, as they stopped trying to trust their own weaknesses but turned to God's strength to renew their lives.

2. Jesus is not only our righteousness before God that deals with our guilt and the condemnation for our sin, but he also clothes us with his righteousness, so we are being transformed into his likeness in our daily lives. The one follows the other. At the time Doug wrote this, ten people who had recently come to faith were taking their first steps in this journey.

3. We absolutely needed to be continually filled with the Holy Spirit in order for us to live, minister, share and serve in this way. It can't be done by relying on our own strength and ability. As St Paul said, "I have been crucified with Christ, and it is no longer I who live, but Christ who lives in me. And the life I now live in the flesh, I live by faith in the Son of God, who loved me and gave himself for me." (Gal 2:19b–20)

New Wine needs New Wineskins

In the third article, Pastor Doug began by focusing on Jesus' teaching that new wine needed new wineskins, because new wine would expand and burst the old skins that were no longer flexible. Therefore, the old wineskin of Judaism could not contain the new wine of Jesus. The history of the Christian Church shows the same thing. The old wineskins that protect the old traditions by trying to find ways to contain and control the new fermenting wine will burst and sadly, some of the new wine will be spilled. Doug wrote:

> The Scriptures constantly call us to recognise the fact that God will not be contained within the narrow space of our minds and our old way of thinking. God's person and activity will always spill out beyond the shallow rims of our limited vision.[158]

It is the nature of human institutions that over time they become controlling and begin to lose their flexibility. That also applies to the church on earth, therefore renewal is a constant need, because human nature wants to conserve and preserve the comfortable traditions that ensure a stable quiet life. God had taken us on a journey with the gift of new wine. In this article, Doug identified four ways this had affected our lives:

1. We experienced a great desire to engage in personal evangelism. We spoke with people about Jesus. A quiet stream of new Christians flowed into our community. Where were they to go for fellowship and instruction towards Christian maturity?

2. That led us to wrestle with the question of genuine Christian *koinonia*, or fellowship in the fullest biblical sense. We tried to nurture young converts in our private homes, but this had its limitations. "Our elder brothers in the church institutions were heavily critical of our attempts to wrestle with this new situation. The only place we could go for help was the Bible."[159] Books like Howard Snyder's *The Problem of Wineskins*, and the writings of Dietrich Bonhoeffer were a great help, even if we didn't agree with everything they said. The result was that something more like a New Testament *koinonia* began to emerge. We sought greater honesty and supportive relationships in our dealings with one another, love that involved actions as well as emotions and words, and letting the Word of God permeate our life together.

3. But even the first tentative steps towards a more biblically lived out life is not something we are capable of achieving. "The third effect in our lives was the discovery of the immediacy and the reality of God's actual presence and power, of God's acting and caring for us in our lives together."[160] God was acting as the Holy Spirit blessed us with daily examples of his activities in our lives. Drug addicts who had been smashed inside came to faith and were healed, transformed and grew

---

158 Douglas Kuhl, **Guided Together into Renewal**, Servant (October 1977), 3.

159 ibid., 4.

160 ibid., 5.

FURTHER BACKGROUND TO OUR STORY

   into maturity. We were conscious of how God was active in our countless daily interactions. "Praise the Lord, he lives, he works, he moves among us, his people."[161]

4. As the new wine poured out of the new wineskins, we were discovering a new passion for working out in the midst of our pagan society. Of course, this wasn't only happening in Adelaide and among us. Thousands of communities had been raised up across the world, fired up by the same convictions, making the same sacrifices, and experiencing the same overwhelming joy of Christ's abundant new life. At a time when worldwide humanism was evangelising the churches, God was giving new wineskins so that his new wine might flow to all corners of the earth.

These articles by Pastor Doug, written in the first half of 1977, provided an outline of the journey of Jakes to that point, as well as being a platform for what was to follow. It also set the theology of renewal in the wider context that is needed for it to be properly understood. God was renewing his church.

The following two pages are taken from the October 1977 edition of *Servant*. Martin Luther encourages us to give priority to prayer, but not to be so focused on our own words that we miss the Holy Spirit speaking to us as we are praying. Better to stop our own speaking and listen to the thoughts that come into our minds because "here the Holy Spirit himself is preaching and one word of his sermon is better than thousands of our own prayers."[162]

---

161 ibid., 6.

162 Martin Luther, **Some of Luther's thoughts on prayer**, *Servant* (October 77), 11–12.

FURTHER BACKGROUND TO OUR STORY

CHAPTER 27

Dear Master Peter,

I give you the best I have. I tell you how I pray myself. May our Lord God grant you and everyone to do it better.

A good clever barber must have his thoughts, mind and eyes concentrated upon the rasor and the beard and not forget where he is in his stroke and shave. If he keeps talking or looking around or thinking of something else, he is likely to cut a man's mouth or nose - or even his throat. So anything that is to be done well ought to occupy the whole man with all his faculties and members. As the saying goes: he who thinks of many things thinks of nothing and accomplishes no good. How much more must prayer possess the heart exclusively and completely if it is to be good prayer!

It is a good thing to let prayer be the first business in the morning and the last in the evening. Guard yourself against such false and deceitful thoughts that keep whispering: *"Wait awhile. In an hour or so I will pray. I must first finish this or that."* Thinking such thoughts, we get away from prayer into other things that will hold us and involve us till the prayer of the day comes to nought.

We have to watch out so that we may not get weaned from prayer by fooling ourselves that a certain job is more urgent, which it really isn't - and finally we get sluggish, lazy, cold and weary. But the devil is neither sluggish nor lazy around us...

It often happens that I lose myself in such rich thoughts. When such rich good thoughts come, one should let the other prayers go and give room to these thoughts, listen to them in silence and by no means supress them. For here the Holy Spirit Himself is preaching and one word of His sermon is better than thousands of our own prayers. Therefore, I have often learned more in one prayer than I could have obtained from much reading and thinking.

I repeat again: If the Holy Spirit should come when these thoughts are in your mind and begin to preach to your heart, giving you rich and enlightened thoughts, then give Him the honour, let your preconceived ideas go, be quiet and listen to Him who can talk better than you; and note what He proclaims and write it down, so will you experience mircles as David says... *"Open my eyes that I may behold wondrous things out of Thy law."* (Psalm 119:18)

The Spirit will and must grant us this, if your heart is conformed to God's Word.

III The Great LSF Debate

At some point around this time,[163] Lutheran Student Fellowship (LSF) hosted a discussion titled *The Last Word on Charismatics* (good luck with that!). LSF Chaplain, Pastor John Sabel presented *The Cons of the Charismatic Movement* and Pastor Doug Kuhl *The Pros of the Charismatic Movement*. Finally, Eric Grace wrote, *Weighing up the Pros and the Cons*. He was generally supportive of the case presented by Doug. John made the first presentation and Doug had therefore heard that when he presented his response. It seems that the exchange was recorded and later transcribed. The style is oral rather than written.

I have smoothed that out a bit in recording it here. To be fair, there is also no indication that John had an opportunity to respond to what Doug said. Eric clearly wrote later, for he refers to a subsequent private conversation with John. For our purposes in this chapter, I am not going to summarise the whole debate, but just use Doug's piece to illustrate Jakes' understanding of Charismatic Renewal.

Pastor Doug begins by referring to Jesus speaking in his hometown Synagogue:

> [16]When he came to Nazareth, where he had been brought up, he went to the synagogue on the Sabbath day, as was his custom. He stood up to read, 17and the scroll of the prophet Isaiah was given to him. He unrolled the scroll and found the place where it was written: [18]"The Spirit of the Lord is upon me, because he has anointed me to bring good news to the poor. He has sent me to proclaim release to the captives and recovery of sight to the blind, to let the oppressed go free, [19]to proclaim the year of the Lord's favour." [20]And he rolled up the scroll, gave it back to the attendant, and sat down. The eyes of all in the synagogue were fixed on him. [21]Then he began to say to them, "Today this scripture has been fulfilled in your hearing." Luke 4:16–21

Doug commented, "I was once oppressed in my life (still am in many ways) but I know a Saviour who comes to redeem me". He then quotes from the LCA statement described in chapter 14. It states that the presence of charismatic groups may be a reminder to the Church of the weaknesses that may be found from time to time

---

163 **The Last Word on Charismatics**. It appears to be from *Lutheran Student*, but the copy I have is undated. The pages are numbered 17–22. The content makes it plain that it is after the LCA published its statement in early 1976.

FURTHER BACKGROUND TO OUR STORY

in congregations. Doug concludes, "All Lutherans will surely agree that a church continually needs the renewing power of the Holy Spirit if it is to be the church that the Lord wants it to be." Further:

> I differ with John that it is a very individualistic movement. It isn't. As a matter of fact it is a very corporate movement, vitally interested in community life, not for itself, but for the whole body of Christ. ... It's my concern ... that we join ourselves to the body of Christ, that we take our place within the body and we share and care and live responsibly the lives the Lord has called us to live together. Then we learn some of the togetherness, which of course is the very nature of the Godhead. ... This life, through the incarnation of the Son, Jesus now offers us. He offers to call us and to usher us into the experience of life of that eternal community, Father, Son and Holy Spirit on an individual basis. Therefore, as you come into this community, you will be empowered and released to love one another as he has loved us. That is how I see it.

On the charge of emotionalism:

> I don't believe the charismatic movement leads you into some kind of emotional "high"; some emotional trip where you live in fantasyland. You are led to face the reality of your lives and your situation. Even if one can say charismatics are emotional in their worship: of course they are. Emotion is part of our total being and God has come to save us, including our emotions. Lutherans, I guess, are probably more guilty than anyone else of wanting to make Christianity a mere intellectual exercise. We somehow think that if we can intellectualise ourselves through our faith, we've got it, and so we eliminate an involvement on the level of all of our life. As I understand the New Testament, the Lord wishes to lead us into an experience of his salvation and life together with the Son of God, which involves our total lives, the full spectrum of all that is us, and hang it all, that's a pretty good salvation! That's what excited me: that I can be involved in this with all that I am, even my ordinary, human, emotional responses, because (let's face it) my emotional responses to things are part of my ordinary human make-up. Therefore, maybe we try to intellectualise our Christian faith to cut out our emotional responses, in order to somehow make it above 'the ordinary', and make it into an intellectual trip.

On his hope for the church:

> What I hope for my church, not just for charismatics and not just for the Lutheran Church (of which I am a pastor and a member) but for the church of Jesus, the body of Christ, is that it will be constantly renewed. That means that people are renewed through the redeeming love of Christ Jesus, through the power of the Holy Spirit, as God reaches down into our ordinariness. ...

That's what I am involved in every day of my life: reaching out to drug addicts and alcoholics and guys who have been blown apart emotionally, and somehow together with brothers and sisters, trying to speak the love of Jesus to all those pieces. We can't do it, only the Holy Spirit can do it; all we can do is to be instruments of the Word.

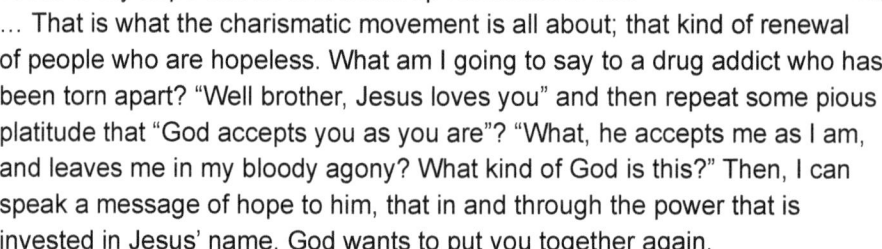

Sure we battle daily with sin, and we always will, but the point is, I do not battle in despair, I do not battle with no hope. I battle as one to whom hope has come, for Jesus is my hope and he has taken up residence in me.
… That is what the charismatic movement is all about; that kind of renewal of people who are hopeless. What am I going to say to a drug addict who has been torn apart? "Well brother, Jesus loves you" and then repeat some pious platitude that "God accepts you as you are"? "What, he accepts me as I am, and leaves me in my bloody agony? What kind of God is this?" Then, I can speak a message of hope to him, that in and through the power that is invested in Jesus' name, God wants to put you together again.

So there is power, but it is powerful life invested in ordinary daily activity. How I relate to my wife, my children, my brothers and sisters around me. God has promised to meet me in all the ordinary circumstances of life. Not in some high quasi-spiritual trip. No sir! I agree with John on that. That's not where God promises to meet us, but rather in the ordinary circumstances of our daily living.

And finally:

What I have personally got out of the charismatic movement is not only an understanding of community I didn't have before, but also an experience of it, which has just revolutionised my whole life and my whole thinking of the life of discipleship to which Jesus has called me. God redeems our brokenness and failures. He comes and he meets us at the point of our brokenness and our spiritual failures. He meets us at that point with the victory of Jesus. That's what I understand the Christian church to be all about; that's what it's always been all about. That's what I understand the message of Martin Luther to be. Luther says that God meets me there, so I don't have to work myself into heaven. Nor do I have to put up with the brokenness either, but as the Lord Jesus said at the beginning of his ministry, "The Spirit of the Lord is upon me, because he has anointed me to bring good news to the poor. He has sent me to proclaim release to the captives and recovery of sight to the blind, to let the oppressed go free, to proclaim the year of the Lord's favour." Praise the Lord!

FURTHER BACKGROUND TO OUR STORY

Conclusion

There are many other documents from this time, including the minutes of the *President's Committee for Pastoral Consultation with Pastor Doug Kuhl and the Elders of Jacob's Ladder* and the undated *A Case for the Outpouring of the Holy Spirit upon our Lives Today* with a response dated 16 December 1975, by Dr EW Janetzki, who was a member of the 'President's Committee'. In addition, there were many articles in our magazines and no doubt other papers. We can't deal with all of them here, or this chapter would be even longer than it is. My intention was just to give an overview and a summary of the main issues. As with the rest of this book, the selection of materials, not to mention the fact that many documents have not survived, means that it is inevitable that mistakes have been made and that the whole story has not been told. I have tried to be fair, but I am also an individual who was a participant in these things, and who has opinions and biases. For that, I apologise, but the alternative was not to tell the story at all.

It is my view that in general, while I respect the Church leaders of the time, they did not respond well to us, and an opportunity was missed for the future of our Church. While we no doubt all had our blind spots and excesses, they by and large, refused to even consider that there was validity in what we were saying. A notable exception was Dr Daniel Overduin, who taught in the community and helped us with our constitution and other documents. All the main players from the Church of that era have gone to their heavenly home, so I have not been able to consult them, for their updated point of view. I considered them all personal friends and had good positive relationships with them going forward into the 1980s and beyond.

There were, of course, also many other church leaders and seminary lecturers from that time who had no involvement in these processes. They are not included in my comments above. Maybe someone else will write another book about the theology of renewal, as it was understood by Jacob's Ladder in the late 1970s, and the Church's response at that time. I have provided only a brief overview.

SECTION VI: THE LASTING IMPACT ON OUR LIVES

CHAPTER 28: Our Individual Stories

We asked each participant in *Jacob's Ladder / Servants of Christ Community* to write a brief reflection on how being part of Jakes impacted the rest of their lives. To keep this manageable, we set a limit of 250 words for individuals and 500 words for couples. Except where noted, each of those who responded wrote their own account. These are their stories.

The 1980 Jakes Reunion

Erika Anear

I started attending Jacob's Ladder as a fifteen year old and was there until the end about seven years later. I only lived in the community for 3 months in the last phase, so I was shaped by the incredible messages from Doug, God filled worship and inspiring people I observed and interacted with mainly on Sundays.

Jakes ignited my desire to know more of God and to be on the cutting edge of what he is doing in the world to bring his Kingdom to earth and I still have that! Jakes ignited my desire to live in community and in recent years, this has been reignited, but because of Jakes I also know that it will come with enormous challenges and opportunities.

The "sold out" for God that I saw in many people then has always influenced my desire to stay sold out for God. Jakes shaped me always to want more of God and to know that he would fulfil that.

The presence of God that was present during our worship times showed me that this was possible—that God could "kiss me" through a song or a sermon that had been written especially for me! Therefore, my life was and is lived knowing that this is possible and being in places where this is happening.

In conclusion the passion, enthusiasm, enjoyment, dedication and love that I saw and experienced among us as we sought and obeyed God has never left me, and I continue this journey that was ignited then.

Knarelle Beard

In early 1974, I visited from Sydney with a busload of other young adult Uniting Church Christians to work in the Kairos Festival. Some of our time was spent in Jacob's Ladder Coffee House where I met local Christians.

Later in the year, I returned for a holiday to hang out with Jakes people—instant friends, crazy fun! They asked me to move to Adelaide to join the community. Someone even offered to find me a comparable job in Adelaide! I said a tentative "Yes…" only to have God whisper inside my head "You come because I call you, not because you're bribed." Three weeks later, having resigned from my job as a graphic artist with no subsequent job in sight, I and my worldly goods moved to Adelaide to join the Jakes community.

I became a Jakes staff member, doing any graphic design and illustration required, including fliers, pamphlets, and *Jacob's Letter* and *Servant* magazines. I also did illustrations for the Uniting and Lutheran Churches.

THE LASTING IMPACT ON OUR LIVES

SECTION VI

CHAPTER 28

Through Jakes I met Rod and Vivi Boucher, who believed in me and encouraged me to put my creativity and faith on the line. We also heard challenging teaching in Jakes (and from visiting speakers) that helped us interrogate our lives and priorities under God.

In 1978 I began work with Adelaide pastor Dr Harry Wendt (Lutheran pastor heading up *Crossways International*) doing the graphics and illustrations for his biblical teaching courses (translated and used throughout the world), work that continued in Adelaide or the USA until 2014.

Richard Berry

I was raised and found the Lord through my parents' ministry in the Salvation Army. I was led into the ministry of outreach through Christian music and travelled to many places in Australia. In 1974, God presented me with the challenge of promoting overseas artists together with those from Oz. Personally, I was active in the local scene with my music and creative ministry and this led to someone contacting me from Jacob's Ladder. From there I spent many happy times with the "Jakes crew", which considerably enriched my spiritual walk. Sharing in meetings at Gawler Place, the houses in Chief Street and the property (old Salvo Church) on Torrens Road, Renown Park. This led to many personal friendships at Jakes being formed, which still blossom today. I would have to say, one such person was the late Julie Anne McBride (née Lambert) who was a personal friend of my family and we were able to be involved in her growing ministry.

God showed me a lot through Jacob's Ladder, which I believe was unique, both then and now. My work broadened over 20 years and I established *Solsound Promotions of South Australia* and was able to bring Barry McGuire and Paul Stookey (of Peter, Paul & Mary) to fellowship at Gawler Place. I am so grateful for the way Jakes ministry (thanks Doug Kuhl) enriched my life! It is a special part of my "ministry memories".

Val and Trevor Brooks

We came into community having already begun working with street kids as we called them. We were married December 1970 and moved into a house with another Christian girl, Meredith Ross, with the express purpose of opening our home to the homeless. The Easter weekend after our wedding we had 27 souls stay with us in our three-bedroom home. When we left our nurture house at Winchester Street, we took David Skeat with us and continued taking in teenagers for about another ten years. What Jakes had taught us was twofold; what was the value of church community and the very necessity of community.

Jakes still remains strong in my mind as a great example of what it means to be church. There was generosity in sharing time and possessions; practical love. Jakes is the nearest I have come to experiencing what we are told in Acts: "and all who believed were together and had all things in common." One of the books I read while at Jakes was *Living Together in a World Falling Apart*, which had as its theme, "Live simply so that others may simply live." This became the motive for the rest of our lives. It engraved in Valerie and me a deep desire to be generous in sharing our lives with others and living as frugally as we could. The spiritual fellowship we knew in Jakes flavoured our understanding of Church, and I have not found a fellowship that has come anywhere near it since. Sometimes I hear brethren saying, "Oh, we are a New Testament church," which normally means we don't want much to do with the Old Testament: a foolish thought. Jakes to me, was the nearest I have come to knowing a church that lived as the New Testament church lived. Jakes affected Valerie and my lives in that we wanted to live this way at all times.

The second thing we learnt from our time in Jakes was the strong necessity that such fellowships have to be supported by the church as a whole. At that time there were three main street communities. Jakes, House of the Rock and The Jesus Centre. Each of these in the end had to close down. I believe the main cause of this was the lack of support that these groups received from the mainline churches. Working with street people was an emotionally draining experience. Christian brethren who couldn't join the intense community lifestyle could have offered support in many ways, but on the whole, it seems they simply backed away. It was akin to sending our missionaries out and then abandoning them.

Valerie and I left Jakes with a deep awareness of the beauty of the Church and also how frail it can be. We were grateful that Jesus told us that he was building his church. How did Jakes influence the rest of Val and my lives? It gave us a blueprint of how church ought to be, and a deep desire to let Jesus build us into his church.

[Val was called home in 1993]

THE LASTING IMPACT ON OUR LIVES

SECTION VI — CHAPTER 28

Monica and Ivan Christian

As I write these words at the age of 71, I look back on my story as a young woman, raised in a Lutheran Manse, with not much knowledge of and experience in anything. Music was my special love, and it was while singing with Brian Loffler and Tim Jaensch at the 'coffee lounge' in the Unley Lutheran Church hall, that I met Geoff Strelan. During the previous years I had also been a youth leader, and perhaps this is why Geoff phoned me, as I noted in my diary, with 'his idea'. He asked me to join him and Milton Eckermann as a founding member of the Dorian Society. It was a small group with big ideas about sharing our faith and encouraging others to do the same.

This story is not about the Dorian Society as such, but without us, perhaps Jacob's Ladder may not have eventuated. We were involved from the very beginning, checking out and agreeing on the available space, finding second-hand and new items, deciding on layout, setting up the kitchen and planning our initial limited menu.

In retrospect, it amazes me how much time and energy we made available for the beginnings of Jacob's Ladder. What a dream, and what an all-consuming project for us, only just out of our teens and some of us newly married! And how many of our friends and siblings were drawn in to help us with the painting, setting up 'the tent', and the layout, especially the kitchen. Thank you all.

Ivan Christian and I were married in August 1969, so Ivan too was very much part of the Jacob's Ladder scene before it began and in its early days. At that stage, Ivan was at Uni doing a Bachelor of Arts as a pre-seminary student. He remembers going downstairs talking to people on the streets and inviting them in. While he later decided to become a high school teacher, he has never stopped sharing the Gospel.

We had a serious car accident on 17 May 1971. We recall visiting Jakes after my recovery, but we were no longer involved. Our memories are a bit hazy from this period, but at some stage our involvement ceased. However, we have continued to serve as a couple, supporting one another as needed in our careers, recognising each other's abilities and sharing our combined gift of hospitality. Perhaps that began with Jacob's Ladder.

Vera Crane

My spiritual walk began as a Greek Orthodox, then a Catholic, but by the age of fifteen, I could not see the point of "Church", so I stopped going. With one thing and another, I found myself divorced with a young baby by 23. Not the outcome I expected.

But God had a plan.

Friends took me to this wild upstairs joint in Gawler Place. I found God's love through a crazy lot of Jesus people. I found my answer, a vision, a family, a community of believers who showed me on whom to build the rest of my life, Jesus Christ, and that is what I did.

I was very sad and wished that it had not ended. I loved the lifestyle so much that I joined Manoah for a few years afterwards.

And now, all these years later, I live in a unit in a group of ten in Clarence Park, and am still trying to capture that "community" spirit. I have taken the role of Presiding Officer and continuing to actively interact and care for those around me in a spirit of service, which we learnt through those years.

My heart is still yearning for that special community connection that we had in Jacob's Ladder. As I ponder my final years, I want to continue to live in close relationship with others. Perhaps it will be a Retirement Village. Perhaps it will be an intentional community in the form of our own retirement village… now there's a thought.

Michelle Gibson

I moved into Winchester Street Malvern community houses with Trevor and Val Brooks and their two children. I was 18 years old and this was my first time living out of home. I loved it! What an amazing adventure I was on with God. Totally naive and idealistic, I observed and learned. I received a good grounding in Lutheran theology from Pastor Doug, which has buoyed me along to this day, and the gentle Holy Spirit who is always with me.

I married Bonny Gibson whom I met in the community. Bonny and I went to YWAM in England to do their Discipleship Training School at Holmsted Manor in West Sussex in 1983. Our outreach phase was in Amsterdam with Floyd McClung and Urban Missions.

We came back with a vision of starting a Christian Motorcycle Club to minister to those who would not consider going into a church. Our two sons Aaron and Zane were born in 1984 and 1988. During this time we worked together with Mac and Jen Hayes and several couples in Melbourne and 1989 saw the birth of Longriders Christian Motorcycle Club Adelaide and Melbourne chapters on the same day.

THE LASTING IMPACT ON OUR LIVES

SECTION VI

CHAPTER 28

I am so grateful for my six years living in Jacob's Ladder Community. The relationships I established there were life changing and in many instances lifelong. It was foundational for me in my faith and relationship with God, which continues to meander through life-giving vistas and wonderful adventures.

Janet Haar

I first came to Jacob's Ladder through the invitation of three young men who lived in the flat opposite mine, in suburban Adelaide. It was during a time in my life when I was cautious and feeling the need for space; having just experienced a breakup with someone I was serious about. I did not know much about the Coffee Lounge or the Lutheran Church. I came from a Catholic background. But later, when I did accept that invite, I found the workers at Jakes were committed to reaching out to street kids and those living on the edge.

I started reading the Bible and still gratefully remember the diverse group of people who led various faith workshops. Eventually I took Confirmation lessons with Pastor Doug Kuhl, and I eagerly embraced the teaching of being saved by grace.

As I got to know the Jakes community, I became part of their journey in an ongoing ministry to whomever walked up the stairs and through the doors. The encouragement, mentoring, times of discovery I received, and the feeling of being valued and understood, shaped and equipped me for a future God-centred ministry with my husband, Stephen, in the Lutheran Church.

I am thankful for the many beautiful people that were part of that journey, and for our God who never gives up on anyone; who through the ministry of Jacob's Ladder and the wider church have grounded and centred me in the faith. The journey continues and I always take the opportunity to share with others what God has done for me, and how a simple invitation reset my compass for life.

Stephen Haar

I was only sixteen when I began pastoral studies at Luther Seminary in 1972. In my first years of study, I discovered that I had an imperfect faith; and, that this was a wonderful thing. As I wrestled with Church teachings, and the writings of theologians, I discovered how much I resonated with the prayerful cry of the man in the gospels: *"Lord, I believe; help my unbelief."*

Our Individual Stories // 223

I was only nineteen when I found myself climbing the stairs to Jacob's Ladder Coffee Lounge. As challenging as those days and conversations were, with people from the street who climbed those same stairs, I learned further lessons about leaning on God's grace in a life of discipleship involving head, heart, and hand.

The bedrock grace of God has been the constant in my service as a pastor, teacher, and leader. More than forty years on, I remember Jacob's Ladder community as forming and informing me about how to stand authentically with people who struggle with faith and doubt, by leaning on grace: the accepting, loving presence of God, in Jesus Christ. Mission and ministry are not based solely on our abilities but on a gracious God who works through imperfect people to achieve the perfect work of faith. What a wonderful thing it was to learn that stepping out in faith begins with our imperfection; and then the Holy Spirit, working through the gospel wrapped in human words and actions, brings the perfect love of God to others.

Peter Jasprizza

There is no question that the Holy Spirit and the incredible Power of God was upon that place and in the lives of the people who belonged to Jacob's Ladder.

When the community dissolved, I was a mess. I had no idea what to do. I took my small family to Sydney and stayed with Doug Kuhl for a time and then returned to Adelaide. Suffice it to say that I did not have the capacity of mind as a family man to make good decisions. I tried studying theology and while I got good grades, I knew after one year that being a Pastor was not for me. My decision not to continue with the study caused our family to disintegrate. I was lost and alone again. God had given me a new life and I had ruined it. Depression loomed and I buried myself in work. It seemed to me that no one from the community wanted to know me anymore, as I was a failure as a Christian. I was a backslider.

Thirty or so years later, I am retired after a successful career in IT. I still feel that glow in my heart from the memories of experiences I had at Jakes but at the same time, I carry a great sadness. My heart is broken over the loss of my family and the damage I caused to my children and others. Without knowing God's forgiveness I would have been gone long before now. I pray and shed tears as I listen to Spirit-filled singers on YouTube. That is what keeps me alive now, together with the love of my new family.

THE LASTING IMPACT ON OUR LIVES

Ava Leitner

Jakes was instrumental in my making a decision to live for Jesus in my late teens.

The teaching of holiness and cost of discipleship remain with me. Along with memories of doing life with such a diverse group of enthusiasts for Jesus, some of whom became lifelong friends. The kind that stick through thick and thin times. After leaving Jakes I had the opportunity of living at Manoah and then YWAM.

Like so many others I had no idea of how wounded I was when I came to Jesus through Jakes. The call on my life never lifted and he has once again brought me to a group of radical Jesus people, passionate about seeing heaven blossom on earth. I am so grateful that he remained faithful wherever I was in relation to him.

The ministry to the streets and outlaw bikers of Jakes holds a special place in my heart. Whilst there is no motorbike these days, the winds of his Spirit are blowing. Just as the songs we sang then created a movement.

Kevin Lieschke

How can one live an "ordinary" life when they have been "spoiled for the ordinary"? Prior to Jakes, I had been impacted by contact with some friends who had been 'Jesus People' at the beginning of 1974 in Sydney, where I had gone to attend the Lutheran Youth Convention. Coming to know Jesus as a real person and then asking him what he wanted me to do, straight after finishing Year 12, was the reason I ended up in Adelaide. I was looking for others who knew Jesus like I did, and I found that in Jakes.

Jakes people took things beyond the traditional religion I had known all my life, to radical discipleship—taking Jesus' words literally and attempting to live them in community. Taking in the homeless, the addicted, the disabled, and the mentally ill. No small feat, and with varied success, at the same time as marriage and kids, holding families together.

When the formal community came to a close and we and a small band of others moved to Sydney, again it was reaching out to the dispossessed, the poor, the socially disadvantaged. It led me to work in the hardest areas of welfare, and to make a difference in the systems of the day. Spoiled for the ordinary—and loving it.

Re-making the connections with those we shared those brief years with in the 1970s is always a pleasure. I also continue to have a love of two wheels and connections with guys who love motorbikes and adventure.

Marcia Lieschke

I feel blessed that I came into contact with the ministry of Jacob's Ladder during those usual years of turmoil in late teens. I had already given my life over to Christ, so it is no surprise that he should lead me into a community where I could learn more of his ways and grow.

I believe I had and have to this day a calling to work among the needy of our world. I engaged in ministry among some very needy people in Jakes. I grew to love community life and this has drawn me to the communities I have been a part of over the last 40 years.

I have a gift to sing and during the years in Jakes, I found a place to gain confidence to sing openly as a soloist and in public. My love to worship Jesus in a creative and contemporary way was supported by those around me. In the 1980s and onward, I became involved in some worship conferences/events in Sydney and later on the NSW Central Coast that we believe brought forth a new sound in worship across this nation. I would never have had the confidence to be a part of this as a soloist singer, and in the administration of these conferences/events, had I not experienced those few years of support from my Jakes days.

To this day, I fondly remember and am grateful to the Jakes community, for it changed my life and forged a pathway for God's plan and purpose for me.

Julie Anne McBride (Lambert)[164]

Julie Anne was born with cerebral palsy. From late 1975 she and her wheelchair were regular features in the life of the community. Getting up the stairs to the Coffee House was a challenge but it happened regularly. She spoke of Jacob's Ladder when she and Neville were interviewed for a story in *Alive Magazine* in February 1999:

> It was through the care of the Jacob's Ladder community that Julie Anne moved from being a nominal Christian to a living relationship with God. … With the support of the community, Julie Anne grew into a new

---

[164] Written by Steen in consultation with Neville.

THE LASTING IMPACT ON OUR LIVES

SECTION vi

CHAPTER 28

independence, and she moved into a community house. She in turn began caring for others. … Julie Anne had a growing desire to set up a community house for people with disabilities. … The simple lessons that Julie Anne had learned at Jacob's Ladder—cooking and washing, interdependence and meaningful existence—she now passed on to others. Over the next four years, 50 people moved through the house.[165]

Julie Anne had been told she shouldn't expect upfront roles because no one would put up with her spasms and speech, yet she spoke at hundreds of meetings over the years.[166] She married Neville McBride in April 1986. Together they established the Koinonia Trust, an outreach ministry that emphasises the needs and the abilities of people with disabilities, their families, carers and friends. She was called home on the 4th August 2019. The Adelaide Advertiser printed her obituary on 16 November 2019, reporting that in 1983 she entered the Miss Australia Quest to challenge people's ideas of what was normal and beautiful.

Constantine (Kon) Michailidis

I became a visitor to Jakes in 1977/78 and loved the vibe. The music was great, especially those out of the Catholic Charismatic Songbook. I became good friends with people like David Skeat, Phil Jefferis and Knarelle Beard. I visited when it moved to Torrens Road and stayed when it became Truth and Light Christian Fellowship, led by David Trudinger, Glen Heidenreich, Ian Wade and others. I would regularly visit Manoah in the Adelaide Hills when it began and received much blessing and encouragement from the Heidenreichs and almost joined that community. In 1979 I taught at Trinity Christian School, Rosewater, where Peter Schubert was principal. Helen Wade also taught there. The Kuhl and Wade children attended.

I then entered Bible College and in 1983 the Lord led me to Redfern, Sydney, to join the Kuhls at the Coolibah Community, which became Elijah Task Ministries. David and Marie Skeat had been there but left to join YWAM by the time I arrived. Kevin and Marcia Lieschke and their girls were there. I became a deacon in that church where Doug was pastor. I left in 1984 and worked with the Department of Community Services. I married in 1992. In 1997, my wife and I began *Yeshua Tsidkenu*, a Russian-speaking Messianic Jewish congregation, under the *Christian & Missionary Alliance* who ordained me as

---

165 Anne Bartlett, **Ready, Willing & Disabled**, *Alive* (February 1999), 26–28.

166 ibid., 28.

a minister. I am retired from secular work, but we still pastor that congregation in Sydney.

Jakes / Servants of Christ / Truth and Light / Manoah / the Kuhls were a treasured part of my early life as a Christian.

Lyn Muller

A chance encounter with Phil Jefferis in January 1976 ... I had just finished my University degree and was enjoying the summer holidays. Would I be involved with a Drama Group going to Tunarama in Port Lincoln on the January long weekend? This group was part of a Christian 'outreach' by Jacob's Ladder. I had been involved with drama and dance groups for some time and enjoyed participating in the creative arts. So I agreed.

On my return to Adelaide after this weekend, I started to attend Jacob's Ladder for their worship sessions, and became involved with the drama group. I continued dancing with an International Dance group, where we learnt folk dances from many nationalities. The Christian Dance Fellowship in Australia was just beginning, and I was among the founding members in South Australia.

I moved into a community house in Croydon, where Peter Muller was the resident 'elder' at the ripe age of 21. I was working full-time by then as a Medical Scientist at the QEH. We had several street kids staying at any one time, so we had some interesting times. After the community disbanded, we moved to Port Adelaide Uniting Church, along with Colin and Chris Tierney-Smith, with whom I remained close friends. We continued our love of music, drama and dance there together. I had dance group and children's dance classes there for another 18 years.

Ruth and Steen Olsen

We got married in May 1974. After six months, we were leading a girls' house in Goodwood, followed by the large house in Queen Street, Norwood, together with Karl Brettig in 1975 and then the Frederick Street, Welland house through 1976. In 1977 we moved to Toowoomba, Queensland, where Steen was assigned to serve his internship as a Seminary student and then our final year back in Adelaide. Steen graduated at the end of 1978 and we served parishes in the Hunter Valley, NSW (1979–85), Tuggeranong ACT / Cooma NSW (1985–1993), and Christchurch NZ

THE LASTING IMPACT ON OUR LIVES

(1993–1995) before Steen served as bishop of the Lutheran Church of New Zealand for twelve years and finally as Director for Mission for the Lutheran Church in South Australia and the Northern Territory for a decade. Now we are retired in North Eastern Adelaide.

Along the way we helped establish and lead the *Kogudus* retreat ministry, Ruth edited an intercessors newsletter, cared for many people and was involved in music in worship, and Steen served on more committees and commissions than he cares to remember. We raised a couple of kids, lived in many different houses and worked with people from many different denominations, backgrounds and ethnicities.

In Jacob's Ladder we were privileged to be part of a missional community before such a thing had a name. We learned that the church was sent by God into his world by being participants in a group of people who were doing it. We were thrust into leadership roles and discovered that involved community discernment, and supporting the roles of others. We saw many people come to discover the love of Jesus and then find that they, in turn, loved Jesus right back. We discovered that it wasn't the end of the world when things went wrong. We made mistakes and found that God still worked and that his promises remained trustworthy. In living and working with kids who were involved with bikie and street gangs and drugs, we were often out of our depth and comfort zone, but we discovered courage and abilities that surprised us.

For Steen, in particular, dealing with church leaders and needing to discuss theology with theologians who questioned our orthodoxy, was an education in itself. Little did he know! For Ruth it was pivotal in beginning to recognise the Holy Spirit as a person, not a neutral 'it', enabling her to begin taking steps she hadn't dreamt possible. That paved the way for discovering much in walking with Jesus and coming to know God as 'Abba Father'. She learnt to break through the fear barrier and use spiritual gifts in serving people over the years since then. Certainly an adventure.

Through it all God was working in and through us at the time, while also preparing us for what lay ahead. That journey is not yet at an end. We are still learning and growing, but we look back on our time in Jakes as foundational.

Lyn and Malcolm Pech

We met with Milton Eckermann and Geoff Strelan. We discussed the idea of a coffee lounge in Gawler Place to cater for the fellowship needs of Lutheran youth coming to the city from the country; for work or study. Malley was in that category, arriving at the Lutheran Youth Hostel in Wayville in January 1969, to begin a Fitting and Turning apprenticeship at Chrysler Australia Ltd at Tonsley Park. The first action that he recalls, after inspecting the premises upstairs in Gawler Place, was to go to an auction at a hotel on Richmond Rd to buy dining furniture and other requirements. We bought lots of square tables and cream-fabric upholstered chairs.

Once set up we needed kitchen workers, waiters and managers. Malley was one of the six or so inaugural managers, along with his flatmates Chris Rothe and Glenn Schultz. Once underway we received help from youth of the Metropolitan South Zone and Metropolitan North Zone. A lot of time was spent getting to know the people who came into Jakes, and the managers realised that we needed people who could just sit at table and talk. We then chose people who were called counsellors.

We were married in May 1973, and we lived in a house in Parkside. On two occasions, we took in folk for the night that we had met at Jakes. One time it was three blokes from Perth, travelling to the East Coast. They had run out of money. The next day they sold their Pontiac car and left us with a toolbox and towrope that they were not able to take with them as they continued by coach.

Another time it was a weedy little guy and his petite girlfriend. They stayed the night—in separate rooms—and when in the morning we found them in the same bed Malley did his offended Christian morals act. They left. With his wallet, he later discovered. They came back to Jakes later and Malley challenged the little guy when he met him on the stairs. He gave Malley a black eye. He never saw it coming. Beware the little guy!

In mid 1974, we decided to move to Port Lincoln where Malley had applied to work for Co-op Bulk Handling as a maintenance fitter. We moved in September 1974, and this was really the end of our relationship with Jakes. When we returned to Adelaide in 1977, we had two sons and Jakes had moved on. As did we. We settled at Morphett Vale and became part of the Calvary Lutheran worshipping community. Malley answered the call to the ordained ministry in 1993 when he began his study at Luther Seminary (then Luther Campus). Our preparation for pastoral ministry had begun long before this, 23 years earlier, when we became part of what was to become known as the ministry of 'Jakes'.

THE LASTING IMPACT ON OUR LIVES

Naomi Rosenberg

In January 1975 my close girlfriend Marcia asked me to Swan Reach where she was cutting apricots. That weekend was my introduction not only to my future husband but also to many new friends who were part of the Jacob's Ladder (Jakes) community. After marrying and spending 17 months living on our own we moved into a community house as the leaders where we had more mature Christians than non-Christians living with us. Our goal was to help the non-Christians emotionally, physically and spiritually.

Living in a community house with others was a full and rewarding experience. It was not always easy but the benefits out-weighed the negative times. The memories I have include eating blue coloured rice, coming home to fish swimming in the bath and my coffee percolator working overtime but not for me!

On Sundays, we had great worship times at Jacob's Ladder. The teaching by Doug was fantastic. It was very good grounding for my life ahead. I have fond recollections of liturgical dances, dramas and talented songwriters and musos/singers.

After the community dissolved, I continued on my Christian walk as part of various denominations. I worked in the field of nursing until the age of 45, and then after 5 years of theological study, I started working as a Pastor in the Uniting Church. Many friends made at Jakes have been life-long, and I am very pleased God took me to Swan Reach all those years ago!

Marty Rosenberg

In 1974, the work at Jakes caught my attention because it was ministering to unchurched people that the church seemed to have no way of reaching. What also attracted me to it was the teaching, both about relationships and the Bible within the context of its culture and history. I also read and listened to teaching that had a current, Christian world view, sociologically and theologically.

There were others my age who were also on this journey and together our faith was strengthened and our relationships deepened. In hindsight, I can say that Jakes gave me the most accelerated growth-spurt to my faith in my entire life. The pre-conceived ideas of my faith were tested, and I was often challenged by people with very different backgrounds to mine, to give an account of my faith and to explain why I believed in Jesus.

Because Jakes quickly became a functioning community that I was proud to be a part of, I could very easily invite people into it to taste and see how we lived our lives as Christians.

I met Naomi from outside of Jakes, and we, along with the other couples in the community had children, beginning a whole new need to develop the "community" aspect, as well as the outreach.

Since Jakes disbanded in 1979, I have been a Social Worker (8yrs), Federal Police Agent (16yrs), Backpacker Owner (3yrs), and a Minister in the Uniting Church (13yrs), with 1 wife, 3 children and 11 grandchildren.

Judy Rosindale-Smith (Fiegert/Peacey)

In 1973, while working for the Lutheran Mission in Papua New Guinea I read in "The Lutheran" periodical that a new venture to reach homeless people and drug addicts, street kids, was starting in Adelaide. Before my return from PNG, I resolved to be involved in this "Jacobs' Ladder" venture. When I got back, I commenced my Midwifery training at the Queen Victoria Hospital and was involved with the Jacob's Ladder ministry one night of most weekends. Each Sunday we had church in the coffee lounge, which I loved.

During the whole time of my involvement with "Jacobs' Ladder" and later "Truth and Light" my knowledge of the Bible and scripture increased as never before or since. Pastor Doug Kuhl took us on a journey basing our lives on the book of Acts. I lived in community houses for a couple of years, with part of that time at Queen Street, Norwood.

At the "Truth and Light" venue, I enjoyed singing in the band for contemporary church. One day at Manoah Christian community Judith Heidenreich prayed for me for emotional healing. So amazing. The healing was like warm oil going down through my veins from my scalp to my feet and it felt like I was walking on a big rubber ball for 12 months after this prayer and my emotional healing was so complete. At that same time, I received the gift of speaking in tongues. In retrospect, my life was richly impacted by a deep and fulfilling Christian experience that I treasure.

Anthea Rothe

The memories and experiences of that short time in community living have had a lasting impact. Soon after getting married in 1978, we bought a house in West Hindmarsh where the Mullers, Peaceys and Tierney-Smiths lived

THE LASTING IMPACT ON OUR LIVES

SECTION vi

CHAPTER 28

within walking distance. This meant we could share resources easily. I learnt to hold possessions lightly. It is easy to give things to people who need them because whenever I need something God provides. The highlight of the week was Community Tea (on Monday night I think it was) at somebody's home. It wasn't tightly organised, just bring whatever food you wanted to share then we would eat together, worship and pray. I loved the free-form worship, and the openness and the love-in-action I experienced there.

Every fellowship group I've been in since then has listened to me profess that a "Second Chapter of Acts" society is possible because I have lived it! I trust Jakes people with my life, and my failures; the connection and commitment is still real. When our son Samuel suffered a major head injury at age 11, Karl Brettig heard about it and mobilised prayer support with people we'd never met. When I finally accepted that my 37-year marriage was over, a 'chance' meeting with Naomi at our grandchildren's school provided me with counselling and support. I am so grateful for the way Jakes people stepped into the new thing that God was doing in the 70s and the courage it gives me to step into a new future.

Chris Schubert

Perhaps most importantly, it was through Jakes that I met Peter (Bert); a significant, wonderful, and ongoing impact indeed. Beyond that? In the early 2000s, I encountered the following, "Faith is *caught* in relationships, usually, but not always, in the family home". This has become my 'mantra for evangelism'. I think it resonated with me, in part, because of my experiences in Jakes. I remember that during my earliest interactions at Jakes, I was struck by the ease with which matters of faith were part of our conversations. We had real—where the rubber hits the road—conversations, with each other, and with those we met in outreach. As I have gone on, and out, from Jakes, I have desired to live grace, and to have conversations like that, so that, perhaps, others might glimpse our amazing Papa God in me, and faith might be caught in my relationships. I have tried to live that 'relationship evangelism', for example, in my parenting; through involvement in various Bible Study groups; living and working for the LCA in PNG; and while working at Scripture Union Bookshop and Scripture Union SA.

A quite different impact of my time at Jakes is that, sub-consciously, I think I took some version of a *Vow of Poverty*, which has manifested as a strong reluctance to spend money, particularly on myself, my home etc. I continue to work through the good and bad of this, and clearly its origins are complex, but I do think it began in the ethos of Jakes.

Peter Schubert aka Bert

In 1972, I was a first-year student at Adelaide Teachers College. While hanging out one Saturday night, someone suggested that we go to Jacob's Ladder. I had no idea that this venture would lead to a pivotal time in my faith journey. I remember ascending the three flights of wooden stairs, walking into a dimly lit room filled with young people, loud music and warm vibes. At evening's end, two announcements were made. One was an appeal for helpers. The other an invitation to people who needed help to make themselves known. I found myself drawn in. I offered my services as a helper. Before long, I was attending training sessions that empowered me to become a "faith sharer" which found me sitting among young people who had come off the streets and sharing the love of Jesus with them. My faith grew stronger as it was being challenged and I wanted to have the answers. It seemed a natural progression to take young homeless people into our homes where we could mentor and nurture their faith. What a joy to have Jacob's Ladder open on a Sunday morning for worship where the Spirit moved through the teaching, the prayers, the fellowship, and the songs.

For sure there were challenges, scary moments, and times when I wondered what God had called me into. But on reflection, I am grateful that God led me up those stairs. The time at Jakes was a touchstone of living life in Christian fellowship; of following God's calling; of being open to his Spirit; being kind, caring and sharing the love of Jesus with others.

Anne Sellers

Raisin toast, grilled cheese sandwiches and hot chocolate were some of the attractions at Jacob's Ladder Coffee House. I joined my church youth group to prepare food and chat with guests at the coffee house. It was the most interesting thing in my life. The Coffee Lounge grew into a community/church. Pastor Doug was a gifted Bible teacher, and I drank in knowledge, prayer, and fellowship. I played piano and flute in the worship band, which played for many "Celebrations", weddings, and large conferences. Leading worship with this band was a highlight of my life.

After SOCC dissolved, I felt sad and lacked purpose. I sought another community of Christians who were impacting the world. I joined YWAM in 1980 and later attended an evangelism program in the USA. I stayed at YWAM Salem and served in various leadership roles and outreach teams

THE LASTING IMPACT ON OUR LIVES

around the world. I enjoyed helping others identify their gifts/talents through an assessment system, which prepared teams for ministry in Mongolia, Mexico and other places. Mongolia now has a thriving church of over 100,000 Christians, which was started by people who trained at YWAM Salem.

After 14 years at YWAM Salem, I was ready for a change, so I attended university and earned a Business degree. I met Tom Callaghan at church and we married in 1999. We lived in Australia for 5 years and enjoyed time with my family, especially my Mum in her last years. Tom's mother had health struggles, so we returned to Oregon in 2015 to stabilize her life. We are active in a Salem church.

David Skeat

The events that surrounded the formation and disbandment of Jacob's Ladder / Servants of Christ Community were extraordinary. Now 40 years on many of us can look back and recognise that this was a time in which God was at work in the lives of a group of people who just wanted to love and follow Jesus. We were all drawn from many different backgrounds and had our own strengths and weaknesses, but we dared to believe that God would use us to change the world, and He did!

The years of prayer, worship and radical discipleship provided a hothouse for this group and we were stamped with an indelible desire to serve Jesus and to fulfil the great commission. There were many prophecies about how we would affect the nations, and when it all ended some of us wondered how these prophecies could come true, but God is always faithful to His word.

For me and my family, we ended up in YWAM, and have been career missionaries. As individuals, our family has travelled to over 30 different nations. Personally, I have either taught or preached the Gospel in over 20 nations, have established ministries that have reached out to the poor, taken on issues that are related to social justice, have established specialist ministries for disaster relief, and medical training interventions that improve health care in remote poor communities.

The values that are behind these ministry outcomes were first instilled in me through the Jakes hothouse. After Jakes, we launched out to find our way. As we followed Jesus, God provided direction and growth; the rest is history! But for me, Jakes was a key factor in helping me to recognize and follow my life's calling.

Geoff Turner aka Scrooge

From a very early age, I have had the personal sense of a closeness with the one I have come to know as 'God', and whom Jesus calls our Heavenly Father. In the early 1980s, Ava and our young family at the time went on a working holiday to Canberra for a Discipleship Training School and then onto Auckland for two years on a Crossway School of Evangelism, both run by *Youth With A Mission*. The highlight was to be involved in a cross-cultural outreach in Tonga. Back in Australia, we built a home in the Adelaide Hills in Lobethal where I began to run a painting and sign writing business from home.

After our marriage broke up, I married Rosalie and for almost the next thirty years, we continued with my vocational career at Lobethal in painting, decorating and sign writing. We remained members of various Lutheran fellowships over this period, with Rosalie exercising a wonderful gift of choral leading and music ministry. We shared a passion for seeing both environs and people 'come alive' again through Christ. I had a speciality in Heritage Decoration and did extensive study to develop this area and then moved into training and assessment of apprentices. My dear Rosalie died in 2017.

My years of experiencing discipleship and leadership in the Jacob's Ladder / Servants of Christ, Christian marriage and at Manoah, consolidated the realisation that our faith walk is best worked out through varied expressions of Christian Community. The image and the character of God in his Fatherly heart expressed in the life and ministry of Jesus has been my inspiration and passion.

Doug Vogelsang

After Jakes I resigned from the State Valuation Office. I took an overseas trip visiting a Catholic rehabilitation community in the Philippines for two weeks. Then onto Hong Kong and stayed with a pastor who was involved in the massive influx of boat people from Cambodia. From there I went into China for ten days, then onto a Christian Community in Ann Arbor, USA for two weeks, followed by Indianapolis to visit Dr Harry Wendt of *Crossways International*.

Coming back to Australia I decided to go to Luther Seminary (1980–1981). This was not for me. In April 1981 I attended the LCA Synod in Sydney and met Prue. We had known each other since the 50s through youth meetings. We then kept in touch (Prue lived in Sydney) and in April 1982 we got engaged and married in December 1982.

THE LASTING IMPACT ON OUR LIVES

SECTION vi

CHAPTER 28

I then went back to the State Valuation Office and worked in various offices. We went to Murray Bridge where I became involved in the Holy Cross Congregation, then returned to Adelaide for a few years, then moved to Port Augusta and worked there for 21 years until I retired in 2009. I served in the Congregation in Port Augusta in several capacities. I enjoyed the country work. We returned to Tanunda and worship at St Paul's Congregation.

My involvement with Jakes has given me a wider vision and understanding of the people who need to have an emptiness filled and young people who do not have their needs met.

Helen and Ian Wade

When we think of Jacob's Ladder, we think of all the people we met, worked with, prayed for and even "struggled" with in many areas. Our memories hold both joy and some sadness.

When we became a part of Jakes we began a life living "by faith", a new adventure in trusting Jesus. We grew differently than we could ever have anticipated. It included testing and growth in many areas of our lives. Ian says we "grew taller in Jesus".

Ian's role as an elder in the Community was established at about the same time as the Servants of Christ Community was formed.

"Servants of Christ" was an apt name for the Community as we aimed to serve the surrounding community. A major area aiming to fulfil this was the establishment of a large number of Community Houses. These "homes" provided safe homes for, as we called them, "street kids". They also provided many opportunities for personal ministry to a wide cross-section of people. Living with previously unknown, mostly young people, was both rewarding and testing. We were enriched through this necessarily intense situation.

Jacob's Ladder, the Drop In Centre, had a strong influence on the Adelaide CBD street scene. It was estimated that up to 200 people had weekly contact with us. Ian had a major part in these first contacts. His position at Jakes was basically to "hold the fort" as it were, to receive visitors, to listen, encourage and be a mentor. He also could refer them on to the elders for possible placement in a Community House or contact with others in the ministry team.

Many varied areas of expertise were established as the Community grew. Ian established a woodworking workshop at the rear of one of the houses.

Some Community members made furniture items. One was a bedhead. Others mended. Due to this, opportunities for growing relationships and Christian witness were promoted.

Music became a strong part of Community life, not only during Praise and Worship during Sunday Celebration times but also in keeping up with Christian music of the day. The group "Second Chapter of Acts" was popular. Helen played piano before the Celebrations at times—a privilege. The Community was involved, along with other church groups and individuals who had been touched by the Holy Spirit during the Charismatic Movement during the 70's, in sponsoring some Christian singers from overseas. We were both involved in these large concerts.

Overall, the Jakes / Servants of Christ Community experience was a deep work of God in our lives. He used this time to teach us about ourselves, how much he loves others, how each one is His "Holy Ground". Most of all, we once again found that we just can't do without Him!

Lindsay Webb

It was June 1979, just after my 21st birthday that I moved into a recently established community house in Aroona Road Kilkenny. The initial residents were me, Peter, Tom, Jeff and Hamish.

The experience, I think for us all, was very dysfunctional. It was an old stone house. Basic facilities such as stove and shower didn't operate properly. We came from vastly differing backgrounds. I was in my final year of a teaching diploma; Peter worked at Mitsubishi; and as I recall, Hamish had a health background possibly nursing; and Jeff a trade background. Tom appeared to have no fixed employment. Our relationship was very disjointed. In many ways we lived separate lives and there was no real house 'leader'. It was more a house full of Christians, rather than a Christian household. Hamish's stay was short lived as he decided the house was too disorderly for him to live in, and Jeff moved out later to get married. The arrival unannounced, of a young single mother with a toddler only added to the disruption and a great deal of animosity ensued between us and her.

In spite of these trials, it was a time of my faith's consolidation, of love and nurturing, when I met many new Christian brothers and sisters in the wider Jakes community.

THE LASTING IMPACT ON OUR LIVES

Sheila and Stan Whittam

Our encounter with Jakes led us to a challenging time in the Lutheran Church at Lowbank. We were new Christians in a very conservative church. This was in 1979. So radical was this exposure that it landed us in hot water, and we were excommunicated. It didn't hurt us at all, as we did not know what it meant! We really just wondered where we belonged. However, it was a freeing time to get more involved in the Waikerie community and with the itinerant workers there. We started a church!

Sheila remembers how we had learned from Doug Kuhl and others to look for guidance from the Lord and believe it, and to look for the accompanying signs by the Holy Spirit. It seemed easy … remember we were new Christians. Many, many times guidance aligned and showed us amazing things about our personal walk and the little ministry we had, which actually turned part of the church life in the Riverland upside down!

Stan recalls that we were stirred to think of the wider picture and through this it became clear that cross-cultural ministry was for us. We left our home and our kids who were then aged 20, 18 and 15. WEC International sent us to Ghana in West Africa. It was the most difficult Christian experience we have ever had! We experienced the loss of our identities and in yielding to the team's demands; we essentially felt a loss of care. Although we stayed for two years of training and then the four years overseas that we had committed to, we arrived home broken.

In hindsight, this was a proving or testing time for our faith. We remembered that many others in ministry also suffered. We see suffering in the Acts of the Apostles and this was also confirmed when we travelled to other parts of the world and saw that Christian ministry is not necessarily a glory trip. The Jeremiah story is another example of this.

We joined the Aldgate Baptist Church on our return in 1992. They had a holistic approach to many things and we learned to understand what had happened to us. It took five years to recover, but while that was going on Sheila was invited to lead a new cross-cultural ministry team. She especially needed to testify that missions and church life can be political and fraught with difficulties that have to be managed while remaining in love with the Lord. Recovery was slower for Stan who remains cautious with church life but he testifies to the Lord of love.

We have both been able to walk in forgiveness and live in the Lord's peace, sometimes confronting difficult situations, especially in Ghana. The Jacob's

Ladder sessions we attended in 1975 and thereafter, when we heard teaching from Doug Kuhl, certainly enlightened us about overcoming these situations. We had observed this in action when the power encounters could only be resolved by focusing on the power of Jesus.

Chris Wills (George)

Life after the dissolution of Jakes/SOC was perhaps kinder to me, in that I continued to live in Chief St after Kuhls departure for Sydney and my decision to stay in Adelaide. For some time we had been joining Camden Christian Centre for worship and this group was able to take over the two Housing Trust houses under the leadership of Pastor Gary Althorp.

Through this group I met my husband John, whom I married in August 1981 and we have 3 children: Michael, Kimberley & Melissa who is married to Ben. After a number of years attending Seacombe Uniting Church, we had several years where we weren't attending church, but still had contact with a few Jakes members, including the Rosenbergs, who were responsible for our becoming part of Sunset Rock Uniting congregation at Stirling.

I retired in 2015 after 15 years at Happy Valley Community Children's Centre, and in 2016 John retired and became a volunteer at *Second Chances* prison ministry, visiting Mobilong Prison weekly. In 2017 we became part of JAUNT, a group ministering to ex-prisoners, drug addicts, bikers and alcoholics, and other broken souls, meeting weekly for a shared meal, singing and sharing testimonies of the incredible way Jesus brings healing. Some of these relationships have become the closest to those we shared in Jakes.

I am encouraged by my weekly fellowship with an incredible group of ladies at Bible Study, where God equips ordinary women for extraordinary service to bring glory to him. It seems like a full circle for me, only possible through the continued love of our Father through the power of the Holy Spirit, sought so earnestly in Jakes and still manifest among us all.

BIBLIOGRAPHY

Major Historical Sources

Box, Greg,
>   *Drop In Centres*, Service to Youth Council Inc, Parkside SA, March 1974.

Brettig, Karl, ed.,
>   *Jacob's Ladder Newsletter*, September 1973, November–December 1973 and January 1974 editions.
>   *Jacob's Letter*, May 1975, October 1975, May 1976 and September 1976 editions.
>   *Servant*, Vol 1 No 1 February–March 1977, Vol 1 No 2 July 1977, Vol 1 No 3 October 1977;
>   >   Vol 2 No 1 January 1978, Vol 2 No 2 April 1978, Vol 2 No 3 July 1978, Vol 2 No 4 October 1978;
>   >   Vol 3 No 1 January 1979, Vol 3 No 2 April 1979, Vol 3 No 3 August 1979, Vol 3 No 4 December 1979 editions.

Brettig, Karl,
>   *Jacob's Ladder—A New Foundation*, Lutheran Student Vol 1 No 1, March 1974, pp. 20–22.

Christian, Monica with Leigh Newton,
>   *Jacob's Ladder Retrospective: In the beginning*, The Messenger, St Stephens Lutheran Church, Wakefield Street, Adelaide, vol. 60 no. 5 (September/October 1998) pp. 5–6.

Graebner, David,
>   *Christ Conversation Coffee*, The Messenger, St Stephens Lutheran Church, Wakefield Street, Adelaide (9 August 1971) pp. 21–23.

Hartwig, Noel,
>   *The Story of Jacob's Ladder*, unpublished Thesis, 1978. Accessed at Lutheran Archives.

Lieschke, Kevin,
>   *Case Study of an Organisation: Servants of Christ Community*, unpublished paper (15 June 1979).

Lohmeyer, Rex, David Southern, Trish Bryce and Karl Brettig,
>   *Jacob's Ladder Retrospective*, The Messenger, St Stephens Lutheran Church, Wakefield Street, Adelaide, vol 60 no. 4 (July/August 1998) pp. 5–8.

Muller, Peter with Leigh Newton,
>   *Jacob's Ladder Retrospective: The Community*, The Messenger, St Stephens Lutheran Church, Wakefield Street, Adelaide, vol. 60 no, 6 (November/December 1998) pp. 5–6.

Olsen, Steen,
>   *History*, Jacob's Letter (October 1975) pp. 2–3;
>   *The Growth of Jacob's Ladder Christian Community as a part of the Lutheran Church of Australia, South Australian District*, Forum 69 (May 1976) pp. 5–9.

BIBLIOGRAPHY

Articles in Jakes Newsletters and Magazines
[Not including news snippets, announcements, etc]

Jacob's Ladder Newsletter

Jacob's Ladder Newsletter (September 1973)
> *After Jacob's Ladder What?*—Doug Vogelsang
> *Spiritual Depression by Martin Lloyd-Jones, Book Review*—Karl Brettig
> *Love Is There*—Peter Bean
> *A Spiritual Detective!*—Leonore Schubert

Jacob's Ladder Newsletter (November–December 1973)
> *More on Involvement*—Peter Bean
> *Full Time Youth Worker*—author unknown
> *A Short Poem: Now the Story*—Ursula Schultz

Jacob's Ladder Newsletter (January 1974)
> *Jacob's Ladder: 1974 and Beyond*—Editor
> *Climbing Jacob's Ladder: Excitement, Weakness, Urgency*—K.B. [Karl Brettig?]
> *Who is the Lord of Your Life*—N.B.
> *Jonathan Livingston Seagull by Richard Bauch, Book Review*—P.B. [Peter Bean?]

Jacob's Letter

Jacob's Letter (May 1975)
> *Looking Ahead*—Doug Kuhl
> *Bike and Street*—Geoff (Scrooge) Turner
> *The Sonshine Centre in Henley Beach*—Peter Schubert
> *Money: God's Gift to Man*—Doug Vogelsang
> *Community Houses*—Steen Olsen

Jacob's Letter (October 1975)
> *History*—Steen Olsen
> *Aims for…*—author unknown
> *What's Happening Currently at Jakes?*—Karl Brettig
> *"Kerux Apostles" Motorcycle Club*—
> > Geoff (Scrooge) Turner
> *The Re-discovery of Jesus by Clergy and Church*—
> > John Hirt (House of the New World, Sydney)
> *Questions We Face*—Peter Müller
> *The Shape of Things to Come*—Doug Kuhl

Jacob's Letter (May 1976)

    Counterfeit Kingdom—Doug Kuhl

    Our Priesthood in Jesus—Peter Müller

    Money, Money Everywhere (and not a drop to drink)—Steen Olsen

    Living as God's Refugee—Peter Jasprizza

    Lutheran Spiritual Renewal—Doug Kuhl

    Christianity or Western Thinking—Karl Brettig

    On the Street—Ian Wade

    Stepping out with the Lord—Brian Proeve

    Yahweh Shalom Christian Community—Ian McLeish

    Stookey Visit—author unknown

    Constitutional Agreement Has Been Reached—Steen Olsen

Jacob's Letter (September 1976)

    An Excellent Model of a Marriage Handbook—Dr Daniel Overduin

    Living Together in the Body—Steen Olsen

    Worship (or don't make the stones cry!)—Karl Brettig

    Current Happenings—Karl Brettig

    House of Milk and Honey Co-operative—John Grimwade and Terry Allen

    Dear Harry and Family—Ian Wade

    My Coming to Jesus—Tony McDermott

Servant

Servant vol. 1 no. 1 (February–March 1977)

    Guided Together into Renewal—Doug Kuhl

    Personal Prayer—Steve Haar

    Family Worship—Peter Müller

    Women in Community—Helen Wade

    Reflection on Christmas Eve—Geoff Strelan

Servant vol. 1 no. 2 (July 1977)

    Guided Together into Renewal (Part II)—Doug Kuhl

    The Seed of Love—Jane Breen

    Renewal of the Mind—Karl Brettig

    Do Not Lie!—Alexander Solzhenitsyn

    Filled with the Spirit (A married couple receives new life)—Glen Heidenreich

    From Weak Threads into a Strong Garment—Brian Proeve

    "She is Precious to Me"—Helen Wade

BIBLIOGRAPHY

Servant vol. 1 no. 3 (October 1977)
  Guided Together into Renewal (Part III)—Doug Kuhl
  The Evangelical Community—Peter Müller
  Some of Luther's Thoughts on Prayer—Martin Luther
  A Look at the International Charismatic Renewal—Gary Seromik
  Report from the Kansas Conference—Doug Vogelsang and Doug Kuhl
  Good News—Gunter Stark

Servant vol. 2 no. 1 (January 1978)
  What is Charismatic Renewal?—LCR Australia
  Show Your True Colours—CH Spurgeon
  Unless the Lord Builds the House—Kathy Vogt
  He Stood at the Door (and I calmly flung it open)—Peter Schubert
  The House We Live In—Larry Christenson
  Prophecy by Bruce Yocum, Book Review—David Trudinger
  Interview with Graham Pulkingham

Servant vol. 2 no. 2 (April 1978)
  Doctors, Medicine & Divine Healing—George Martin
  Anointed with Oil—Judith Heidenreich
  A Healing Reviewed—Jay Hutchinson
  Jesus the Great Physician—Mary Bates
  Divine Healing—TA Hegre
  Conference Reports—Dave Trudinger
  Do You Know What You Are Asking?—Dennis Mattiske
  The House We Live In (Part 2)—Larry Christenson

Servant vol. 2 no. 3 (July 1978)
  Growing in Unity—John Carroll
  Interview with Pastor Bruce Kilpatrick
  The House We Live In (Part 3)—Larry Christenson
  Why Do We Need Spiritual Gifts?—Don Basham
  Developing Effective Prayer—Karl Brettig
  From Bomb Shelter to Christ—Rudolf (Rudy) Oestmann
  The Charismatic Renewal among Lutherans by Larry Christenson, Book Review—Matt J Colwell

Servant vol. 2 no. 4 (October 1978)
  The Acts for Today—Charles Ringma
  Loving One Another (in God's House)—John Carroll
  Using the Word of God during Prayer Meetings—Geoff Strelan
  Conference Reports—Glen Heidenreich and Marty Rosenberg

It Happened on the Line—HJ Noack

Search for a New life—Sheila Wittam

A Time for Intercession by Erwin Prange, Book Review—David Trudinger

Servant vol. 3 no. 1 (January 1979)

Overcoming in Christ—Doug Kuhl

God at Work in Indonesia—Dato

Intercession and Warfare—Lance Lambert

The Gift of Tongues—Larry Christenson

The Lutheran Tradition—Theodore Jungkuntz

Servant vol. 3 no. 2 (April 1979)

It's a New Day!—Alan Langstaff

Developments in Lutheran Charismatic Renewal—Karl Brettig

Praying Together—Geoff Strelan

Interview with Johnson Seimo

Personal Testimony—Phyllis Schubert

Servant vol. 3 no. 3 (August 1979)

Peter and Company—Dave Andrews

Reaching out with the Gospel—Rob McCarthy

Thoughts—Helmut Thielicke

A Word—Jane Breen

Becoming a Christian—Peter Jasprizza

Servant vol. 3 no. 4 (December 1979)

Treasure in Clay Pots—Geoff Strelan

Emotions: Resources for Christian Life—Steve Clark

Notes from Los Angeles—Doug Vogelsang

Reflection on Jesus—Helen Wade

Rags to Riches—Graham (Bonnie) Gibson

BIBLIOGRAPHY

Other Key Documents

Manager's Report Book

    3/3/1972 to 13/10/1973

AGM Agendas: Reports/Minutes

    1975   Pastor's Report

    22/2/1978 AGM—
- Agenda
- Reports
- Minutes

    21/4/1978 Community Gathering—
- Agenda

    9/3/1979 AGM—
- Agenda
- Reports
- Minutes

Constitution

    16/3/1976

    10/1976

Covenant

    1/3/1978

A look at the Servants of Christ Community

    undated

LCA SA/NT District President's Committee for Pastoral Consultation with the Pastor of Jacob's Ladder

    The minutes are in the Lutheran Archives.

    1975: 29/4, 15/5, 9/6, 21/7, 11/8, 22/9, 1/12, 10/12, 18/12

    1976: 5/2, 11/3, 18/3, 6/5, 22/7, 22/10

www.ingramcontent.com/pod-product-compliance
Lightning Source LLC
Chambersburg PA
CBHW061132010526
44107CB00068B/2914